OFFICE FOR STANDARDS
IN EDUCATION

Secondary
1993-97 **Education**

A REVIEW OF SECONDARY SCHOOLS IN ENGLAND

ΓIONERY OFFICE

Office for Standards in Education
Alexandra House
33 Kingsway
London WC2B 6SE

Telephone 0171-421 6800

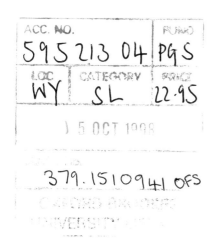
ISBN 0 11 350099 8

Contents

INTRODUCTION

In 1992 the Education (Schools) Act established the statutory basis for the inspection of schools with the aim that all secondary schools in England (including middle deemed secondary) should be inspected on a four-yearly cycle beginning in September 1993 and ending in July 1997.

This target has been met, and inspection reports have been made available to parents, prospective parents and other interested parties. At the same time a large amount of data and inspectors' judgements became available for the first time on all secondary schools. **A statistical annex** to this review shows the data upon which aspects of the review are based. However, it should be noted that, as the Framework for Inspection and the criteria for making inspection judgements were amended in 1996, there is a discontinuity between the data arising from first three years of inspection and the fourth. Where criteria remained constant, the full four years of data have been used, but where there was a discontinuity in the criteria only data from 1993-6 or 1996-7 have been used. This evidence from OFSTED inspections of schools, together with findings from HMI surveys carried out during the same period, provides an overview of secondary education in England.

This review looks in depth at the standards achieved by schools, the contributory factors, and the wider aspects of school life. In so doing it acknowledges success, citing examples of good practice, but it also raises issues which schools need to address if they are to improve further.

In 1988 HMI produced a similar survey arising from a sample of inspections undertaken in the years 1982-6. Although that report contained more information on some aspects of schooling, such as the detail of curriculum structure, it gave far less prominence to the analysis of standards and the factors influencing them. The report did, however, make an overall judgement.

Nearly three quarters of the schools inspected were performing satisfactorily in general and half had some notably good features. Fewer than one in ten was judged poor or very poor overall, but a further fifth had some major areas of weakness. Standards were unacceptably low in a very small number of schools.

SECONDARY SCHOOLS, AN APPRAISAL BY HMI, 1988

Although the criteria for judging schools are not identical, this report finds that there are more good schools and fewer with major weaknesses, although there remains a small group of schools which are not providing an acceptable standard of education. In spite of this clear evidence of improvement, there is considerable scope for raising of standards in very many schools.

This review is intended to provide an overview as well as an agenda for schools as OFSTED begins the process of reinspecting all secondary schools over the next six years.

Statistical Annex to the Secondary Review, available free from Research, Analysis & International Team, OFSTED, Alexandra House, 33 Kingsway, London WC2B 6SE,

MAIN FINDINGS

- Over the four-year period of the inspection cycle, the overall quality of education provided by secondary schools in England has improved.

- Two out of five secondary schools are consistently good. Many others are satisfactory overall with some good features. However, one in ten schools has significant weaknesses, and just over one in fifty fails to provide an acceptable quality of education. More broadly, given comparable intakes, schools perform very differently. There is a very wide gap in the standards attained between the most and least successful schools; this gap has widened during recent years.

- More pupils are leaving schools with better qualifications than was the case four years ago. The number of pupils achieving success in the GCSE and A level has risen steadily. There has been a similar improvement in results in the National Curriculum tests in Key Stage 3.

- However, two out of five pupils are failing to achieve the national expectation in English and mathematics at the end of Key Stage 3. One in nine pupils fails to get 5 GCSEs at grade G or above and one in fourteen pupils leaves school without any formal qualification to show for their eleven years of statutory education. While schools have had some success in raising the achievement of the lowest achieving pupils, the very wide gap between highest and lowest attaining pupils has increased since 1991.

- Certain groups of pupils perform far less well than others, and than might be expected of them. The under-performance of boys is a matter of serious concern, as is the fact that pupils from some ethnic minority groups often achieve below their potential.

- Two in five pupils have inadequate skills of literacy and numeracy, which impedes their progress across the curriculum. Information Technology skills remain underdeveloped in half of all schools.

- Overall, leadership and management are good in three out of four schools. Heads and governors have generally risen to the challenge of the greater responsibilities that have accompanied changes in governance and local management of schools. In one in ten schools leadership is weak and provides little clear direction or a sufficient focus on standards.

- The weakest aspect of leadership and management is the monitoring and evaluation by schools of their own performance. This is improving, but could be further improved in two out of three schools. The exercise of the role of middle manager is increasingly effective, but remains uneven in most schools.

- The majority of schools create a climate in which teaching and learning can successfully take place. Schools promote a set of values which contribute to the effective running of the school, to pupils' personal development and to the standards they attain. Behaviour is at least satisfactory in the great majority of schools. However, the proportion of schools where behaviour is good has declined over the four years of the inspection cycle, while the number of pupils excluded has risen.

- The quality of teaching has improved over the four years of the inspection cycle. The majority of lessons taught in most schools are at least satisfactory. The main area of weakness is the failure to provide appropriately for the range of ability in the class, enabling lower attaining pupils to be fully involved while at the same time maintaining high expectations, good pace and challenge to ensure that all pupils make acceptable progress.

- The marking of pupils' work often fails to make the best use of pupils' responses in order to comment on strengths and weaknesses and promote improvement. In general, assessment is one of the weaker aspects of teaching.

- The setting of homework has great potential for raising standards, yet continues to be a weakness in many schools. Some teachers take great care to set appropriately challenging homework on a regular basis, but often homework fails to enthuse or challenge pupils as it might.

- Schools have responded well to the considerable changes in the curriculum, examination courses and syllabuses imposed in the last few years, and in implementing the Code of Practice for pupils with special educational needs.

- Schemes of work are generally much improved. However, curriculum planning for continuity between primary and secondary schools is not given sufficiently high priority in many secondary schools.

- Most schools comply in most respects with the statutory requirements to teach the National Curriculum, religious education, sex education and careers education. It is a matter of concern that some schools ignore or fail to plan effectively to ensure that some subjects, particularly information technology, are treated as laid down in the National Curriculum Orders. There is also significant non-compliance in religious education.

- The majority of schools have developed a curriculum which meets the needs of most of their pupils. However, many schools fail to provide a suitable curriculum for low attaining pupils in Key Stage 4.

- The introduction of GNVQ has extended the range and style of study available in sixth forms, and has enabled an increasing number of students to achieve Advanced-level standard in a choice of general vocational areas. At Intermediate level GNVQ has provided a more worthwhile experience than was previously the case for students on one-year courses.

- The level of resources available adversely affects teaching the National Curriculum in some subjects in a significant number of schools. Common deficiencies include a lack of textbooks available for homework, and inadequate equipment to support the teaching of practical subjects. Such shortages limit the range of work that can be undertaken. Some of the resources prepared by teachers to remedy these deficiencies are of low quality and have a negative impact on standards. However, it is also the case that in some schools there are major weaknesses in the management of resources, for example the use of major central resources such as the library and IT facilities.

- In one-quarter of schools, accommodation is poor in significant respects, and inhibits teaching of the National Curriculum in particular subjects.

1 SECONDARY EDUCATION IN ENGLAND

In 1996 there were 3,010,000 pupils in the 3,594 maintained secondary schools in England. There has been a small but steady decline in the number of schools in recent years - a fall of 5 per cent between 1993 and 1996. In the same period the number of pupils increased by 1.5 per cent. In 1986 there were 19 per cent more schools, 13 per cent more pupils and 18 per cent more teachers than in 1996.

Charts 1 and 2 illustrate the diversity of the secondary sector. The majority are schools which cover all or most of the secondary age range. A minority cater for only a part of this range. Of

these, about 400 are middle schools which cover a significant part of the secondary age range, usually 9-13 years. There has been a significant decline in the number of middle schools over the last four years as several LEAs have reorganised their schools, in part to match their provision to National Curriculum key stages. About half of all secondary schools have sixth forms. This proportion has increased slightly as a small number of 11-16 schools have recently established sixth forms. Many of these schools have sensibly concentrated on developing vocational rather than academic courses in their sixth forms.

The vast majority of secondary schools, nine out of ten, are non-selective comprehensives (Chart 2). There are 160 selective grammar schools, only 5 per cent of all secondary schools. There are a similar number of secondary modern schools for those pupils not selected by the grammar schools. Many other secondary moderns have developed into comprehensive schools.

The Education Reform Act 1988 established, as separate admissions authorities, grant maintained schools and City Technology Colleges. It also promoted more open enrolment by requiring admissions authorities (LEAs, dioceses and schools) to meet parental preferences unless a school was full.

The main result of these policies in the last five years has been the growth in numbers of grant maintained schools which are directly funded through government grants (Chart 3). The proportion of grant maintained schools increased sharply from 1993-1994 but the growth has levelled off since then and grant maintained schools now form just under one-fifth of all maintained secondary schools. The distribution of

Chart 1 Types of school by age range of pupils

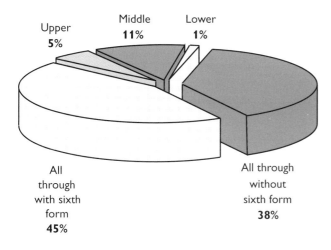

Chart 2 Types of school by admission

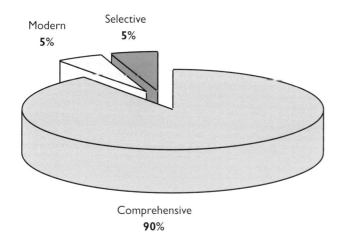

Chart 3 Growth of grant maintained schools

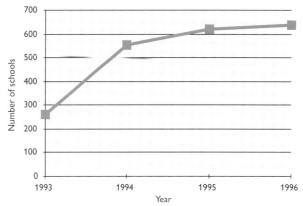

grant maintained schools is patchy, with more in the south of England and in urban areas, particularly outer London. Just over two-thirds of schools remain fully maintained by LEAs (Chart 4). About one-third of LEAs have no grant maintained schools, while in one-tenth of LEAs more than half of pupils are educated in grant maintained schools.

Since 1997 four types of Specialist School have been established. There are now 196 Technology, 47 Language, 6 Sport and 3 Arts Colleges. These schools draw on additional funding from the government and from sponsors and are intended to be centres of excellence in their specialist subject.

Voluntary schools (Chart 5) are usually church schools. They are funded, at least in part, by LEAs but their assets reside with the trustees. Roman Catholic schools form just under half of this group and Church of England schools about one-third; the remainder are run by other foundations and trusts. Special Agreement schools include the 17 City Technology Colleges, which are funded directly by government but also receive sponsorship from business.

Girls' schools form five per cent of schools overall and boys' schools four per cent (Chart 6). There has been a slight decline in the number of both boys' and girls' schools and an increase in the number of mixed schools since 1992. There are wide variations nationally in the distribution of single sex schools. They tend to be mainly concentrated in urban areas. A higher proportion of grammar than comprehensive are single sex schools.

The average size of a secondary school is 838 pupils (Chart 7). One-sixth of secondary schools have less than 500 pupils and almost a quarter have more than 1,100. There has been a continuing shift away from very large schools and there are now only 15 schools with more than 1,800 pupils. Almost one-third of sixth forms have less than 100 pupils and half have under 150 pupils. The size of the sixth form greatly affects the range of courses that it is able to offer cost-effectively (see page 111).

Secondary schools have very different types of intake in terms of both the attainment of pupils on entry and the level of disadvantage of pupils in the school: these two intake measures are closely

associated. There are no national data sets at present for attainment on entry. The best available indicator for level of disadvantage is the proportion of pupils eligible for free school meals. On average, in 1997, 18.3 per cent of pupils were eligible for free school meals (Chart 8). Over 200

Chart 4 Type of school by status

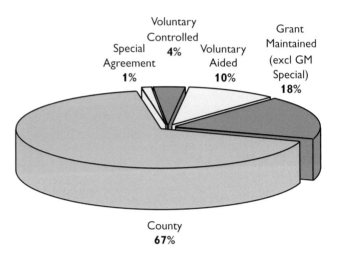

Chart 5 Voluntary schools

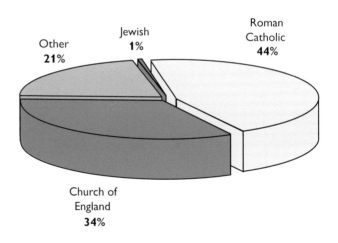

Chart 6 Types of school by gender of pupils

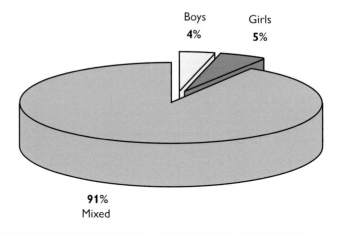

secondary schools (almost 6 per cent) have more than 50 per cent of pupils eligible for free school meals.

The overall picture over the last five years is of downward pressure on resources provided for secondary schools. Schools have been subjected to a reduction in expenditure in real terms and have sought to improve efficiency and provide improved value for money. Chart 9 shows unit costs for secondary schools, that is, the amount spent by the LEA per pupil. A real terms index is used which is set at 100 for 1991/2 when the unit cost for secondary schools was £1,773 per pupil. This

overall index shows a decline of 5.2 points since 1991/2. Looking at the components of the budget in more detail, the sharpest decline has been in expenditure on repairs and maintenance. The expenditure on books and equipment has remained static in real terms. The cost of teachers has fallen slightly whilst the unit cost of support and administrative staff has increased.

Pupil teacher ratios (PTRs) have risen from 15.8 in 1992 to 16.8 in 1996 (Chart 10) with significant variations within and between LEAs. The most favourable PTRs were in inner London. These LEAs had the highest proportion of pupils eligible

Chart 7 Secondary school sizes

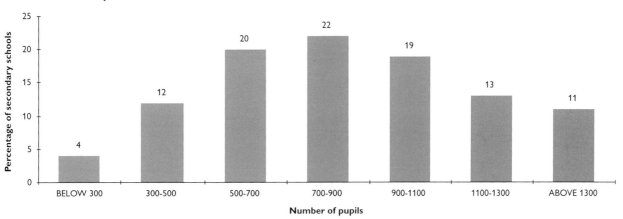

Chart 8 Percentage of secondary school pupils who are eligible for free school meals

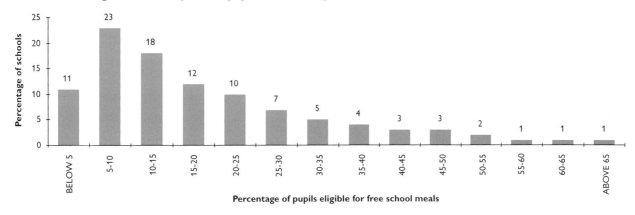

Chart 9 Funding of LEA maintained schools

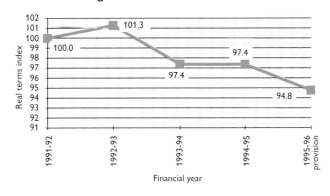

Chart 10 Pupil/teacher ratio

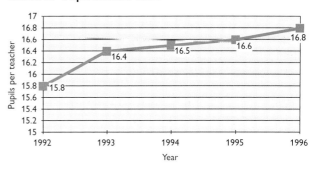

for free school meals and therefore the highest levels of educational disadvantage. They also had the highest proportion of pupils identified as having special educational needs. Average class size has risen from 21.5 in 1992 to 21.9 in 1996 (Chart 11). Over the same period the proportion of classes with more than 31 pupils has risen from 4.4 to 5.7 per cent.

Since 1993 there has been a 7 per cent fall in the number of male teachers and a 2 per cent rise in the number of female teachers. There are now more female than male teachers in the secondary sector. However, in contrast there are 795 female headteachers (22 per cent) against 2,799 male (78 per cent). The proportion of female headteachers recently appointed to schools serving disadvantaged areas is higher than for schools nationally.

The class contact ratio represents the proportion of the teacher's week that is spent teaching classes of pupils (Chart 12). All teachers are provided with a certain amount of non-contact time for lesson planning, marking and administrative purposes. Teachers with posts of responsibility are generally given additional non- contact time in order for them to carry out their duties. The chart shows a small but steady increase in the proportion of class contact time and therefore an associated fall in the amount of non-contact time available for teachers. This has to be set against the growing demands, particularly on middle managers, to engage in a range of activities including data collection, target setting and teacher appraisal which require non-contact time.

The average hours of lesson time in the week have also increased slightly from 24.15 hours in 1992 to 24.6 hours in 1996 (Chart 13). The DfEE recommended minimum time is 24 hours for Key Stage 3 and 25 hours for Key Stage 4.

Over the period of this review the proportion of schools with adequate accommodation has remained at about three-quarters. In the remaining one-quarter the accommodation is judged poor in significant respects, including deficiencies which inhibit the teaching of the National Curriculum in particular subject areas including science, design and technology, art, music and PE. Some schools have poor or inaccessible study facilities, including libraries and computer rooms. Some schools are poorly

decorated. Some are heavily dependent on 'temporary' accommodation, which can be of poor quality.

Chart 11 Average class size

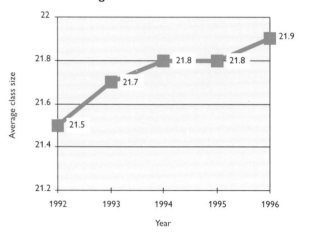

Chart 12 Class contact ratio

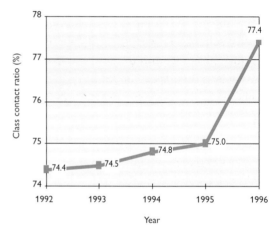

Chart 13 Hours per week at Key Stages 3 & 4

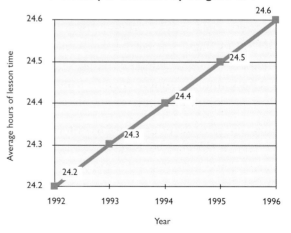

2
STANDARDS IN SECONDARY SCHOOLS

2.1 Overview of standards

Evidence from inspections indicates a gradual improvement in standards over the inspection cycle. The proportion of departments where inspectors judged that standards were good increased from 1993 to 1996, while the proportion of departments where standards were poor decreased. Using the new inspection Framework in 1996/7, inspectors judged that pupils made good gains in knowledge, skills and understanding across the subjects of the curriculum in nearly half of secondary schools. However, pupils made unsatisfactory progress and therefore achieved substantially less than they should have in one in ten schools in Key Stage 3 and one in sixteen in Key Stage 4.

There are significant variations in pupils' achievement as they move up through secondary school. Although problems of continuity from Key Stage 2 remain (see 6.2, page 104) pupils generally make a sound start in Year 7, often motivated by the challenge provided by the higher level of resourcing and by the specialist accommodation in practical subjects. There is then a dip in progress in Years 8 and 9 (Chart 14). Progress then improves in Key Stage 4 where pupils respond well to the demands of GCSE and where teachers have clear syllabus and assessment requirements to focus their work and pitch the level of demand.

Inspectors' judgements of progress in different subjects, shown in Chart 15, confirm in most cases the general picture of better progress in Key Stage 4 than in Key Stage 3. A number of other specific points stand out. Schools have struggled with the relatively new demands of information technology and half of schools fail to comply with statutory requirements. As yet, the standards achieved, the spread of attainment and rates of progress in IT are wider than in any other subject. The revised National Curriculum has helped teachers to raise

Chart 14

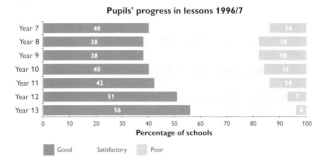

Pupils' progress in lessons 1996/7

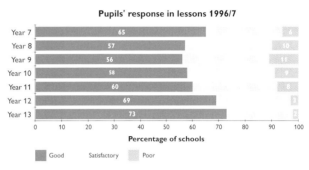

Pupils' response in lessons 1996/7

Chart 15 Progress at KS3 & KS4 by subjects 1996/97

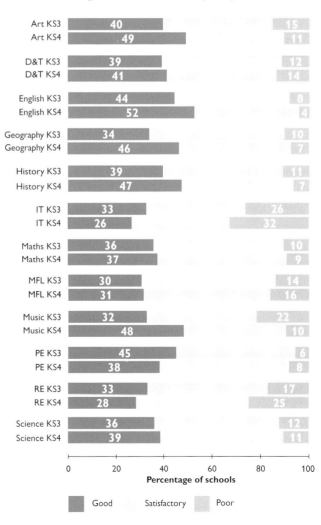

standards in design and technology. As teachers have gained in confidence and made better use of support materials, so pupils' knowledge and understanding and skills have improved. There are continued weaknesses in religious education where a lack of time and use of non-specialist teachers often limit progress, and in modern foreign languages where increasing numbers of pupils are now taking the subject in Key Stage 4.

The progress made by pupils with learning difficulties is satisfactory in the majority of schools and in some schools they make good progress. The introduction in 1994 of the Code of Practice on the Identification and Assessment of Special Educational Needs has contributed to an improvement in pupils' progress over the last four years. Individual education plans (IEPs) identify literacy as the main focus for improvement, although numeracy and behaviour are priorities in many cases. The emphasis in schools on a narrow diet of basic skills exercises explains the weaker progress these pupils generally make in other areas of the curriculum. In secondary schools the subject department structure and the large number of different teachers who teach each pupil can present logistical difficulties in the implementation of IEPs.

Achievement in schools' sixth forms is generally good. Students make good progress in both GCE A level and in GNVQ courses. Students often achieve impressive standards; underachievement is uncommon.

Inspection shows that, overall, many pupils achieve high standards and that these standards are rising steadily. There are, nevertheless, continuing concerns. Too many pupils still achieve too little. The tail of low achievement is too long. The gap between high attaining and low attaining pupils shows no signs of narrowing. The substantial weakness in one in ten schools in Key Stage 3 requires urgent attention. Even in the majority of schools where inspectors judge that pupils make sound progress, there is room for improvement. Those schools where achievement is good demonstrate what schools in similar circumstances can achieve. At present there is still too much variation in the achievement of pupils in different schools.

2.2 Standards achieved in national tests and GCSE examinations

Chart 16 shows the percentage of pupils achieving level 5 or above in the statutory Key Stage 3 national tests for the core subjects in 1997. English test results show a small fall in the proportion of pupils achieving this standard compared with 1996. In mathematics and science the test results show an improvement on previous years. Girls do significantly better than boys in English, but there is little difference in mathematics and science. The fact that two in five fourteen year olds failed to reach the national expectation in English and mathematics reinforces national concerns about standards of literacy and numeracy.

Chart 16 National Curriculum test performance 1996-1997

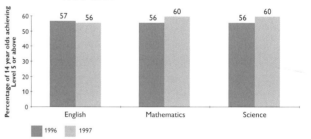

The performance of pupils in public examinations has improved steadily over the last five years. The greatest improvement has been in the proportion of pupils gaining 5 or more GCSEs at grades A* to C (Chart 17). In 1992 this figure for 16 year olds in maintained schools was 35.6 per cent and in 1997 it was 43.1 per cent, an improvement of 7.5 percentage points. The proportion of pupils gaining 5 or more A* to G grades has improved more slowly; from 83.6 per cent to 88.4 per cent – an increase of only 4.8 percentage points. It remains a matter of very considerable concern that one in nine pupils fails to gain this basic set of qualifications, and that the proportion of pupils leaving school with no GCSEs has remained at about 1 in 14 pupils.

Chart 17 GCSE performance 1992-1997

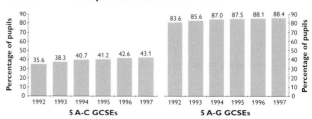

While these figures provide useful benchmarks, they do not take account of any changes in performance within these bands; the average points score per pupil, where grade G is worth 1 point and A* is worth 8 points, is a better indicator of overall attainment. The average point score has increased from 30.7 in 1992 to 36.9 in 1997, an increase of 6.2 points (Chart 18). However, this overall increase masks very unequal rates of improvement. The increase for the lowest performing quarter of pupils has been very much less than for others. This is shown in Chart 19. The lowest attaining quarter of pupils scored, on average, only 8.2 points per pupil, while the highest attaining quarter scored over seven times higher. The very wide gap between these groups of pupils has increased since 1991. Thus, while schools have had some success in raising the achievement of the lowest achieving pupils this has done nothing to close this gap.

The improvements in examination performance have been attributed in some quarters to a shift in the standards set by examination groups. A joint study by OFSTED and SCAA[1] concluded that between 1985 and 1995 there was little evidence of any significant change in examination standards in GCSE English. In chemistry and mathematics, however, changes in the syllabus requirements made comparison less secure, and although overall they too were judged to be of about the same level of difficulty, there was a clear need to keep the demands of the examinations under review in order to ensure that standards were maintained.

There have been a number of other recent changes in GCSE: new criteria for syllabuses; tiered examinations; altered regulations for coursework; and short courses. It is, however, too early to say what effect, if any, these may have on standards of performance.

2.3 Standards achieved in sixth forms

GCE A level continues to be the major qualification pursued by students in school sixth forms, but the GNVQ has been a significant innovation in this phase.

Examination results at GCE A-level have shown a small but steady improvement. This is shown in Chart 20. The number of students in maintained secondary schools entered for A levels increased from 106,059 in 1995 to 118,573 in 1997. Overall, girls outnumbered boys by 5,700. Pass rates have improved from 81 per cent in 1993 to 87 per cent in 1997. The numbers entered for AS courses in 1996 amounted to approximately 8 per cent of those for A level. The pass rate for AS examinations fluctuated at just above 70 per cent. The average points score per student taking 2 or more A levels has increased from 15.9 in 1995 to 17.0 in 1997. Girls achieve slightly better than boys, but the difference is less marked than at GCSE. Boys have a wider spread of attainment, with higher proportions of boys than girls achieving less than 5 points and more than 30 points.

While most A-level syllabuses have evolved gradually over decades, there has recently been a marked change with the introduction of modular syllabuses as an alternative to traditional linear syllabuses in most subjects. Such syllabuses were introduced in a significant way in mathematics,

Chart 18 GCSE average points score, 1992-7

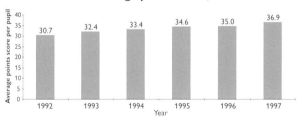

Chart 19 GCSE points score of all pupils by quarters 1991 and 1996

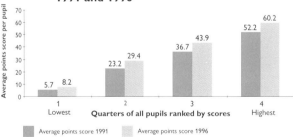

Chart 20 GCE A-level points score for students taking two or more A levels 1992 to 1997

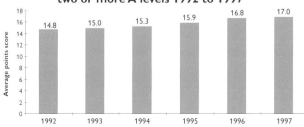

[1] *Standards in Public Examinations 1975 to 1995,* SCAA, 1996.

followed by new syllabuses examined for the first time in 1996 in English and the sciences, and other subjects from 1997. In 1996, modular examinations were taken by 59 per cent of all A-level candidates in mathematics, and slightly smaller proportions in biology, chemistry and physics. Numbers were significantly lower in English. Modular syllabuses accounted for 15 per cent of all A-level entries in 1996; in 1997 the proportion had risen to 30 per cent. The introduction of modular syllabuses has been accompanied by significant improvements in the take-up of mathematics, though not yet in other subjects. A-level results have improved considerably in some of the schools which have introduced modular A-level mathematics syllabuses. Results in modular physics have also been good.

The 'standards over time' report referred to on page 17 also focused on A levels in English, mathematics and chemistry. Here, too, the standards set in English in 1985 and 1995 were judged to be comparable. The standards set in mathematics and chemistry were judged to have varied only slightly. Further evidence of the consistency of examination standards was given in an HMI inspection of the quality and standards of GCE A-level examinations in six subjects during the period 1994 to 1996. This found minor variations in the standards set. As with the GCSE, there is a need for continued vigilance in order to ensure that the level of demand is maintained. There is no evidence so far to suggest that modular courses provide an easier option. Improvements in results may arise from other factors associated with these courses: students' increased motivation, more consistent effort throughout the course, and better awareness of their own capabilities. However, OFSTED will be completing a detailed inspection of modular A levels during 1998 to ensure that standards are secured in this significant new provision of A-level courses.

The introduction of GNVQs has extended the range and style of study available in sixth forms and has enabled an increasing number of students to achieve Advanced-level standard in a choice of broad vocational areas. At the same time, Intermediate level GNVQ has enabled one-year sixth-form students to achieve more than would normally have been the case on a GCSE resit programme. Chart 21 shows the number of students on GNVQ courses in the last two years

and highlights the sharp increase in the number of students taking Advanced courses.

Chart 21 Number of students taking GNVQ courses in sixth forms

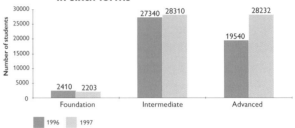

There is evidence that GNVQ results have also improved in the short time since their introduction. An analysis of results is more complex than for GCE or GCSE because courses do not have to be completed in a fixed time. In 1997 at Advanced level almost 50 per cent of all candidates in sixth forms and in FE colleges achieved the full award - an increase of 10 percentage points over the previous year. A further 20 per cent achieved at least six accredited units. In a sample of school sixth forms inspected in the summer of 1997, many achieved higher completion rates than this, with relatively high proportions of merit and distinction results.

2.4 The differential performance of schools

Standards achieved in schools of different type

Comparisons between schools of different type require the consideration of a wide range of variables including intake, location, age range and size. Neither is any group of schools entirely homogeneous. For example, there is a considerable difference of 20 points between the highest and lowest average GCSE point score achieved by pupils in grammar schools. LEA maintained schools, by far the biggest group of

Chart 22 Comparison of average GCSE points score per pupil in LEA and GM schools against eligibility for free school meals 1997

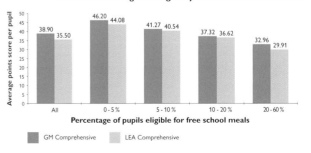

schools, include some of the highest and some of the lowest performing schools. Even so, some generalisations can be made in comparing achievement in specific types of schools against achievement in schools overall.

Grant maintained schools have consistently achieved higher GCSE scores than LEA maintained schools. In 1997 the average point score per pupil for GM comprehensive schools was 38.9 compared with 35.5 for LEA maintained comprehensive schools. However, GM schools overall have a lower level of disadvantage; when schools with similar intakes are compared this difference between the sectors is reduced.

Inspection evidence shows that the quality of teaching in GM and LEA maintained schools is very similar. Inspectors also judge that the progress made by pupils in lessons is very similar. GM schools are judged to be better managed overall and more provide good value for money than LEA maintained schools. GM schools also tend to have better resources and a more positive ethos. However, this has yet to be translated into significantly higher standards of achievement in the case of most schools.

Results achieved by pupils in denominational schools are higher than the average for all schools. Roman Catholic schools do particularly well, given that levels of disadvantage in these schools, as indicated by free school meal entitlement, are also slightly higher than average. Results in Church of England schools are also high but they tend to serve areas with less disadvantage.

Overall, City Technology Colleges (CTCs) score a significantly higher GCSE points score than maintained schools and have improved more in the last four years, particularly in 1996-7. There is, however, quite a wide variation in the points score of the different CTCs. Post-16 the picture is very mixed. CTCs generally give a stronger emphasis to vocational courses, and some CTCs have still to establish a full sixth form. Inspection reports on CTCs have generally been positive. CTCs generally benefit from very good accommodation and resources, a longer teaching day and a highly qualified staff. The recent improvement in GCSE scores shows that most CTCs have taken advantage of these circumstances and have produced good and improving standards. The process, however, has taken time. Moreover, a minority of CTCs have yet to properly exploit these benefits.

Pupils in middle schools make slightly slower progress than pupils in secondary schools overall. This is a reflection of poorer teaching in some subjects, particularly English and science, including weaker subject expertise, assessment practice, and use of homework.

The impact of competition between schools

During the years 1993-97 secondary schools changed considerably in response to a series of legislative measures, including the effects of the Education Reform Act 1988. A main thrust of government policy at this time was to devolve decision-making to the local level - that is, to schools and parents - while retaining and in many ways reinforcing the capacity of central government to intervene where it deemed appropriate.

Chart 23 Achievement of pupils in denominational and other schools

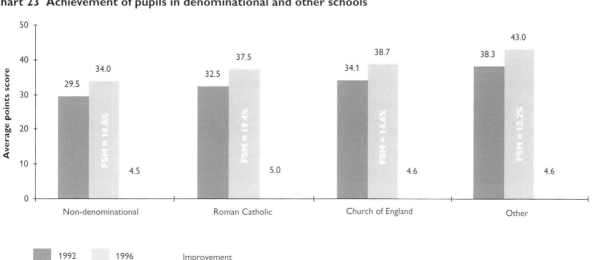

In 1992, the White Paper *Choice and Diversity* spelled out both the detailed rationale for measures taken in the years immediately preceding and the government's plans for the education system for the future. That rationale had at its heart a market theory. Local management of schools and GM status, coupled with more open enrolment of pupils, gave schools both the freedom and the motive to compete for pupils. Parents would, acting in the interests of their children, choose good schools, which would expand. Unpopular schools would lose pupils and funding and ultimately would close. Standards overall would be driven up through competition and the exercise of local decision-making.

The secondary sector already was, even before 1988, very diverse. During the years of this review that diversity increased, largely because of the growth of the GM sector, but also because of the introduction of City Technology Colleges and the success of the specialising schools initiative. Schools differ in many other ways which can be equally telling in influencing parental perceptions. Parents may, for example, choose a school for its location, or the school uniform, or because it is perceived as having good discipline, or for many other reasons.

The principle of parental choice has, however, been frustrated because there have not been enough 'good' schools; and such schools have not been able, for the most part, to expand very greatly. Parents do not in fact have the right to choose schools, merely to express a preference. In some areas parents have been subject to some aggressive marketing, particularly where schools are competing for 'better' pupils. This tends to raise expectations among parents that cannot always be fulfilled. It is frequently a source of some local irritation that parents are drawn to particular schools by glossy advertising, only to find that no place is available for their child. On the other hand, there is no evidence of widespread malpractice. Admissions policies are generally applied fairly, and covert selection of pupils appears to be rare. The resulting pattern is complex. In some areas a clear hierarchy of schools has emerged, defined by parental perceptions of quality. In other areas no such hierarchy exists.

The purpose of providing choice and diversity was, at least in part, to raise standards. Nationally, on the published measures, standards have risen during the years in question, but the part played in that rise by competition between schools is obscure. What can be said is that some schools have become fuller (or more oversubscribed) while others have had increasing difficulty in filling their places. Some LEAs have relatively large numbers of surplus places, or are net exporters of pupils to neighbouring LEAs. These are self-evidently indicators of the relative popularity of their schools, but there is no correlation between either and the standards achieved across the LEA or the rate of improvement attained.

Some secondary schools have become locked into a vicious circle. The fact that their examination results are modest has meant that few parents outside their immediate catchment area indicated a preference for them. As a consequence they have unfilled places and have been regularly confronted with the demand that they admit difficult pupils. The difficulty of assimilating such pupils has rendered some schools even more unpopular with parents.

Nationally, the gap between the top 10 per cent of schools and the bottom 10 per cent in terms of GCSE point scores widened between 1992 and 1996. The percentage of pupils leaving with no graded result also increased. This is a problem which requires urgent attention. Sixteen year-olds who leave schools with no qualifications face a future which offers them little chance of fulfilling reasonable aspirations.

2.5 Basic and key skills

Standards of literacy and communication across the curriculum

HMCI's Annual Report in 1994/5 stated that 'underachievement in reading in Key Stages 3 and 4 results from weak teaching which leaves many pupils unable to use books, libraries and other media sources effectively and to understand different kinds of text. In at least one-fifth of schools, reading skills need to be taught in a more sustained and well-planned way'. Chart 24 shows that while standards of reading are good in around six out of ten schools, they remain unsatisfactory in around one in seven.

Chart 24 also shows that writing is weaker than reading. Overall, standards of writing by pupils in Key Stages 3 and 4 were judged to be good or better in over half of the schools inspected. At the other end of the scale the standard was judged to be poor or very poor in about a fifth of schools. The main features of poor-quality writing in Key Stage 3 are a failure to write good-quality formal prose and weak spelling, grammar and punctuation. Many pupils cannot produce sustained, well-structured writing which expresses what they are trying to say. Too much writing is inappropriately informal in that it strongly resembles the pupils' speech. Some 'drafting' is sometimes not genuine drafting at all but making neat copies of what was roughly scribbled down at the first attempt. Low-attaining pupils often do not finish their work and lack the support to enable them to produce worthwhile pieces. Many pupils have problems in writing quickly, neatly and with accuracy.

Standards in speaking and listening are rather higher than in writing and reading, but are less well developed in Key Stage 3 than in Key Stage 4. Speaking and listening were judged to be at least good in about two-thirds of the schools inspected during this period. The percentage of schools where standards were unsatisfactory or poor reduced over the three years for which data is available.

In general, pupils with learning difficulties make greater progress in improving their basic skills in core subjects than they do across the curriculum as a whole. The improvement across both Key Stages 3 and 4 in reading skills and spelling reflects the emphasis in the provision for these pupils in most schools, whether through special teaching in small groups or through targeted support in the classroom.

The quality of writing in GNVQs varies considerably, particularly at Intermediate level. The best written work, at Advanced level, is very good, with students well aware of the audience for whom they are writing and of necessary conventions, for example in producing business correspondence and full-scale reports of a technical nature. Less satisfactory work, usually but not entirely at Intermediate level, is typified by technical inaccuracies in spelling, punctuation and grammar, and by an excessive use of colloquial expressions.

Because of the strong emphasis given to oral work in GNVQ courses, students' speaking and listening skills are often very good, at both Intermediate and Advanced levels. The need to act independently and to present ideas to others in situations designed to simulate the real world of the workplace and business environment has proved to be a powerful stimulus for development of skills in speaking and listening. The communication skills of Advanced GNVQ students are usually satisfactory, and in some cases very good. Standards are satisfactory overall in Intermediate GNVQ, but with particular weaknesses evident in some schools.

Chart 24 Pupils' competence in literacy and communication skills, Key Stages 3 & 4 1995/96

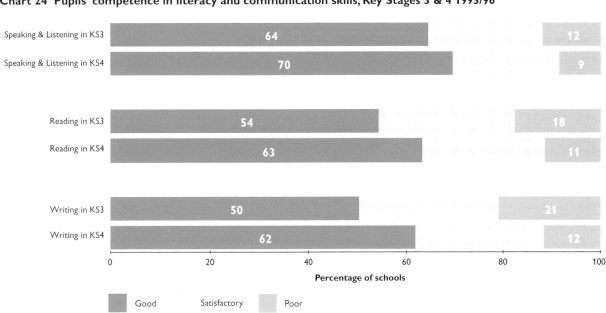

Raising standards in reading

It is self-evident that pupils do more reading in English than in other subjects, with an emphasis on imaginative texts rather than information books. However, in responding to the very broad requirements of the National Curriculum Order and the consequent reading expectations presented by Key Stage 3 tests and the new GCSE syllabuses, English departments are broadening the range of reading for pupils to include more non-fiction (see also pages 126–128).

Reading is the crucial key to high standards in other National Curriculum subjects. History provides a good example of a subject where skills in reading are an essential component of subject progress. Some history departments have become increasingly successful in fostering reading for different purposes. Pupils read a variety of written evidence for understanding and to enable them to make valid connections between discrete items of information. In the best work students go beyond what is in the actual text of a document, using their understanding of the origins, style and intention of the author to evaluate its reliability and decide on the appropriateness of the source to support an argument. Particularly at GCE A level, students scan text in order to locate relevant information, drawing on a range of sources to produce a cogent argument. In a minority of history lessons where standards are low the use of sources tends to be mechanistic and does not further pupils' understanding of the subject; in such work there is a tendency for the teacher to rely uncritically on a single textbook or inadequate worksheets. Overall, however, history teachers understand that pupils need to go beyond the superficial and literal when analysing and using texts, and to cope with written materials which demand increasingly complex language skills.

The study of texts in English lessons ensures that pupils have a sound basic diet of fiction. Many pupils do not go further than this by reading more widely, even though schools encourage them to do so in a number of imaginative ways such as special promotional events and incentives. Too often, however, these have only a limited, short-term impact, and a range of problems persist for the majority of pupils who do not manage to engage with fiction in a way which prompts them to want to read more. For many their interpretation is limited to the literal and does not extend to making important inferences; some do not move on to more sophisticated authors and texts after enjoying favourite stories and authors in their early years, whilst others develop attachments to particular genres or popular series and fail to explore different and more challenging material; boys, who tend to have more negative attitudes towards reading than girls, have as a result narrower experiences of fiction and in particular find novels which explore personal relationships difficult; pupils from disadvantaged backgrounds, regardless of gender, read with less accuracy and comprehension than their more socially advantaged peers; bilingual pupils, who often master the mechanics of reading, struggle with comprehension, especially where contexts are unfamiliar. Despite these problems the reading of fiction is often popular with pupils, especially in Key Stage 3, and there are many who, in school and at home, read and appreciate a variety of imaginative literature, including poetry, and whose interest continues to develop and deepen in later life.

Despite good work in some departments, especially recently in English, many pupils have weak skills in using non-fiction. One problem is that departments fail to provide tasks which challenge pupils as readers or offer reading experiences which extend and enrich the subject beyond the confines of the textbook. Furthermore, pupils are not taught how to make effective use of information from books, or the CD Rom. This problem is compounded for those pupils who arrive at school with reading difficulties, particularly boys of low attainment who do not receive SEN support, and whose progress is seriously hampered because the reading which they are required to do across the curriculum is too demanding. This can lead to disaffection and the disruption of lessons.

Schools thus need to have clearly defined practical approaches to reading across the Key Stage 3 curriculum. At **Honywood School, Essex,** approaches to reading are part of a broader policy framework for language development.

A language policy has evolved since 1994 as a result of the high profile given to language in the curriculum linked to regular INSET sessions for the whole staff. A number of members of staff, including key middle managers, have had strong involvement throughout. The language policy provides a consistent set of starting points which departments can use to improve aspects of their work.The school is currently attempting to improve pupils' higher order reading skills since it was discovered that some pupils in Year 8 scored less well in reading comprehension than they ought, given their abilities as tested in Year 7. The humanities department is fully conversant with the school language policy and has worked hard to link progression in its programmes of work in history, geography and RE with progression in the language expectations made of pupils in these subjects. Lessons have explicit 'language' elements such as purposeful reading with clear challenge.

HMI INSPECTION, 1997

At **Wallasey School, Wirral,** training of identified teachers and students was an important strategy in furthering a whole school approach.

Science and humanities teachers and school librarians took part in literacy training provided by the LEA. Additionally some Year 13 students were trained in paired reading, and they in turn trained their peers. The school's approach to literacy is twofold. Whole school strategies include explicit approaches to subject-specific vocabulary and concepts by subject departments and the provision of appropriate dictionaries in all rooms. Specific interventions aimed at specific groups of pupils include paired reading, with fifty sixth-form students working one to one with Year 7 pupils identified by staff; the targeting of pupils with a reading age of around 7.5 years for small group work three times weekly with trained staff using National Literacy Project and Reading Recovery strategies; and workshops and printed advice for parents to help them help their children.

HMI INSPECTION, 1997

All teachers need to recognise why wider reading is essential to the raising of standards and why pupils' skills in reading for different purposes cannot be taken for granted. Programmes for reading should build on practice in earlier key stages, and ensure that the reading of fiction and non-fiction is given appropriate weighting and is equally rewarding for girls and boys. English departments need to review their selections of texts for class use, and judge whether they provide sufficient literary or linguistic challenge. They should also review the effectiveness of their monitoring and support for pupils' wider, self-chosen reading.

All subject departments should ask themselves to what extent they require pupils to read widely in their subject; it remains the case that for very many pupils, reading is confined to use of standard class textbooks which, although designed to be attractive, offer a limited reading experience, especially for the more capable pupils. There is a tension in that many class texts are designed to make learning easier for the pupils, but in so doing they sometimes reduce pupils' engagement with the text at any great depth. For it is only through such engagement that pupils' interests, understanding and critical analysis of the text will be increased.

Reading is a time-consuming activity. Schools need to consider carefully the amount of the school day that they can allocate to such activities, and promote a culture in which pupils and parents recognise the need for a high proportion of reading to be done at home.

Raising standards in writing

Some pupils fail to mature sufficiently in their writing, and in particular to develop greater independence in organising their writing . The ability to write extended prose, essential for high attainment in subjects such as history, geography and RE, is often undeveloped. When given the opportunity to respond to open-ended questions, for example, pupils lack strategies to organise their writing and sustain an argument. Too often they are not given sufficient opportunity or guidance to explore historical events and issues, geographical patterns and processes or religious and philosophical questions through writing.

Good teaching provides assignments which give pupils a real purpose for writing, and perhaps even a real audience; moreover, it frequently provides a supportive framework that recognises the difficulties inherent in written composition - so that pupils plan, draft, edit and proof-read their work before considering it finished. Such approaches are essential for all pupils, and especially, for example, for those learning English as an additional language. Inspection reports commonly cite instances of good-quality writing with flair and imagination in a wide range of forms and for different purposes. In the very best work pupils develop a distinctive personal style and confidently structure their work; and good writing also has qualities such as the use of a wide vocabulary combined with accurate use of technical terminology.

Pupils' writing skills undoubtedly need improving in a variety of subjects. Writing is by far the most difficult set of language skills to acquire. For many pupils writing is all too often regarded as a tiresome task. Some have not mastered the technical skills sufficiently to be able to write fluently: they struggle with spelling and sentence construction and in so doing are unable to focus on the message and meaning in their writing. Where they lack technical writing skills but demands for complex writing are made of them, it is unsurprising that they seek to write as little as possible. Writing must be made more rewarding for these pupils and that requires a concerted effort by teachers in all subjects to help them acquire writing skills.

All schools, but particularly those with identified weaknesses in these areas, should consider carrying out an audit of pupils' writing across the curriculum to inform the school's literacy policy and practice. The audit should identify, for example, the balance between creative and factual writing.

St. Paul's RC Secondary School in Greenwich received an audit by the LEA inspectorate as part of the Borough's literacy initiative. This resulted in a detailed report on the basis of which targets were set. Pupils are now succeeding in meeting 'performance indicators' across the curriculum including evidence of redrafting and increased accuracy in writing.

HMI INSPECTION, 1997

Such an audit should seek to identify whether pupils are given sufficient opportunities to use writing in order to establish meaning, and to 'think through writing' in order to develop understanding. It is also important to know whether the writing skills needed in different subjects are explicitly and consistently taught by all the teachers in a department so that the demands made of pupils are raised year by year; whether the teaching of writing clearly demonstrates to the pupils exactly what the expected standards are; and whether pupils' writing is effectively assessed, with the marking establishing new targets which have been identified from assignment to assignment and which will further challenge the pupil.

Raising standards in speaking and listening

Overall, there has been an improvement in schools' provision for oral work. Talking about a topic is widely understood by teachers to be a useful part of most learning, whether as preparation for some planned work, as an essential part of carrying out the work or perhaps in evaluating how well or poorly an assignment has been done.

Despite this broadly positive picture, for some pupils, particularly those of below average ability, speaking and listening skills are underdeveloped, especially in Key Stage 3. Many pupils lack confidence in speaking, especially when asked to justify a point of view or to communicate more complex ideas. Lower attaining pupils in particular are able to offer only brief responses in class; their discussion skills are poorly developed. In schools where standards are low pupils are often confident in describing their own experiences and in stating opinions - but this is as far as it goes. They are sometimes inattentive, have a narrow, restricted vocabulary and are unable to elaborate ideas or develop arguments. They find it impossible to talk in other than their largely colloquial language, making it difficult for them to feel confident about taking part in events which call for more formal speech.

In English lessons pupils take part in a range of activities such as whole-class, group and paired discussion which provide opportunities for talking formally, for example making presentations, and standards are often high. In drama, pupils develop confidence, a sense of audience and improve their capacity to concentrate and to listen carefully.

In lessons other than English and drama many subject teachers encourage pupils to ask questions and engage their classes in discussion, the quality of which can be high at times.

A Year 8 history lesson on the English Civil War proved challenging and stimulating for a mixed ability group. In the previous lesson, pupils, in pairs, had discussed key issues covered so far. On this occasion the teacher, referring to an information worksheet, challenged the pupils to explain clearly some of the more difficult points; key concepts such as 'Parliament' were thoroughly addressed. Some pupils made extended spoken responses to the questions and were pushed to do so by the teacher, and to be exactly clear about what they were saying. The second half of the lesson involved the pupils in reading aloud from their textbook; again, understandings were clarified by good questioning, and glossing of difficult language. The overall level of thinking in this session was well above average, and the weaker pupils benefited from the well-judged interactive oral work supplemented by a carefully conceived worksheet containing a mixture of information and questions.

HMI INSPECTION, 1996

Pupils generally enjoy discussion and are positively motivated when they take part in well-managed sessions. In most subjects examples can be found of teachers' planned incorporation of some aspect of spoken language. Subject teachers increasingly insist upon correct usage of technical terms. Where the teaching is skilled and attentive to detail, pupils learn to discuss the subject using the appropriate language. As a result they learn better. However, in subjects other than English a full range of talking activity is less common and opportunities for use of talk are often missed. In science, for example, teaching often fails to capitalise on opportunities to develop conceptual understanding. Where teachers do manage to do this it is generally by means of questioning that challenges misconceptions and re-shapes the basis of pupils' understanding so that they are in the best position to approach new work. This kind of oral work is not often seen. Even rarer is good classroom discussion which builds bridges between topics or explores the wider significance of work in hand.

One of the most significant messages from inspection is the variation in standards between classes in the same school. For example, some teachers talk too much themselves, so preventing much discussion or spoken exchange; some fail to provide opportunities for group or paired discussion or for problem-solving and investigation, which are often a stimulus for high quality listening and learning. Overall, expectations of pupils as speakers and listeners rarely increase as they move through the school.

Teaching that develops and makes good use of speaking and listening requires considerable skill. Providing opportunities for speaking and listening is not enough; pupils require to be taught the various skills and disciplines explicitly by all subject staff. It is important, therefore, that this issue is addressed at whole school level, and not, as is so often the case, left only to the English department. Central to such a policy is the recognition that competence in speaking and listening at all stages of school life is an essential prerequisite not only for the development of good reading and writing skills but for all learning and, ultimately, understanding.

Pupils learning English as an additional language make most progress across a range of subjects where there are plenty of opportunities for speaking and listening. Where pupils are not given opportunities to develop their language and to work actively with new and specialist subject vocabulary in an appropriate context, they find it difficult to improve their understanding of what is being taught and to handle the concepts necessary for progress.

Standards of numeracy across the curriculum

Chart 25 shows that pupils' competence in numeracy across the curriculum was judged to be poor in about one in six schools. The performance of Year 8 and 9 pupils on the written mathematics tests in the Third International Mathematics and Science Study[2] was generally disappointing in number and related topics and the relative position of England has deteriorated since previous studies were conducted. However, the performance of 13 year-olds in a range of practical tasks in mathematics was more positive. Pupils were generally successful at carrying out the mathematical procedures involved, more so than they were at reasoning and problem-solving.

---

[2] *The Third International Mathematics and Science Study* (TIMSS), National Foundation for Educational Research, 1996.

Chart 1 Types of school by age range of pupils

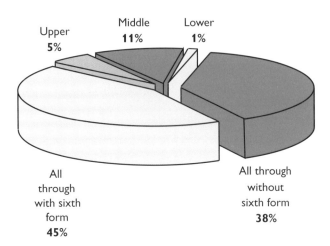

Upper
5%

Middle
11%

Lower
1%

All through with sixth form
45%

All through without sixth form
38%

Within GNVQ courses, application of number has consistently been the most problematic of the three key skills, at both Advanced and Intermediate levels. Standards achieved in application of number were less than satisfactory when GNVQ was first introduced. There has been some improvement over the four years up to 1997, but there remains an unacceptably wide spread in performance across schools, ranging from poor to good. It remains the case that, with very few exceptions, numerical skills do not make a strong enough contribution to students' vocational studies.

Although skills in numeracy are used and developed across a number of subjects the main focus, in terms of both the teaching and inspection of numeracy, is inevitably on mathematics. Here, inspection evidence has shown that in many schools, pupils demonstrate serious numerical weaknesses. These most often relate to a lack of speed and accuracy when undertaking calculations and an over-dependence on calculators. Pupils also lack confidence when asked to recall number facts and do not have the requisite fluency with numbers needed to develop and use mental strategies in arithmetic. For example, pupils continue to count on to find 7+19 rather than use key facts and alternative methods such as 7+20-1 or 19+1+6. Pupils' poor mental strategies often reflect the lack of attention teachers give to oral and mental work. In many schools, mathematics teaching does not provide pupils with sufficient opportunity to sharpen their mental skills and techniques. Too often the focus is only on the practice of skills in Key Stage 3; little attention is given to strategies, and practice only occasionally

continues into Key Stage 4 even though it is often needed. Often calculators are used randomly and it is rare for schools to teach pupils how to use the full range of facilities available on the calculator (see also pages 27–8, 132).

Schools often use tests to assess pupils' strengths and weaknesses in mathematics early in Year 7. However, when schools have identified that a high proportion of pupils have poor numeracy skills the mathematics department does not always have the necessary teaching programme in place to remedy this serious deficiency. For example, some departments with a topic-based scheme of work which follows a one- or two-year cycle do not give sufficient attention to keeping pupils' numeracy skills sharp when they are working on other topic areas.

Raising standards of numeracy

In mathematics departments where standards in numeracy are high, there is a good balance between time spent on mental and pencil-and-paper methods. Pupils are taught to use and apply different approaches depending on the complexity of the problem, the scale of the numbers involved and the degree of accuracy required. Pupils develop their skills in estimating before they compute in order to judge whether their answers are reasonable. Some schools, for example, ban calculators for a period of time in Year 7 and spend time on basic number work; they are introduced at a later stage to solve more complex calculations. Additionally, where practice is good, pupils are expected to discuss and to explain their methods and reasoning, to compare approaches and to learn new and more efficient strategies.

In a Year 8 lesson on multiplication, pupils were given a number and challenged to find consecutive numbers whose product equalled the given number. They were estimating and checking results and developing strategies that later involved knowledge of multiplication tables, factors and digital roots. The teacher used good questioning of pupils to generate discussion and to encourage pupils to share and evaluate their approach. The lesson generated enthusiasm and good mental work with number.

HMI INSPECTION, 1997

Mathematics teaching and assessment bear the brunt of criticisms about real and perceived weaknesses in numeracy skills. However, the development of numeracy is only part of a mathematics curriculum and an over-emphasis on numeracy, particularly in its narrowest form, can distort the development of the subject. It has, therefore, to be a whole school matter to establish a clearer vision of what numeracy is, and how to develop numeracy skills both in mathematics and other subjects. Pupils need to be helped to recognise that skills developed and reinforced in mathematics can help their learning in other subjects.

Progress in numeracy in subjects such as science, geography and technology is sometimes hindered by pupils' poor computation skills, though not their graphical and data handling skills, which are often better developed. Standards of numeracy are poor where demands across subjects are ill-matched to the pupils' competencies and previous experiences. Pupils are confused when they are introduced to alternative calculating methods in different subjects. Few schools successfully operate a clear whole school policy on the teaching of numeracy and there is too little effective liaison between departments to determine consistency in the use of calculating and other techniques. Increasingly, schools are aware of the need to develop such a policy and to audit the use of numeracy skills in other subjects, but for many schools the immediate need is to raise standards of numeracy in mathematics.

In the short term, there is a need to bring the great majority of pupils up to the level expected at the end of Key Stage 3. The current emphasis on improving students' key skills in the application of

number in Key Stage 4 and post-16 is an admission of failure at earlier key stages. Establishing strategies for the teaching of numeracy in relevant subjects in Key Stage 3 is a matter to be resolved urgently. An important first step is for mathematics and other relevant teachers to plan for the development of numeracy skills.

Such planning must have a clear focus on teaching methods, and be stated clearly in mathematics and other departmental handbooks and schemes of work. Teaching, using both oral and written activities, should aim to develop in pupils a strong feel for number by boosting their knowledge and recall of number facts and ensuring that they can use a range of approaches to numerical computation. They also need to have an understanding of the concepts underlying these approaches which enable decisions to be made about the selection of number operations appropriate to particular problems. The precise activities in which the required skills are to be developed must be identified clearly, as well as the necessary time allocations. The need to reduce inconsistencies in approach between teachers and across different subjects and year groups will be vital if progression in numeracy skills is to be established and implemented consistently throughout Key Stages 3 and 4.

Clear guidance on the role of the calculator will be required, with more teaching of the use of the range of functions and further consideration of the use of scientific and graphical calculators. Teachers must understand when calculators should and should not be used, with more guidance given as to what constitutes sensible use, rather than the random or pupil-directed use. Many pupils now have scientific calculators which are cheap and readily accessible. The capability of these calculators has increased, but often is not used. For example, the random number generators are rarely used in place of dice or coins to extend pupils' understanding of randomness. Alternative modes of representation of numbers to introduce and contextualise standard forms or to discuss precision and approximations get little attention. Sophisticated tools are being used for relatively simple calculations such as 'look up' tables. Occasionally schools recommend a particular calculator and spend time during Key Stage 3 tutoring pupils on its use. This successfully prepares pupils for using a wide range of the available facilities in mathematics and other curriculum subjects. Finally, schools need to consider the use of computers to develop and enhance numeracy skills, which requires both greater access and planned and appropriate use of the available software.

Standards in information technology across the curriculum

Competence in IT (Chart 26) is a particular weakness in many schools. Pupils' IT capability is not as well developed as other key skills, and is poor in two in five schools. The 1995 National Curriculum Orders placed a general requirement on all subjects except PE to make appropriate use of IT in their teaching of the Programmes of Study. However, less detail was provided in most subjects than in the original Orders. The dearth of specific references to IT in the subject Orders has discouraged its use across the curriculum, particularly in Key Stage 4, and for many pupils this has resulted in a lack of coherent development of their IT competence. IT-related approaches had already begun to find their way into commercially published schemes of work in a number of subjects in the early 1990s and guidance was issued by SCAA and NCET in 1995/6 to illustrate how IT could be applied in each subject to strengthen teaching and learning. So far, only a minority of departments have incorporated such approaches in their schemes of work.

Extensive use is made of IT within GNVQ courses because the style of working, with its emphasis on coursework, particularly lends itself to the use of computers. Achievement in the use of IT has been good in approximately half of the GNVQ courses

inspected in recent years, with frequent examples of extremely effective use being made to enhance the quality of vocational assignments. However, in a quarter of courses attainment in IT skills has been unsatisfactory. This has often been because students were not encouraged to use a sufficiently wide range of software applications, so that the quite demanding key skills specifications were not fully met. In other cases, students had insufficient access to computers or to teachers with the necessary expertise and experience.

Raising standards of IT capability

Good planning of IT is invariably associated with pupils' success in both IT competency and subject understanding. An IT application requires thorough preparation by the class teacher to ensure maximum relevance and impact on learning the subject.

In a Year 10 GCSE geography class pupils presented their fieldwork investigations as wordprocessed documents which combined digitally scanned photographs with an electronic analysis of the data gathered, using a spreadsheet's graph drawing facility.

HMI INSPECTION, 1997

In a Year 9 science lesson a blank spreadsheet, already prepared by the teacher and stored on the computer network, had to be downloaded by pupils into their machines, and completed with data about the planets in the solar system. The pupils had been given a worksheet with addresses of Web sites containing data on the planets and the solar system. Pupils then had to access the data at these various Internet addresses in order to answer some of the

Chart 26 Pupils' competence in information technology in Key Stages 3 & 4 1996/97

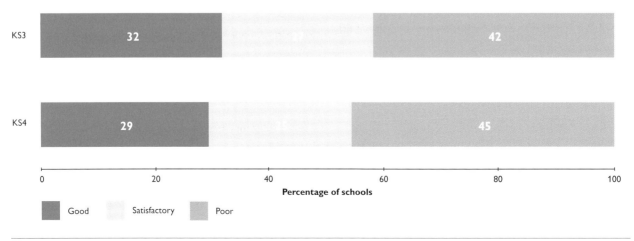

questions on the worksheet. They had to ascertain the values of certain variables, for example the size of a planet and its distance from the sun. They copied and pasted parts of the information gathered from the accessed Web sites into their spreadsheet, where these were considered relevant. Finally, pupils had to scrutinise and analyse the data so gathered, identifying patterns and relationships between variables, for instance, length of day and diameter of the planet or length of year, surface temperature and distance of the planet from the sun. The motivation for this work and the reality of the data greatly enhanced the achievement of the pupils.

HMI INSPECTION, 1997

Where pupils are given such opportunities to use IT applications regularly, they quickly develop familiarity with them and can acquire high levels of skill which allow productive use of the application in subject learning.

Such investment in preparing resources, however, is costly in teachers' time and requires a substantial commitment. Many teachers are not convinced that this produces sufficient benefits in terms of raising standards and therefore many subject departments remain largely untouched by IT. Even in departments which make some use of IT, many teachers lack awareness of what constitutes acceptable standards. For example, many English teachers have used computers for creating electronic newspapers, which pupils produce with desktop publishing software. Good English work is sometimes produced, and the pressure of working to a tight production timetable throws into sharp relief the advantages of text and image handling by computer. Often, however, expectations of layout and visual attractiveness of such class publications are not high. Opportunities are rarely taken for involving teachers from art and design departments in jointly supervising and assessing such work. The application of IT to designing and making a product, such as a newspaper, offers opportunities for teachers with different subject backgrounds to be seen to work together in order to raise expectations and standards overall.

A significant problem for the application of IT across the curriculum is access to appropriate IT facilities in the subject rooms as well as in specialist areas such as a computer room or library. A minority of secondary schools are very well resourced for IT. There are many more schools at the other end of the scale, where unsatisfactory equipment provision or accommodation hinder pupils from developing their skills in IT. Availability of sufficient equipment on its own, however, is no guarantee that the progress of pupils in IT will be good. For example, a number of schools have begun to invest in integrated learning systems to promote pupils' literacy and numeracy. Inspection has shown that much planning is required to ensure that use of such systems is consistent and well articulated with other work in English and mathematics, and that skills acquired are transferable.

2.6 Aspects of underachievement

The relative attainment of boys

In Key Stage 3 tests girls achieve considerably better results in English than boys, though there is little difference in mathematics and science. The performance of both girls and boys at GCSE has steadily improved in recent years, but girls' performance is significantly better and the gap between boys and girls shows no signs of narrowing (Chart 27). In 1997 the average points score for girls was 39.2 compared with 34.7 for boys. This difference of 4.5 points is equivalent to nearly an extra GCSE at grade C. Girls now perform better than boys in most subjects, often by very large margins: in English the girls have an advantage of 18.1 per cent at A*-C grades. Girls have caught up with boys in mathematics, and now gain proportionally more A*-C grades. At GCE A Level girls now have a slightly higher average points score than boys.

Inspection reports identify significant variations in attainment or progress between boys and girls in six out of ten schools. Concern about boys' achievement was a main finding in around one-quarter of reports. In some schools weaknesses in boys' attainment are linked to poor motivation and unsatisfactory attitudes to work. Many teachers identify some boys' relatively poor ability to organise themselves and their work as a crucial failing.

Chart 27 GCSE average points score for boys and girls 1992-1997

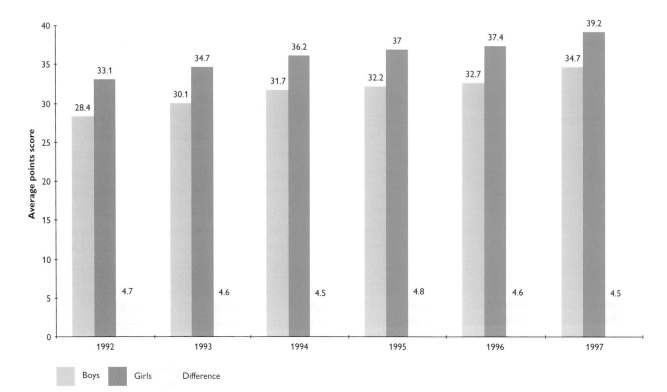

Boys   Girls   Difference

Schools, however, are generally better at identifying that they have a problem with boys' achievement or attitudes than they are at knowing what to do about it. They are often anxious that any action they might take could be to the detriment of the progress of girls: there might be a levelling down rather than a levelling up.

Despite these complexities, some schools have taken effective action to promote boys' attainment within the context of their efforts to improve overall standards.

*At **All Saints' Roman Catholic School, York,** in 1993 and 1994 the proportion of boys achieving five or more higher grades was above the national average, but the proportion of girls at this level was far above the average. The 1995 OFSTED inspection identified this disparity as the first Key Issue in the inspection report, giving further weight to the school's continuing work in this area. An already very strong system of pastoral support in Key Stage 4 was improved so as to give very close attention to pupils (usually boys) thought to be seriously underachieving in academic performance or behaviour: the Year Head now interviews these pupils and their parents, and agreed targets are established. In addition, every Year 10*

pupil's progress is compared with their potential as indicated by Year 7 and Year 9 standardised tests, and middle ability underachievers (again, mostly boys) are invited to the weekly after-school Achievers' Club to discuss their progress and to devise methods of improving it. A third group are seen regularly by senior management to review their self-identified priorities. Across this range of schemes staff find themselves focusing continually on some boys' classroom effort, homework diligence and general readiness for work. Very close links are maintained with the parents of the pupils supported, and all parents of Year 10 pupils have been informed both of the implications for GCSE success of the Key Stage 3 testing, and that boys are more likely to underperform in Key Stage 4. The school attempts to use assembly and tutorial time to encourage each pupil to "be your own person". A glossy school magazine celebrates a range of successes achieved by pupils and classes compete to acquire merits. Issues which challenge the ethos of the school are taken seriously: the headteacher suspended Year 10 lessons for an hour after an out-of-school fight between two boys, in order to convene a forum, attended voluntarily by half the year group, at which the implications of the fight were discussed openly. The school has now shifted from its immediate response to the OFSTED report of devising specific strategies to raise boys' achievement to a rather broader approach which attempts to raise achievement overall, but whilst maintaining an awareness of boys' particular needs.

HMI INSPECTION, 1997

Such effective programmes to improve boys' achievement are planned carefully; the schools recognise that the performance of either sex at GCSE can change considerably from year to year and so they review achievement over several years to inform their action. Initiatives to boost pupils' progress are most successful where they are based on evidence to show that the individuals targeted are capable of doing better; this requires the use of assessment data to estimate potential. Additionally, some schools have analysed the relationships between gender, ethnicity, and ability, to determine whether their focus should be on all boys, or just boys from one ethnic group or ability group. Some schools look carefully at a range of measures of performance in order to judge where intervention is best justified; others have restricted their initiatives to a group of pupils estimated to be on the GCSE C/D borderline.

Overall, there is considerable evidence that the attainment of some boys begins to fall off more sharply during Year 8. Schools which concentrate on what is essentially remedial action in Key Stage 4 are likely to be acting too late to have a major impact. More schools need to monitor carefully the relative progress of boys and girls, and take early action to improve boys' diligence, basic skills, and commitment to academic success.

The attainment of pupils from ethnic minorities

The pattern of relative achievement of different ethnic groups is complex, not least because of the interaction of ethnicity with the factors of social class and gender[3]. The lack of national data on the achievement of pupils from different ethnic groups makes it difficult to form a clear overall picture.

Evidence from small-scale studies, however, indicates that African Caribbean pupils are relatively less successful than their Asian and white peers, with African Caribbean boys in particular having the lowest rate of improvement. In attempting to gauge the relative standards of achievement of Bangladeshi, Indian and Pakistani pupils issues of location, social background and gender are of considerable significance. At best, pupils from each of these groups, but particularly pupils of Indian origin, achieve excellent results often leading to university entrance. In contrast, Pakistani and Bangladeshi pupils are less likely to achieve five or more higher grade GCSEs and more likely to leave school without any qualifications. There are, however, exceptions to these general patterns. An example is in the London Borough of Tower Hamlets, where Bangladeshi pupils now achieve higher average GCSE scores than both white and African Caribbean pupils. Nevertheless, although the situation is improving, large numbers of minority ethnic pupils continue to underachieve.

The achievement of Traveller children is a further cause for concern. Relatively little data is available on the attainment of these pupils, but in general their achievement is unsatisfactory. Poor standards are exacerbated by patterns of irregular attendance, although this is improving slowly. It is estimated that as many as 10,000 Traveller children are not even registered with a school.

Many pupils with English as an additional language make good progress at school and some attain high standards. However, many are held back by their inability to gain full access to the curriculum and do not achieve their full potential, particularly in subjects which are very dependent on English. Specialised support teaching can be very beneficial to these pupils. Where support is of good quality, and is not withdrawn too early, good progress is often made once proficiency in English has improved.

Schools and LEAs have become increasingly conscious of the differential performance of ethnic minority pupils, and some have developed specific strategies to raise their achievement. A starting point has frequently been the closer evaluation of data to identify the specific patterns of achievement in a school or LEA area. In a West Midlands school, for example, ethnic monitoring confirmed that there was a marked difference in performance between different ethnic and gender groups, in that only 25 per cent of African

---

3 *Recent Research on the Achievements of Ethnic Minority Pupils*, D Gillborn and C Gipps, OFSTED Reviews of Research, HMSO, 1996.

Caribbean boys gained 5+ A*-C compared to 77 per cent of Asian boys and 42 per cent of white boys. The school would have been in a better position to pursue this analysis further if the category 'Asian' had been subdivided to show the performance of Indian, Pakistani, and Bangladeshi pupils.

Such data can be useful in targeting initiatives and resources. General strategies include homework clubs, often run by language support teachers, which can make a major contribution to improving pupils' confidence and attainment. Similarly, the use of target setting and personal action plans can provide pupils with manageable learning steps with periodic review used to ascertain whether the targets have been met. Some specific projects targeted at African Caribbean pupils seek to improve motivation as well as offering individual support.

Unsurprisingly, strategies for raising the achievement of ethnic minority pupils are also good for raising the achievement of all pupils. The **St Thomas the Apostle College** is a popular, multi-ethnic boys' school in a disadvantaged part of South London. One-half of the pupils are of African Caribbean heritage; their reading skills on entry are generally low, as are those of many other pupils. This is an improving school: the number of pupils gaining five or more higher grade GCSEs rose steadily from 21 per cent in 1993 to 53 per cent in 1997; the African Caribbean group of pupils achieved an even greater rise in achievement than the overall cohort.

The school has a strong ethos and gives high priority to its corporate activities. It is keen to strengthen pupils' self-esteem: it gives pupils a range of opportunities for achieving success and emphasises their achievements at prize days. Its links with parents are good, particularly in its attempts to enlist parental support in monitoring their sons' homework and in helping them with it where they can. The school keeps parents well informed of its initiatives and policies.

The school's current improvement initiatives derive from a senior management with clear vision for the future. A Head of Research, Development and Teaching post has been created within the senior management team to review classroom work across the school and to

devise staff development strategies for weaker departments. The acknowledged need to raise standards of literacy, and aspects of numeracy, has led to the establishment of specific programmes across the school, using Basic Skills Agency funding. Staff have identified key vocabulary essential to each subject and the teaching emphasises this knowledge; reading support is available for pupils at lunchtimes; numeracy competitions are held for tutor groups. Additional staff are employed to work intensively with Year 9 boys whose progress is very weak. Pupils in Year 11 have a lengthy meeting with a person employed by, but external to, the school to discuss action planning and to identify ways forward in preparing for examinations. The school has begun to collate the outcomes of these discussions and to analyse them systematically to see if any trends are emerging for particular subjects or groups of pupils.

The timetable has been extended to support pupils nearing GCSE examinations: they have opportunities to attend after-school lessons on examination techniques and half-term revision sessions. The mathematics department helps 70 per cent of pupils to set action plans for their development in the subject; this department achieves good standards at GCSE.

Senior staff are now concerned to monitor pupils' progress more carefully from entry to GCSE. The school is introducing a broader range of standardised testing in the belief that the tests currently used may under-estimate the potential of pupils from some ethnic groups. The school intends to use the new data to evaluate the effectiveness of its current initiatives and to determine whether the needs identified, and analysed according to ethnic grouping, are indeed being met.

HMI INSPECTION, 1996

Some schools are able to point to areas of general improvement as a result of their initiatives. These include improvements in attendance, behaviour and overall GCSE entries, as well as upward movement of minority ethnic pupils through sets and rising attainment in the GCSE. In other cases, however, statistics indicate a stubborn lack of improvement despite such initiatives.

The performance of schools in disadvantaged circumstances

Taking eligibility for free school meals as the indicator, Chart 28 shows that there is a strong association between socio-economic disadvantage and pupil attainment. In those schools where there are low levels of disadvantage the pupils on average score almost twice as many GCSE points as those in schools where pupils are the most disadvantaged. Nevertheless, there has been steady improvement in schools across the full range with the biggest improvements in the most disadvantaged and in the least disadvantaged schools.

The scatter chart shows the wide range of attainment in different schools in the 1996 GCSE examination (Chart 29). Each point on the graph represents an individual school. As disadvantage increases, average points scores fall. The inverse link between the level of entitlement for free school meals in a school and the proportion of pupils attaining higher grade GCSEs is well established. Particular schools and LEAs consistently appear at the lower end of norm-referenced performance tables. However, for schools with the same level of disadvantage average points scores differ widely. For example, schools with one-fifth of pupils eligible for free school meals (the national average) have average points scores ranging from 20 to 45 points.

Schools in disadvantaged areas often receive pupils who have well below the national average attainment on entry. Additionally, some of these schools serve populations that are very mobile and as a result lose and admit many pupils during the course of a year, increasing problems of educational discontinuity. Some of the pupils admitted may well have experienced difficulties in their school careers, in particular having been

Chart 28 Schools' performance 1993-6: average GCSE points score against free school meals

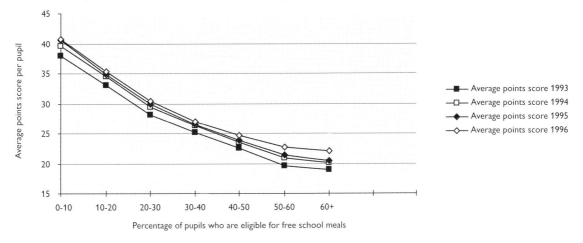

Chart 29 School performance: average GCSE points score against eligibility for free school meals, 1995/6

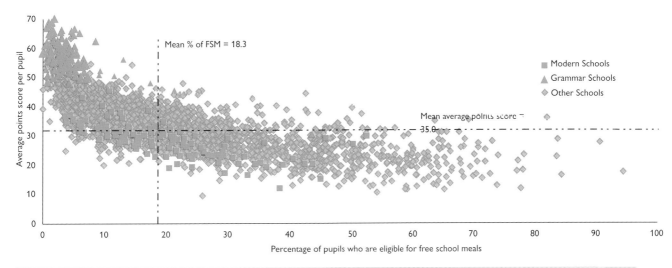

excluded from other schools. Other pupils may be newly arrived in Britain, with little or no English. Some of these pupils who are refugees may be traumatised, and others may lack any previous experience of school.

It is notable that schools with the highest eligibility for free school meals have made the greatest proportional improvement, but they have been more successful in establishing a consistent pattern of improvement in lower GCSE grades, and thus in average points score, than in higher GCSE grades. In 1996, of the one hundred schools with the highest eligibility for free school meals (all above 58 per cent compared to a national average of 18.3 per cent), only three, all girls' schools, achieved the national GCSE average points score of 35 or more. Even though sixty-two of these schools had rates of improvement above the national average rate, they have so far largely failed to narrow the absolute gap in performance between more and less advantaged schools.

Schools which have demonstrated sustained improvement in standards of achievement have generally also brought about improvements in the school as a whole. In particular, initiatives in the management of the school, in teaching, in the curriculum, in shaping pupils' attitudes to school including attendance and approaches to learning, and in the involvement of parents have been important elements in school improvement. Two schools, Stoke Newington and Litherland, in the contrasting locations of Hackney and Sefton, provide examples of successful approaches to school improvement.

Stoke Newington School in Hackney has many of the characteristics of disadvantage with 59 per cent eligibility for free school meals. Sixty-six per cent of the pupils are from minority ethnic groups including 24 per cent who are Turkish/Kurdish, some of whom are refugees. Over 30 different first languages are spoken at the school. The school receives pupils across the ability range, but with a higher proportion of average to less able students. At the time of the OFSTED inspection in 1994 the school was taking a large number of mid-term entrants including non-English speakers, pupils with learning difficulties, and more than 50 pupils who had either been permanently excluded from their last school or had left to avoid exclusion.

*The 1994 OFSTED report on **Stoke Newington School** commented on the improving performance of the school, but indicated variation in standards by subjects, by minority ethnic group, and by gender. Even so, the report stated that 'planning in the school is good. There are systems and structures in place with due regard to curriculum, management and finance, aimed at raising achievement. A range of other indicators suggest a firm determination on the part of staff to improve the opportunities of pupils at Stoke Newington School.' Since that time, the number of pupils achieving 5 or more GCSE grades A*-C has risen to 30.5 per cent. An analysis undertaken by the school shows that the average points score of all pupils is 32.2, and that of pupils eligible for free schools meals is 30.0, a figure significantly above that normally found.*

Several factors can be seen to have contributed to this improvement. The development plan is a key instrument, with the first objective 'to inspire and empower all of our students to fulfil their full potential'. To this end specific objectives are defined with targets and performance indicators. Many of these are whole school targets including literacy and homework, but there are also targets for planning, teaching and assessment in individual departments.

A focus on teaching methods has involved whole school discussion of differentiation and a grouping policy. The predominant number of boys over girls in the school has caused the school to create some classes of boys only. There is some setting, but the tendency of setting to stratify the school by ethnicity has led to a focus on group needs within classes. Thus, for example, African Caribbean pupils were identified as underachievers and so their progress was monitored in various ways, including classroom observation, to identify effective and ineffective teaching strategies for this particular group of pupils as a basis for future lesson planning and classroom management. The average points score for this group in 1997 was 27.8, although boys continue to do less well than girls.

A focus on learning has led to the development of closer academic monitoring and mentoring of pupils. Heads of year have been given the role of curriculum leaders. The role of tutors has been enhanced to give them a responsibility for oversight of pupils' progress. In order to monitor progress effectively termly assessments are to be made of all pupils. These will be used with tutors to establish tangible short-term targets; will be sent to parents; and will provide data for monitoring the performance of girls and boys and different ethnic groups. The database will also contain information from Key Stage 2 to act as a baseline for measuring progress; it will also provide information on relative performance across subjects, and it is intended to use this to target Section 11 support.

HMI INSPECTION, 1997

Litherland High School, Sefton serves an area of high unemployment, and 45 per cent of pupils are eligible for free school meals. Fewer than 1 per cent of the pupils are from minority ethnic groups. The intake is heavily skewed towards the less able, but the full range of ability is represented. A new headteacher was appointed in 1991. At that time the school suffered from low morale. The proportion of pupils gaining higher grade GCSEs was 17 per cent. The intake of the school was at its lowest for a decade; vandalism was a severe and persistent problem; and the school was regularly subject to break-ins and arson.

The school was inspected in 1993. Inspectors commented on the positive ethos of the school, the high levels of pupil motivation, and the good quality of teaching. The report concluded:

Under positive and imaginative leadership, the school has developed a shared vision and sense of purpose. There is a clear set of priorities for developments in the immediate future...The governors are involved in many aspects of the life of the school and their decision to refurbish and redecorate most of the school has provided an attractive learning environment. There has been a major investment in information technology and pupils have the opportunity to use this as a tool for learning in many subject areas.

OFSTED INSPECTION REPORT, 1993

In 1997, when the school was re-inspected, attainment remained below average, although the number of pupils gaining 5 GCSEs at grades A* to G was in line with the national average and the average points score was improving faster than the national average. The 1997 report comments on several features of the school which have been significant in its improvement.

Almost all the teaching (98 per cent) is of satisfactory standard with over half the lessons being good or very good. This is a higher figure than in the last inspection. The teaching of pupils with special needs is nearly always good. Teachers plan well and their management of pupils is good, relying on mature and well developed relationships. The use of good resources, including information technology, by teachers in many lessons across the curriculum is very effective.

Recent improvements to the accommodation... and to resources generally have added to the effectiveness of teaching and to pupil motivation. The library has been transformed into an excellent resource...and is now the hub of much research activity by pupils.

There is still work to be done, but the opening paragraph of the report makes clear what a school can achieve against the odds.

Litherland...is a school with significant strengths and few weaknesses. There is dynamic leadership. Pupils are proud of the school and this is reflected in the way they relate to staff and to each other. They are well motivated and most of them are making good progress in a positive climate for learning.

OFSTED INSPECTION REPORT, 1997

The need for sustained and consistent action if standards are to be raised in disadvantaged schools was emphasised in the OFSTED publication *Access and Achievement in Urban Education*[4], which concluded that

> *the unique blend of difficulties, and also of strengths, in each institution and each locality means that strategies have to be tailored to need, well managed, and sustained over long periods of continuing educational change... the most successful initiatives occur when a particular need is precisely identified, strategies are designed and resources deployed specifically to meet it, and sustainable structures and processes are put in place.*

Success over time brings with it greater confidence on the part of the pupils and teachers in the school, and of parents considering where to send their children. Schools which are unpopular are vulnerable. Full schools are much more likely to be able to build on success and sustain their improvement.

Numbers of disadvantaged schools find difficulty in sustaining improvements in the proportion of higher grade GCSE results over a number of years, and often experience a switchback of rises and falls. For many schools serving areas of disadvantage, success is short-lived, with the gains of one year lost in the next. The OFSTED publication *Access and Achievement*, the 1993 National Commission on Education Report, and the 1995 House of Commons Select Committee on Education report *Performance in City Schools* have all pointed up the difficulties of consistently raising educational standards in disadvantaged areas. As shown in the examples cited above, some schools have in themselves the capacity to bring about improvement. Beyond this, the report of the National Commission argued that some schools are unlikely to improve without external support, and that 'a concerted national policy' would offer the prospect of raising standards in these areas, and might include a new approach to funding, attracting good teachers and encouraging local innovation. The present government's proposal to establish 'Education Action Zones' promises just such an approach.

[4] *Access and Achievement in Urban Education*, HMSO, 1993.

Schools requiring special measures

A feature of OFSTED's work that has attracted particular public interest is the action taken to deal with 'failing schools'. Between 1993 and 1997, 85 secondary schools which were failing to provide an acceptable standard of education for their pupils were placed in special measures. Additionally, around ten per cent of secondary schools were identified by OFSTED inspectors as having serious weaknesses.

Most of the schools in special measures are in urban or inner city areas, often serving socially and economically disadvantaged communities. Mixed schools predominate; there are no girls' schools in special measures, but three boys' schools. Although the schools vary in size, their roll is usually smaller than the national average and often falling. The proportion of pupils entitled to free school meals is frequently well above the national average; only one school has less than the average proportion of pupils entitled to free school meals. A high proportion of these schools has an intake which is ethnically diverse, although there are also some mainly white schools.

Standards in these schools are low and there is significant under-achievement. Low levels of literacy are common to virtually all the schools, and difficulty with reading and writing hinders progress across the curriculum. Levels of numeracy are also low: in the Key Stage 3 national tests, results in mathematics are, on average, just below half the national average. In GCSE examinations the average points score of 20 is well below the national average of 35. Very few pupils attain five or more higher grades at GCSE and almost three times as many pupils do not achieve a graded result compared with other schools. The proportion of pupils attaining five or more graded results is closer to, but still below, the national average. In about one-fifth of the schools the progress of bilingual pupils is a concern.

Attendance often falls below 85 per cent despite strenuous efforts by the school; raising levels usually proves time-consuming and the effort by the school is not matched by the pupils and their parents. Standards of behaviour are often satisfactory. However, in a small but significant number of schools, behaviour in classrooms and around the building is poor and pupils are vulnerable: here, inconsistencies in teachers' approach to behaviour management from lesson to lesson gives pupils too much scope for disruption. Levels of exclusion are, on average, three times the national average. Even where behaviour is good, pupils' attitudes and willingness to work are often poor.

The schools share common weaknesses in the quality of education provided. Leadership and management have been weak in the years or months before the inspection and in some cases continue to be so. There is insufficient emphasis on raising standards of achievement or on ensuring that the requirements of the National Curriculum are met. Systems for monitoring the quality of teaching and the performance of pupils, and for assessing the strengths and weaknesses of the school, are inadequate. There is also a high level of unsatisfactory teaching. Weaknesses centre around poor planning of the lessons and pupils' work. Far too often the teaching fails to capitalise on pupils' positive attitudes towards their work. Often the tasks are not appropriate for the pupils' age and ability, teachers' expectations are too low and the pace of work in many lessons is too slow.

For schools to improve from such a low ebb, four prerequisites are necessary:

● accepting the judgement;

● knowing what to do;

● knowing how to go about it;

● securing the support of all parties: the governors, teachers, pupils, parents and the LEA.

Seven of these schools have improved and are now providing a satisfactory standard of education; they were subject to special measures for between two and three years, far less than the five-to seven-year period which was cited by some researchers as the length of time required to turn a school round. The majority of schools in special measures have made and continue to make reasonable progress in implementing their action plans and remedying their weaknesses. The schools that have made most progress, most quickly, have resolved to work together to tackle their weaknesses and have ensured that everyone connected with the school is determined that it will succeed.

All of the seven secondary schools which have successfully negotiated the route out of special measures are in urban settings with higher than average proportions of pupils entitled to free school meals. Two are mainly white schools; three have more than 50 per cent of bilingual pupils. All have high numbers of pupils with special educational needs, but one has a particularly high proportion. In this respect they are no different from the majority of schools in special measures.

Four of the seven appointed a new headteacher early on in the process; all made significant changes in the management structure. Changes were made to improve the quality of teachers' planning and the curriculum, and rigorous systems for monitoring the quality of teaching were implemented, but not always sufficiently early to provide the impetus for rapid change.

The support given by the LEA in the six maintained schools played an important part in the schools' development. The appointment of additional governors with specific expertise helped to refocus the schools' resources and energies. The provision of advice and consultancy, particularly in preparing the action plans, monitoring the schools' progress towards their targets, and evaluating the quality of teaching, was a crucial factor. Provision of significant funds for staff development programmes and substantial alterations and repairs to buildings made major contributions to improving one school. One of the seven schools is grant maintained, and this school gained additional governors appointed by the Secretary of State; senior managers sought support from outside the school, but it took longer than other schools to produce an appropriate action plan and get the recovery underway.

Where schools have failed to make sufficiently rapid improvement it is because of a failure to address a number of key problems, some of which are deep rooted. Firm leadership is vital for improvement. In the majority of schools where weaknesses are identified in leadership and management these issues are addressed very soon after the inspection, often involving a change of headship. However, in a significant minority of schools the period of special measures has seen several changes of headteacher and it is only when a permanent appointment is made that improvement becomes secure. Also, initially, the governing bodies of these schools are usually well-intentioned but lack sufficient knowledge and expertise to assist with strategic planning and evaluation.

Where teachers do not recognise the need to change, or where the impact of professional development is low, the quality of teaching remains unsatisfactory. Schools which do not have the internal resources or expertise to monitor teaching effectively are in a weak position to identify targets for improvement and insist that they are met. Recruitment of specialist teachers presents an added difficulty, especially in shortage subjects such as design and technology and modern foreign languages. In a significant number of schools where recruitment is difficult, a reliance on agency and supply teachers affects the quality of teaching and the continuity of pupils' education.

A major obstacle to raising standards in these schools is the low literacy level of the intake, yet there is often no suitably structured and organised specialist teaching programme to identify and remedy these difficulties. Teachers lack the expertise to deal with these problems. Although some special educational needs teachers are adept at dealing with pupils who need specific help with reading and writing, the numbers of pupils involved and the depth of their need is too great for one or two teachers to tackle alone.

Eleven secondary schools with particular difficulties were designated by the Secretary of State to be in need of additional help to speed up progress. They have subsequently moved more rapidly towards closure or recovery. Six schools have closed.

3 LEADERSHIP AND MANAGEMENT

3.1 The quality of leadership

Good leadership and management are fundamental to the success of a school. At least three-quarters of secondary schools enjoy good leadership; in over half of schools the leadership is very good or outstanding. In many schools the governing body, headteacher and senior management team work together to provide clear direction. These schools show commitment to high achievement, create an effective learning environment and promote high standards of behaviour and good relationships. The introduction of the National Curriculum and national tests, regular inspection of all schools, published performance tables, and more recently, benchmarking and target setting, have brought a sharper focus on standards in the vast majority of secondary schools. Even so there remains a significant minority of secondary schools which fail to provide an adequate quality of education and where standards are unacceptably low. Management in one in ten secondary schools fails to promote the ethos and sense of purpose that underpin school self-improvement. The number of schools with poor leadership has declined from 14 per cent since the first year of the inspection cycle to 10 per cent, and those with very poor leadership

from 6 per cent to 3 per cent. Although low, these figures are a cause for serious concern because of the clear link between ineffective leadership and a poor quality of education leading to inappropriately low standards. The initiative to require training for all new headteachers is to be welcomed as part of a renewed drive to raise the quality of leadership and management.

The day-to-day management, administration, financial controls, internal and external communications, and working relationships in schools are generally good. School self-review has improved since the beginning of the OFSTED inspection cycle but it is still the weakest aspect of management in nearly one in three of all secondary schools; it is good or better in only two in five schools. Where there are weaknesses, they include longer-term planning, the evaluation of their own cost-effectiveness, the setting of priorities, the consistency of the implementation of plans and policies, and most importantly, the reviewing of the school's work through effective monitoring and evaluation.

Secondary schools are complex organisations and the majority have coped well with the changes introduced by educational legislation over the past decade. Most show many strengths in ensuring they give value for money. Both LEA maintained and grant maintained schools have considerable discretion over how they manage their affairs and deploy their resources, and the best use their allocated funding and resources efficiently and effectively to achieve both high academic standards and a high quality of education. Nearly two out of three schools give at least good value for money, with one in three judged very good or

Chart 30   The leadership of the school

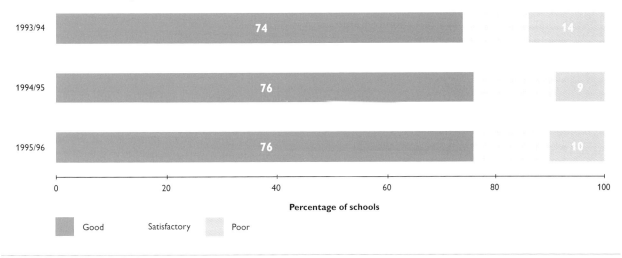

1993/94	74 ... 14
1994/95	76 ... 9
1995/96	76 ... 10

Percentage of schools

Good   Satisfactory   Poor

excellent. However, schools are rarely successful in all they undertake, and the value for money of one in four schools, although satisfactory, leaves much room for improvement. One in ten schools currently gives poor value for money.

The daily administration and organisation in nine out of ten schools are good or very good. This provides an ordered context within which good teaching and learning can take place. The financial control and administration of delegated budgets are now firmly established as part of schools' organisation and administration. Good systems and procedures for financial control are evident in the vast majority of schools, with less than 3 per cent experiencing difficulties. Communications both internally between staff and pupils, and externally with parents and the wider community, are rarely less than satisfactory. More open enrolment and parental choice have given rise to the production of many high-quality prospectuses and schools' aims are generally clearly stated. Usually, parents are kept informed about the school's activities and achievements, though there is less openness about targets for improvement and in only a few schools are parents consulted about priorities and planned developments. The level of activity and commitment shown by senior managers in schools to ensuring effective administration is often greater than that given to enhancing the quality of education provided and securing the highest possible standards of achievement.

3.2 The role of the head-teacher and governors

Most successful schools benefit from leadership of the headteacher and governors which is strong, consultative and has clear vision. Over the last decade the demands upon headteachers have grown and many have risen to the challenge. For example, the inspection report for **Hampstead School, Camden** states:

Hampstead is a good school with many strengths, where the good quality of teaching is the major factor in contributing to high standards...The headteacher provides strong, purposeful leadership and clear educational direction for the school. The school's ethos

reflects a strong commitment, not only to high academic attainment, but also to the establishment of an environment in which staff and students are learning together and achieving together. The headteacher is well supported by the senior executive team and by the governing body which takes a very active role in the life of the school. Through attachment to subject departments and year groups, governors have increased their understanding of how the school functions and have offered their expertise to assist developments. Consultation procedures are good, and the governing body operates effectively.

The high quality of development planning is a strength of the school and makes a significant contribution to the quality of education. A three-year development plan was produced after extensive consultation with staff, parents, students and governors, and evaluation of the school's progress towards implementation of previous plans. This wide consultative process identified both strengths and weaknesses of the school. The three-year plan focuses on appropriate whole-school objectives that are addressed through shorter-term action plans. These action plans are very thorough. They specify staff responsibilities and have clear, manageable targets with deadlines for completion, and are costed.

The school has also set realistic targets for improving examination results, increasing attendance and raising the number of students in the sixth form. Good progress is being made towards the objectives set for this year...Departmental action plans are of similar high quality. Priorities for departments to address are linked to whole school objectives and most targets are being met effectively.

Procedures for support and monitoring of teaching have been developed through a programme of lesson observation managed by a task group of teachers with varied length of experience and a variety of subject expertise.

There is considerable scope for this group to

identify and disseminate good practice, and to make recommendations for further development. ...Other task groups, which have a subsidiary purpose in giving all staff the opportunity to contribute to decision-making, have explored relevant school issues such as curriculum and day structure, IT development, and the school environment.

OFSTED INSPECTION REPORT, 1996

The relationship between the headteacher and the governing body is a significant factor in the success of many schools. Despite some difficulties in responding to all that is required of them, the role of governors in maintaining and improving the quality of education and securing high standards of achievement is becoming established in an increasing number of schools. In a significant number, however, this is still not the case. The governors of effective secondary schools often give very positive support to their school's professional staff and are heavily committed to the school's success. Governors have gained in confidence in their knowledge of the National Curriculum and in their capacity to contribute to school initiatives to monitor and raise standards.

Governing bodies are increasingly aware of their role in strategic planning and gaining expertise in monitoring progress towards the priorities identified in the school development plan. In the most effective schools the governing body has already begun to review the school's achievements against agreed performance indicators, both quantitative and qualitative. Increased involvement in the analysis of examination results has begun to focus attention upon monitoring of individual subject departments and of their teaching. The assessment of the performance of individual headteachers and deputy headteachers against

agreed criteria is now a statutory duty of governing bodies (DfEE Circular 4/96). Through a better understanding of the strengths and weaknesses in the management and leadership of their school and the knowledge of what makes an effective school, headteachers and their governors should be better placed to identify targets and areas for development for themselves and be strongly placed to provide the quality of leadership necessary to achieve these.

Many of the duties which governors undertake are complex and require time, managerial skill and specialised knowledge, altogether amounting to a great deal of pressure on a group of volunteers. Nevertheless, if the intentions of the legislation are to be carried out, governors must tackle these tasks. All LEAs are providing governing body training, but this is not always taken up, leaving governors less well equipped than would otherwise be the case for the tasks they face.

3.3 School aims

How far the aims contribute to the direction and work of a school varies and not all schools review their aims on a regular basis. Most schools, however, formulate their aims carefully and promote them in the daily life of the school; in the majority of schools the prevalent ethos, a reflection of the school's aims, provides a favourable climate for learning and for pupils' development. Section One of the Education Act 1988 places a statutory responsibility upon schools to provide a balanced and broadly-based curriculum which "promotes the spiritual, moral, cultural, mental and physical development of pupils at the school and of society and prepares pupils for the opportunities, responsibilities and experiences of adult life". The vast majority of schools take these responsibilities seriously; they are often explicit in school aims, and are implicit in their ethos.

Chart 31 The implementation of schools' aims, values and policies

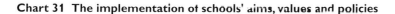

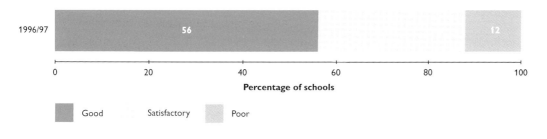

| 1996/97 | 56 | | 12 |

Percentage of schools

Good   Satisfactory   Poor

Claverham Community College in East Sussex, expresses its aims as follows:

To help its pupils:

- to develop fully their individual academic, emotional, physical and social potential;

- to develop self-respect, self-discipline, adaptability, concern for others and the ability to live as independent adults while at the same time contributing to the community;

- to acquire insight, knowledge, skills and practical abilities and the will to use them in the following areas of experience: scientific, technological, mathematical, linguistic, aesthetic, creative, commercial, moral, spiritual, economic, political and recreational;

- to appreciate human achievement of every kind;

- to acquire understanding of the social, economic and political order and a reasoned set of values, attitudes and beliefs;

- to prepare for their adult lives at home, work, leisure and in society as consumers and citizens.

The school's inspection report identified some areas of school life for further development, but provided clear evidence of success in putting its aims into practice.

Standards of achievement were average to high in 80 per cent of lessons... Pupils are mostly well motivated, anxious to make progress...Excellent classroom relationships, the dedication of staff and good behaviour of the pupils form the basis for an effective learning environment....Pupils respect each other's property and are taught the difference between right and wrong. They respond to a variety of needs within the community and are given opportunities to take responsibility...Pupils behave well...are polite and respond well to visitors and teachers...There is an even balance between self-discipline and teacher direction....The college promotes equal opportunities for all racial groups. The college prepares young people for an ethnically and culturally diverse society...The college aims...place the development of academic, emotional, physical and social potential of pupils as a priority.

There is a strong and shared sense of purpose in the College and these priorities are being met.

OFSTED INSPECTION REPORT, 1994

Effective schools define clear aims and attainable goals which have been developed through consultation with governors, staff, parents and the wider community served by the school.

In South Dartmoor Community College, Devon, the staff and governors sought to involve the whole community in deciding upon the aims for the College and how these might be realised. Meetings were held in both the College and a variety of other locations across the College's catchment area in order to ensure that all members of the community could take part in the debate. Draft aims were formulated and again shared with the community before being formally adopted and implemented by the College.

HMI INSPECTION, 1996

Aims act as a starting point for development planning and an instrument for measuring the success of the school over and above relative success in terms of academic measures such as GCSE performance tables. Aims are therefore crucial in determining the direction of the school and in demonstrating what it stands for. The implementation of aims and values has improved: it was judged to be good or very good in over half of schools and satisfactory in almost one third more. However, in nearly one in eight schools aims were judged to be tokenistic, vague and ultimately not mirrored in the life of the school or featured among its priorities. In the great majority of the better schools the senior management has clear responsibilities and works together cohesively as a team to deliver the agreed aims with a focus on improving achievement. However, in the one school in ten where leadership is weak there is little vision or sense of purpose, and senior managers are ineffective in establishing and implementing school policies; in most cases poor leadership is associated with low standards of work and behaviour and with inadequate progress by pupils.

Whole school aims often relate to the personal, social and academic achievement of pupils and enable subject departments to formulate curricular aims and objectives which reflect those of the school as a whole: better departments evaluate their progress in achieving them. New head-teachers are well placed to reassess the impact of the school's aims and some have taken advantage of the process of reviewing aims to create the sense of direction and purpose necessary to support improvement.

*In the **Kings of Wessex School in Somerset** the aims were reviewed through consultation with staff which helped to establish collegiality and a common, shared ethos and enabled departments to reconsider their aims and their contribution to the work of the school as a whole. Objectives which took into account maximising pupil achievement were turned into action through guidance given on schemes of work and policies for assessment and marking. Subject departments were expected to develop strategies for monitoring and evaluating their work and their progress in meeting the objectives derived from the aims: an emphasis upon sustaining improvement in the achievement of pupils was beginning to be established.*

HMI INSPECTION, 1996

Effective schools not only place importance upon aims such as 'to reach the highest academic achievement', but establish specific objectives to translate their aims into action in order to enhance pupils' academic, social and personal development.

3.4 Planning for school development

The capacity of schools to manage change and maintain a clear sense of direction varies widely. Schools have had to set their own priorities within a context of policy changes at a national level, including the curriculum, funding, governance and inspection. Effective schools have managed this well, and are skilled at planning to achieve their goals. Overall, schools' ability to plan has improved: three in five plan well or very well. However, nearly one in five remains ineffective. In many schools much greater attention is now paid to planning so that new policies and practices can evolve as required. However, a few schools attempt to change too much too quickly, priorities are not sufficiently established and the co-ordination of different policy strands is poor and leads to patchy implementation. The weakness of many school development plans is that they do not consider from the outset how progress is to be monitored. Too many plans are not developed on the basis of a thorough evaluation of previous progress. Good school development planning depends on wide consultation with staff and governors, carefully chosen and prioritised objectives, a realistic number of achievable targets, and a mechanism that enables progress to be monitored. The involvement of governors in establishing a strategic view of a school's direction, and its progress or performance in meeting its goals, still needs to improve in many schools.

In most schools where curriculum planning is good, the school development plan is supported by

Chart 32 Planning and priority setting

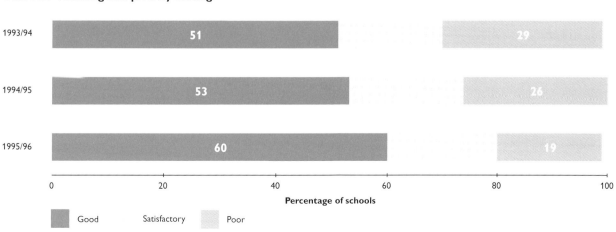

effective departmental strategic planning, and regular review procedures enable all staff to contribute to planning and policy-making.

*In **King Edward VI Upper School**, a 13-18 school in **Bury St Edmunds**, a comprehensive school development plan is drafted annually in the spring term, largely by the senior management team. The draft is discussed by faculties, who evaluate previous performance and check continuity with previous years. Using an in-service training day at the beginning of the summer term, time is given to all staff to discuss the development plan and for faculties to formulate their targets. Following formal discussion with the governing body and their agreement the plan is implemented in the autumn term with review of progress scheduled for the beginning of the spring term and further opportunities for heads of faculty to raise issues.*

HMI INSPECTION, 1996

Good subject development planning takes account of both departmental and whole school priorities. The senior management team ensures that an understanding of priorities is shared at different levels of management in the school. Many schools arrange for regular meetings between middle managers and linked members of the senior management team. These meetings enable some monitoring of departmental or pastoral team progress and often lead to a review of departmental practice in line with whole school policy. An increasing number of schools require departments to write an annual report which records their achievements and progress. This form of monitoring is most effective when linked to the setting of clear targets and where evidence is drawn from classroom observation.

In some schools departmental reviews are identified as part of the school development plan. On occasions formal reviews are carried out by subject inspectors under contract as an alternative to the senior management of the school. This is likely to occur where there are special circumstances, such as preparation for in-service training on classroom approaches, where a department is under-performing, or where senior managers do not have the required subject expertise.

3.5 Financial planning and management of resources

The effective management of schools makes sure that available resources - financial, staffing and accommodation - are targeted on achieving the highest possible quality of education. Efficiency in the use of resources has improved: it was good or very good overall in two-thirds of schools inspected. It was poor or very poor in one in nine schools.

The effect of making schools directly responsible for a much greater proportion of their budgets has undoubtedly been an improvement in financial planning. It is satisfactory or better in almost nine schools out of ten, and at best is integral with whole school strategic planning. Governing bodies often make an important contribution to strategic planning through the committee structure, with individual governors offering support based on their own professional expertise. Some schools, however, have not found it easy to cost their planned developments and fail to link financial planning with whole school and subject development planning. Where financial planning is good the costing of development plans is based on the evaluation of current provision and so enables accurate budget projection. Such detailed monitoring and review are rare and the practice could be adopted more widely to improve the financial efficiency of schools more generally.

Schools receive widely varying levels of funding. This has, unsurprisingly, a significant effect on the quality of teaching materials and resources for learning. Some of these variations can be explained by factors such as London weighting or a high proportion of pupils with special educational needs. However, schools in similar circumstances receive different levels of funding reflecting the variation in the funding levels LEAs receive from central government, and because LEAs in turn devolve different amounts to schools. Additionally, grant maintained schools are funded on a different basis from LEA schools.

On average, 80 per cent of a school's budget is spent on staff salaries, so relatively small-scale changes in staffing can make a considerable difference to the funding available for other resources. Schools also face very different costs for the maintenance of premises. Schools have only limited control over these major areas of spending, and so spending on learning resources varies widely: for example, in 1995/96, spending per pupil on learning resources in secondary schools without sixth forms ranged from £93 to £132. The proportion of secondary schools' budgets allocated to learning resources varied from 4.4 per cent to 6.5 per cent.

Since the introduction of local management of schools there has been a steady increase in teacher contact time (see Chart 12, page 14). In some schools teaching staff have chosen to increase contact time to achieve lower class sizes. However, in 1996-7 alone at least one school in ten reduced the number of teaching staff: where pupil numbers remained constant or increased this resulted in rises in both contact ratios and pupil:teacher ratios, so reducing the amount of time teachers have for preparation and marking

and the time for those with subject management responsibilities to monitor the work of their departments. Although there is insufficient evidence to show any immediate direct effect on standards, increased pressure on teachers and a reduction in schools' flexibility inevitably take their toll.

Most schools have managed the appointment of staff to ensure an appropriate balance of age, experience and gender. In a small number of schools, under one in ten, the stability of staffing leads to a higher than average staffing cost. A well-established staff has some benefits, for example contributing significantly to the ethos and sense of order of a school. However, the higher staffing costs create difficulties for schools in meeting other resource demands. In one school in twenty-five this has a detrimental affect on standards because of the resulting inadequate quality and quantity of learning resources that can

Chart 33 The efficiency and effectiveness with which resources are deployed and used

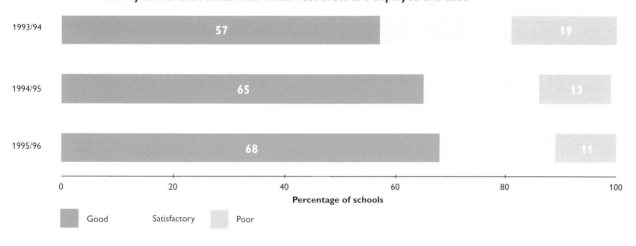

Chart 34 The quality of financial management and decision-taking

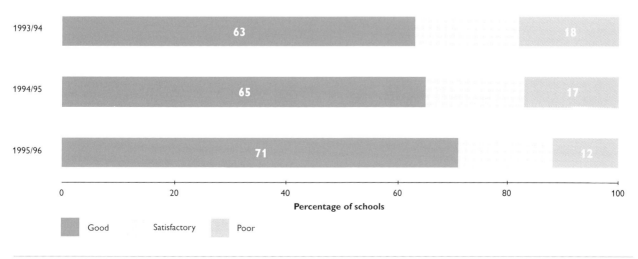

be afforded. Additionally, a lack of staff mobility can affect the ability of a school to react to changing curriculum requirements and its ability to recruit teachers with the skills required to deliver new courses such as GNVQs.

Most schools are aware of the need to maintain a cost-effective sixth form. However, in some schools analysis of staff deployment costs is insufficiently accurate to make informed management decisions. In most of a sample of 70 schools visited by HMI in 1994-95, the proportion of staffing allocated to the sixth form closely matched the proportion of income received for these students. However, in a number of schools with small sixth forms staffing costs exceeded income quite considerably, and here the sixth form was being subsidised by the main school. In a few schools the sixth form subsidised the main school, for example at the cost of low time allocations for A-level subjects.

There are wide variations in the sizes of sixth form teaching groups within and between schools. Average A-level group size in a school can be as low as 2 and as high as 13 or 14. Most schools feel justified in maintaining some costly small groups in minority subjects because of their contribution to the overall sixth-form curriculum, and for the benefit of the whole school, for example in music. A range of sensible strategies is used to reduce the costs of maintaining small group sizes, including joint timetabling of Year 12 and Year 13, and reducing taught time allocations whilst compensating with designated study periods.

Over the course of this review, schools in general have become more effective in financial administration and control. The school office and those associated with finances work efficiently, particularly when roles are clearly specified. In many schools a finance officer or bursar manages the budget well; where they are particularly effective, financial reports for the senior management team and governors are regularly prepared to support budget monitoring. In many schools budget outturn statements are also prepared monthly to enable departments to monitor and check their own spending. Generally schools have set up secure checking procedures and have responded positively to any recommendations made by auditors. Many schools make effective use of dedicated information technology systems to facilitate their procedures

and record-keeping and to monitor expenditure.

However, even in the many secondary schools where the overall level of funding and learning resources is not a major concern, there still remains scope for improved financial management, better prioritisation, and more effective use of the funds for the provision of learning resources and to improve access to them. For example, many schools fail to link the budget to proposals in the school development plan, ensuring that expenditure is focused upon clearly identified needs. A minority of schools have accumulated substantial budget surpluses with no clear rationale for their future use other than for contingency purposes. Many secondary schools fail to undertake a sufficiently rigorous audit of needs for learning resources: this is often related to weaknesses in curriculum planning. A few maintain poor financial records and governors are not fully aware of how the budget is allocated. The level of delegated budget or resources may be seen as insufficient in a significant proportion of schools but increases in funding to improve levels of resourcing are only part of the solution. Without better financial and resource management in many schools the potential of the currently available resources will not be maximised.

The criteria for allocating funds to learning resources are often unclear in schools. For example, expenditure on computers and computer software accounts for a large proportion of total spending on learning resources in many schools even though there are clearly identified shortages of books, materials or other equipment. Very few schools monitor how well resources are used and many are therefore unaware of whether spending has helped to improve the quality of teaching and learning, and thus whether they are getting value for money from existing resources. This lack of audit and planning in many schools makes it difficult to prioritise expenditure. As a result, in many secondary schools funds for learning resources continue to be allocated either on a historic formula or on the basis of ' who shouts the loudest'. Where schools have attempted as a first principle to allocate funds equitably they are often spread thinly across subjects but without really meeting the long-term needs of any.

3.6 School self-review

The Annual Report of HMCI in 1993/94 stated that "the monitoring and evaluation of the curriculum, the quality of teaching and standards of pupils' work by headteachers were weak in many schools...". Over the period 1993-7 there has been some improvement, but reviewing of schools' work remains weak overall in one in three schools and all schools need to continue to address this issue in order to promote further improvement. Some schools, for example, analyse their examination results annually, but do not then consider sufficiently the action necessary to improve them in future years.

Many schools need to monitor much more carefully: the standards achieved; the progress pupils make against baseline data; the performance and attendance patterns of different groups of pupils; the implementation of agreed policies; the quality of teaching; and the effectiveness of expenditure by departments. Where such monitoring occurs schools are in a much better position to evaluate outcomes and plan change accordingly. There is evidence that schools are making progress in this area. However, even in those schools where management and leadership are otherwise very good, there is often a resistance to monitoring the quality of teaching by observing classroom practice.

In the most effective schools there is a common understanding by the staff of the purposes of monitoring and evaluation. Through systematic and purposeful monitoring of the quality of teaching and the standards of work of pupils, good practice is identified and shared. The classroom monitoring of teaching also helps to focus upon

weak or poor practice; this is remedied either by support or by competency procedures taken against the ineffective teacher.

Systematic monitoring of teaching by classroom observation, whether formal or informal, is still relatively rare. In many schools senior managers therefore lack key knowledge essential to fulfil their responsibility of raising standards. Most are aware in general terms of the relative strengths and weaknesses of their teaching staff and most, but not all, take steps to deal with the weakest teachers. However, such action is too rarely informed by the detailed analysis of strengths and weaknesses that systematic classroom observation can bring. Often, headteachers fear that classroom teachers will see such observation as threatening and that good staff relationships will suffer. Even where the job descriptions of heads of department include the 'monitoring of the quality of teaching', it is rare that procedures have been established, and particularly that sufficient time has been provided, for this to be carried out regularly. Nevertheless, an increasing minority of schools have successfully initiated formal monitoring of the quality of teaching, including direct classroom observation.

The more effective strategies for monitoring and evaluating teaching involve a balance between classroom observation by the headteacher or other members of the senior management team and the head of department.

*At **Notley High School**, an 11-16 comprehensive, a formal system of monitoring subject departments has been introduced. Each department is reviewed in turn as part of an eighteen-month cycle. For each review a focus is agreed which is linked to the school*

Chart 35 Reviewing of the school's work

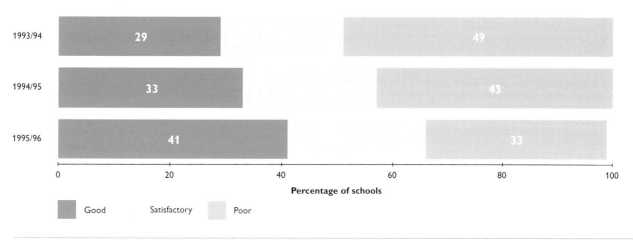

	Good	Satisfactory	Poor
1993/94	29		49
1994/95	33		43
1995/96	41		33

Percentage of schools

development plan, for example, the effectiveness of differentiation in teaching and learning in Key Stage 3. The review is conducted mainly by members of the senior management team but also includes the head of department and a non-specialist teacher from another department. The review includes an analysis of recent examination results and a scrutiny of a sample of pupils' exercise books from each class. However, the main purpose of the review is the observation of teaching and learning in each class and for this a detailed proforma has been agreed. Following the review the head of department and the linked deputy headteacher write an overview which is discussed with the senior management team and at a department meeting before it is circulated to other subject departments and the governing body. A plan of action is then prepared and new targets are set for examination success. The reviews have enabled departments to share good practice, to rectify weaknesses such as an imbalance in the teaching programme, and to draw up plans for in-service training. The reviews have enabled school development planning to be more closely targeted, identified resourcing needs, such as a lack of books for low-attainers. They have also identified those weak teachers for whom support is now provided. Subject heads in this school have a good understanding of strengths and weaknesses in their departments, and are better able to address issues and deploy resources appropriately.

HMI INSPECTION, 1996

Some schools are beginning to evaluate their work using as a basis the OFSTED *Framework for Inspection*. An increasing number of headteachers and senior managers have undertaken OFSTED inspector training. A few schools have adapted OFSTED lesson observation forms and inspection criteria to support their monitoring and evaluation procedures. Where headteachers have established a favourable ethos, lesson observations by senior management on a day-to-day basis promote open dialogue which is perceived as supportive rather than threatening.

However, the evidence from the first inspection cycle of the readiness of schools to undertake self-review is disappointing. If schools are to succeed in using self-review to improve teaching and raise

standards they need to establish monitoring and evaluation strategies which are carried out effectively and attract public confidence in their rigour. Inspection plays a crucial part in the cycle of self-review. For schools to continue to improve, a combination of self-review and external inspection is essential.

OFSTED inspection provides school managers with an objective evaluation of school performance and a platform for further development. While inspections cannot, of themselves, improve schools, there is overwhelming evidence that for the majority of schools they provide the catalyst for change because of their diagnostic and informative power. Knowledge that an inspection is impending acts as a spur to improvement in very many schools. In the light of inspection, most schools become much more successful in identifying their strengths and their weaknesses[5]. In the majority of schools inspection is seen as an aid to school development; as providing a valuable whole school educational audit; as recognition of achievement; as confirmation of good practice; and as providing specific diagnosis of weaknesses in teaching. New headteachers find inspection particularly useful.

Further evidence of the value of inspection for schools has come from the reinspection of secondary schools, which began in the autumn term of 1997. Inspectors are required to assess the extent of the school's progress since its last inspection, including how well it has responded to the previous inspection, and whether the school has the capacity to secure improvement and maintain high standards. Of this first group of schools, albeit a relatively small sample, four in five have been judged to have responded effectively to their previous inspection. Amongst the key features of their success, inspectors identified an improvement in development planning with clearer success criteria, and a much stronger focus on effective teaching and learning, involving the use of formal classroom observation, scrutiny of pupils' work and analysis of performance indicators to raise awareness by teachers and involve them more closely in planning improvement. In the remaining one in five schools, inspectors judged that insufficient progress had been made. One of the key limiting factors in many of these schools was weakness in leadership and management.

[5] *School Evaluation Matters*, OFSTED, 1998.

Additionally, a few schools use specialists external to the school to assist them with the monitoring and evaluation of teaching, for example where there is insufficient expertise within the school to tackle the problems of a weak department. The increased involvement of many schools in initial teacher education often has, as a by-product of mentoring students, a twofold effect: mentors learn and practise the techniques of lesson observation; and the discussions to which this gives rise often cause them to reflect on their own practice.

Good practice in the monitoring and evaluation of attainment focuses upon both the outcome of examinations and the progress pupils are making during their courses. Almost all secondary schools analyse their external examination performance. The complexity of this analysis varies between schools, but at best includes analysis by gender, ethnicity and teaching group. In the great majority of schools, heads of department are interviewed by the headteacher or a member of the senior management team about their department's examination performance. In some schools only those subjects where there are perceived problems are targeted, rather than having the across-the-board discussions which provide both commendation and expressions of concern and ensure that lessons are learned from the departments whose results are especially good. In a few schools, these discussions form part of the formal appraisal system. Numbers of schools are beginning to exploit the more sophisticated analyses of examination and test data that computers can provide.

Gaywood Park School, Norfolk, uses a computerised analysis to enable the evaluation of pupil and departmental performance. This enables comparisons to be made against the potential of pupils and, retrospectively, between different departments in the school and with other schools and departments in the LEA. This has been a powerful tool for raising expectations. For example, the analysis showed that the performance of pupils in an apparently successful department was lower than might have been expected, and that the department was in fact under-performing: this had been concealed by the fact that the subject cohort was predominantly more able, and justified a higher level of demand.

HMI INSPECTION, 1997

Initiatives at national level, such as the annual publication of school performance tables, and at LEA level, such as comparisons with schools of a similar kind, have helped to encourage the use of data by school managers. In many schools, however, there has been an over-concentration on outcomes at whole school and departmental level with insufficient attention to subsequent action, for example to improve the performance of sub-groups of pupils or of individual teachers.

Schools often record trial GCSE results against predicted GCSE grades in order to target individual underachievement. This is sound practice, although the widely adopted specific focus on pupils performing at just below the C/D boundary is inequitable, if understandable in the context of national performance tables. A minority of schools track pupils throughout Key Stage 4, by regularly comparing predicted and potential GCSE grades, so keeping track of pupils' effort and attainment in a well-focused way both across and within subjects.

At Southlands School, Chorley, an LEA initiative using standardised test scores as the basis for analysing GCSE results has been harnessed to provide an analysis of individual and departmental performance for monitoring purposes. The investment of time and resources by the senior management team has paid off in a number of ways. Principally, the school now has a tangible evidence base upon which achievement can be demonstrated. This has contributed towards a rising reputation in the area: the school has moved from a falling roll to being oversubscribed. Implicit in this are perceptibly rising standards. Data are used to identify both departments where there is underachievement, and groups of pupils. More specifically, data are used to identify individual underachievement in time to do something about it. Estimated GCSE grades are used to identify pupils across the attainment range whose performance is lower than might be expected. All such pupils are then monitored by members of the senior management team. They are interviewed fortnightly, targets are set and checked, and class teachers, tutors and parents are involved in the process.

HMI INSPECTION, 1995

Most secondary schools have realised that baseline data are necessary in order to make the analysis of examinations more reliable, to make comparisons year on year, and to set targets for improvement. In many secondary schools, there is, however, a lack of confidence in the quality of primary school assessments of pupils' performance, and so relatively few have made effective use of Key Stage 2 statutory assessment data for analytical purposes. Some schools use instead standardised test scores and internal test and examination results. Commercial software is frequently used in the production of analyses from these databases, although many schools are only just coming to terms with the range and use of available software. Some schools have used staff training days to introduce teachers to the interpretation of the data and the analyses provided by such software. Such training will be needed more widely if the full potential of assessment data is to be realised.

Schools vary considerably in the extent and quality of their monitoring and evaluation of the effectiveness of their sixth forms. Amongst the most useful strategies employed are: use of value-added indicators and analysis, setting performance targets for various courses, sampling of students' work by senior management, auditing the use of resources, and feedback from students and parents. About three-quarters of schools have made effective use of some form of value-added analysis of GCE A-level results. Too few, however, have made full and systematic use of this information to set targets for individual students, and as a basis of departmental review. National value-added data, from GCSE to A level, published since 1995 by the DfEE, make such analysis straightforward and reliable, but awareness of its existence and its potential is still patchy in sixth forms.

Although the majority of schools now have policies and plans for developing their SEN provision most schools do not have sufficient expertise in monitoring their impact within the context of the school development plan. Moreover, schools often have difficulty in evaluating the success of their SEN policy, and do not always report to parents on this, despite the requirement on them to do so. A further weakness is that schools do not always ensure that the provision specified in SEN statements is actually made available to pupils.

Some schools have difficulty in identifying that portion of the budget share included as an indicative amount to be spent on special needs provision by the LEA or the Funding Agency for Schools. Some find it difficult to establish if it has been spent appropriately, and to what effect. An increasing number of LEAs are beginning to develop methods to monitor and evaluate how allocated monies for special educational needs are spent. However, in many LEAs there is little or no support at Stage 3 from the LEA support services for pupils with learning difficulties or other specific disabilities. As a consequence there is increasing pressure to move straight to referral at Stage 4.

3.7 The role of middle managers

Although headteachers, other senior managers and governors can work hard to develop good leadership, vision and a strong sense of purpose within a school, a committed and effective middle management is also essential.

Effective delegation of responsibilities and strategies for ensuring accountability are clearly evident in the best managed and most effective schools. While there has been a steady improvement in the management of schools as a whole over the period of the first inspection cycle, the improvement in subject leadership and management has been less marked. For example, HMCI's Annual Report for 1994/95 reported that "about one-fifth of schools have weaknesses in middle management which frustrate developments". Little improvement is evident in subsequent years.

Where there is a strong partnership with senior management, departmental planning is generally well linked to whole school developments, and subject and pastoral heads are held accountable for their teams. However, where lines of communication with senior management are not clear, the roles of middle managers are not sufficiently defined, and where senior managers do not monitor the implementation of whole school policies at department level, departments tend to act autonomously, set vague or unrealistic targets, and progress towards raising achievement is patchy and uncoordinated.

The role of subject and middle management in schools is crucial: the day-to-day responsibility for ensuring good planning and promoting better teaching in order to secure and sustain high standards across the curriculum lies with those with subject leadership responsibility. The following example describes how a science department, already comparable with other subject areas in terms of examination results, was able to raise the profile and popularity of the subject and achieve improvements in examination performance.

*The science department at **Magdalen College School, Northamptonshire**, has made significant improvements as a result of effective management and good teamworking. A new head of department initiated a three-year development plan, using a school INSET day to establish priorities and deploy sub-groups; all teachers in the department were given an opportunity to contribute to groups and take on specific responsibilities. Staff then addressed agreed targets in areas such as pupils' practical and investigatory skills. One outcome of this strong but responsive leadership was much more collaborative planning and decision-making. This contributed towards raised professional self-esteem and improved quality of classroom practice. In turn, standards as indicated by examination performance have been raised, and science is increasingly popular with an improved uptake post-16.*

HMI INSPECTION, 1997

Inspection has shown that there is a strong positive correlation between schools where the overall management and leadership are very good and good departmental management of National Curriculum subjects, especially the core. Nevertheless, even in well-led schools it is rare for all subject departments to be well managed.

Schools with the best developed middle management structures emphasise the following aspects of the role of the head of department and embody them in job descriptions: the management of people (including pupils, teachers and ancillary staff); the management of curriculum development and implementation; the management of resources (equipment and accommodation) and finances. The best job descriptions also emphasise the importance of communication about their own

area with pupils and parents, with teachers within the department as well as across the school, and with the primary or tertiary sectors. More importantly, the job description sets out the contribution of middle managers to the development and direction of the whole school through their involvement in planning, policy-making and implementation, and departmental review.

Increasingly, the best schools make explicit the role of middle managers in the monitoring and evaluation of their subject, set expectations of review and action planning within the department and ensure a clear understanding by middle managers of their role in target setting and raising standards in the subject. For example, the job description for heads of departments in **Rainham School for Girls** includes as the first of the duties and responsibilities "Quality Assurance: To be responsible for, and monitor and evaluate the work of the staff within the department". However, there remains in many schools a reluctance on the part of subject and department managers to monitor systematically the quality of teaching within their department. All too often the emphasis of subject leaders is on ensuring effective administration of their department and not on tackling the management issues which would have a direct impact upon the quality of teaching and standards in the subject.

Accountability is developed most effectively in schools in which there is clearly specified line management with the head of subject or faculty reporting directly to a member of the senior management team. In some of the schools with good subject leadership and management, regular timetabled meetings between a line manager and head of subject take place. These meetings enable issues to be flagged for departmental discussion and progress in meeting departmental action plans can be assessed.

In many schools, heads of department regularly monitor pupils' work, but not always to agreed criteria. The detailed monitoring of the quality of pupils' class-work takes a variety of forms. In some schools a more systematic approach has been initiated where the headteacher gives guidance to heads of departments about frequency, year groups, sample size and the criteria to be used: written reports and points for action by the department are also often expected. In schools where the headteacher and senior management team review samples of pupils' work from subject departments, the consistency of implementation of policies and improvement in standards can be more readily assessed. As well as being able to monitor standards, any action required to be taken at either whole school, department or individual teacher level can be identified.

Many heads of department are assiduous in monitoring aspects of their department's work, such as exercise books and teachers' planning and records, which provide important but indirect evidence of the quality of teaching. They recognise that more should be done but are sometimes reluctant to report formally on the classroom performance of their colleagues. However, in a climate of good leadership and mutual trust, once well-planned observation has been initiated, many teachers come to see its benefits. For example, in some departments a particular problem is the uniform approach taken by individual teachers, even when they are using a scheme of work which promotes a variety of teaching styles and activities. In a science department, for instance, an audit showed that some teachers made far greater use of IT than others; social and technological aspects of science featured in the teaching of some but by no means all of the department. Having identified the problem, the head of department was able to develop those areas shown to be effective but least employed.

All systematic monitoring, and especially direct lesson observation, is costly in time. The non-contact time which heads of department typically have is barely enough for them to carry out their traditional, administrative functions - and it is often further eroded by coping with staff shortages or mentoring student teachers. If heads of department are successfully to undertake a genuinely managerial role, then they need adequate time to monitor the work they manage. Schools must calculate the cost of this, decide what can realistically be afforded, and then ensure that the expectations laid on heads of department match the time that can be given to them. Timetables have to be constructed so that heads of department are available when colleagues are teaching. The responsibility for monitoring which is written into many job descriptions will remain a

dead letter unless sufficient time is made available and appropriately structured for it to be undertaken.

The headteacher of Warlingham School, Surrey, was concerned that contact time was at a premium within the school and alternative strategies to provide time for monitoring and evaluation were needed. To complement whole school monitoring by the senior management a system of "quality management time" has been introduced. This allows departments to bid for release time and teacher cover to undertake specific departmental management activities such as monitoring and evaluation of departmental practice. Action plans and targets for the use of this time are expected. Time for monitoring is being used productively by a number of departments to begin lesson observation on a systematic basis.

HMI INSPECTION, 1997

The further training of subject managers and those with whole school responsibilities remains a key issue yet to be addressed sufficiently by schools, LEAs and other training providers. In the most effective schools, management training does occur and headteachers are sensitive to the specific needs of their middle managers. But, unlike the training for headteachers and aspiring senior managers, there is very rarely systematic consideration given to subject or pastoral management training.

3.8 Appraisal of staff

Maintaining the effectiveness of teachers is a central responsibility of the management in schools: appraisal is a key element in reviewing an individual teacher's performance and developing strategies to improve it. Teacher appraisal as required by the Education (School Teacher Appraisal) Regulations (1991) has been implemented, at least in spirit, in the majority of schools (Chart 36). The findings from HMI inspection of nearly 300 schools over the period from 1991 to 1996 were, however, disappointing. Overall, appraisal has had minimal impact on teaching and learning in the majority of these schools. In only one in five of schools visited had appraisal led to observable improvements in teaching, and then on a minor scale for the most part. The report concluded that the system:

is functioning below its full potential. There is too little evidence that appraisal is contributing as much as it should to raising pupils' standards of achievement and to improving teachers' levels of performance.

Few schools have capitalised, to any significant extent, upon the appraisal process to identify strengths and weaknesses in an individual teacher's capabilities and improve his or her effectiveness. Appraisal is not adequately informed by classroom observation in the vast majority of schools and very few schools have established links between professional development and needs identified through appraisal. In many schools appraisal is not yet fully effective in achieving the intended purpose of legislation, in particular, to improve the quality of education for pupils. Overall, appraisal has had little impact so far on the quality of teaching in many schools and it is unlikely to do so until it is focused more sharply on the essential features of an individual teacher's performance.

There is a lack of systematic evaluation of appraisal arrangements by schools, which means that many of them cannot give a clear account of their impact or effectiveness. The challenge for schools is to identify how the appraisal system can be developed to improve teachers' performance. There is a need for targets for individual teachers to be more sharply focused on improvement in classroom practice, linked to closer monitoring of the process and follow-up by headteachers. There

is a need, too, for outcomes of appraisal to be linked into school development planning and for school governors to become more involved in the process.

Appraisal was introduced at a time when schools needed to respond to significant changes in education. These include the transfer of responsibilities from LEAs to governing bodies with the introduction of Local Management of Schools; the introduction of the National Curriculum and assessment procedures as well as its revisions; senior management's access to detailed information from OFSTED inspection; better information from which to derive baseline assessment and value-added measures; and more recently the introduction of legislation to establish 'target setting' for the performance of managers and their schools. These changes have altered the context in which appraisal takes place. To take account of this, and also to secure more effective management of the performance of teachers and managers in schools, changes are needed to the way in which appraisal is carried out in the vast majority of schools to ensure it is more effective.

3.9 The management of staff development

There has been a steady improvement in the effectiveness of senior management in schools in providing appropriate professional development opportunities for their staff. Ensuring well-targeted staff development, nevertheless, remains an issue to be addressed by a large number of schools. In

Chart 36 The arrangements for staff appraisal

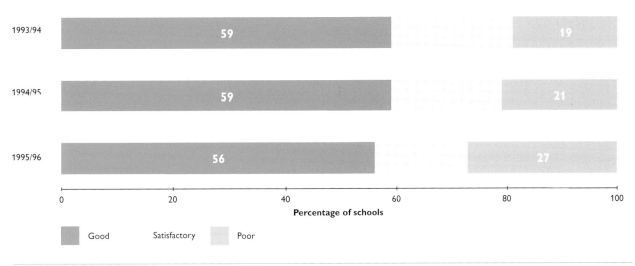

1993/94	59			19	
1994/95	59			21	
1995/96	56			27	

Percentage of schools

☐ Good   Satisfactory   ☐ Poor

1995/6 the arrangements for professional development were judged good or better in half of schools, but were unsatisfactory in one in five (Chart 37).

Nearly all schools have staff development policies and a member of the senior management team is usually responsible for identifying in-service training needs and arranging for them to be met. However, the potential of the appraisal process and in-service training to improve the quality of management in the school, teacher confidence and competence in the classroom, and to raise the standards of work is often only partly realised. In very few schools is there any systematic evaluation of the long-term benefits of professional development upon classroom practice or on the standards of attainment of pupils.

To build on their initial qualifications teachers need professional development during their careers which both enhances and updates their subject knowledge and develops their understanding of the processes of teaching and learning.

'In all subjects, the knowledge required of teachers evolves continuously; in some, maintaining a sufficient level of skill demands opportunities for practice beyond the teaching situation. Changes in the curriculum content also need to be understood and applied. Rapid technological change, particularly in IT, likewise demands that teachers keep abreast of the possibilities these offer to improve the teaching of their subject. For all these reasons, regular and systematic subject-specific staff development through in-service training, for both specialists and non-specialists, remains a major concern if schools are to maintain and improve their effectiveness.'

SUBJECTS AND STANDARDS (OFSTED, 1995)

The content of the National Curriculum and GCSE and A-level courses has changed over recent years affecting some subjects more than others. Regular updating is needed in subjects such as IT and design and technology, where the state of knowledge is changing rapidly. Particular pressure has been placed on teachers of modern foreign languages, where the fluency they require to use the target language as the medium of instruction requires substantial opportunities for real-life practice outside the classroom. Similarly, teachers of vocational courses need periodic direct experience of the workplace if work in school is not to become insulated from developments in their specialist area. In GNVQ courses such as health & social care and leisure & tourism, which cut across conventional school subject boundaries, there are commonly particular staff development needs. Here staff are often able to tackle some units competently, but lack the expertise and experience necessary for others. Greater emphasis thus needs to be given to extending and updating staff expertise in these areas if the courses are to be well taught.

It is understandable that senior managers and teachers will generally use limited in-service training resources to target teachers' main specialisms. However, this falls into the trap of failing to provide training for non-specialists in subjects which they teach in a minority of their time. But it is precisely here that weaknesses in

Chart 37 The arrangements for and impact of staff development

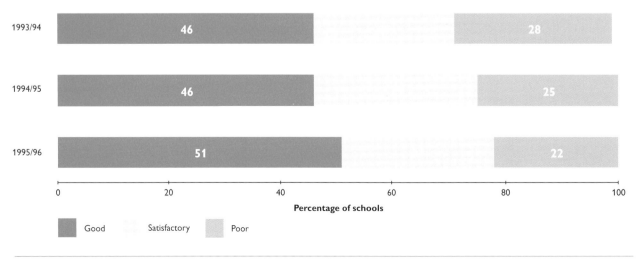

Percentage of schools

Good   Satisfactory   Poor

subject knowledge tend to show themselves most and with the most serious effects. This issue is often more acute in small schools and in middle schools where non-specialist teaching is most likely to be found.

The identification and meeting of staff development needs is not consistent across subjects. For example, IT and RE are the two subjects where the match of number, qualifications and experience of teachers to the demands of the subject curriculum are least favourable, and yet these are the subjects that are most often judged unsatisfactory for arrangements for professional development of staff.

The benefits of training include better subject knowledge, the acquisition or reinforcement of teaching skills, improved curriculum documentation, the more effective use of resources, improved collaboration with SEN support staff and better subject co-ordination. In general the training received on school closure days, at sessions after school or via similar activities organised outside the school at higher education institutions or professional centres, is mostly taught well and received positively. However, a significant weakness is that the quality of planning by providers is not always good enough to ensure that the training actually improves teachers' performance, with a consequent impact on the quality of pupils' learning and achievement.

Overall, schools give too little attention to evaluating the impact of training on the performance of individual teachers, or on the standards achieved by pupils. The appraisal of teachers generally has had little effect on schools' staff development practice. To ensure that staff development is worthwhile and expenditure is used efficiently there is a need for senior management to link more effectively job descriptions of their staff, target setting, and evidence from staff development interviews and from appraisal:

In Southfields School, Kettering, formal monitoring linked to appraisal uses lesson observation and feedback to teachers by the headteacher. The quality of teaching and professional development is linked to the central theme of learning skills and looking at how pupils learn. Overall a clearly structured

system of staff development is in place. The school had seen a considerable improvement in standards at GCSE A*-C grades, which the headteacher attributed to the planned development of the skills and awareness of needs related to effective teaching and learning.

HMI INSPECTION, 1995

Turves Green Girls' School, Birmingham, provides an example of the value of time set aside for in-service training related to course development. Training days are provided for writing assignments in collaboration with specialist colleagues with whom teachers discuss their ideas and review teaching and learning strategies. This was the case during the planning stage of a Part 1 GNVQ Engineering course. Finances were identified at an early stage to support the freeing of the teacher's time to attend a three-day planning course linked to a local industrial partner.

HMI INSPECTION, 1996

LEAs continue to be the main providers of in-service training for schools, but they operate in an increasingly competitive environment, with growing private sector provision. Here, as with LEA provision, schools report a wide variation in quality. Staff development resources are finite; it is therefore important that senior management ensure value for money from the staff development opportunities undertaken. There is a need to ensure that INSET is directed more specifically at improving the quality of teaching and learning and thereby at raising pupils' achievements. Increasing numbers of schools are becoming involved in the 'Investors In People' initiative and seeing staff development as an integral part of their strategy to raise standards.

4 ETHOS, BEHAVIOUR AND PUPIL SUPPORT

4.1 Ethos

The ethos established and articulated by the headteacher and senior management team is manifested in the 'tone' of the school, its coherence, stability and the mutual confidence between staff and pupils. It is demonstrated in shared values and a common purpose. At best, it centres on a clear set of aims, linked to achievable objectives, is translated into all of the school's thinking and documentation, is monitored, is sustained by forward planning and INSET, and promotes high expectations for and by each individual in the school. Ethos was judged to be satisfactory or better in almost nine schools in ten; it was good or very good in three-quarters.

Woodhouse School, Tamworth, is typical of many of the schools where the ethos is judged to be positive.

The school is effectively led by its headteacher; it successfully fulfils its aim to create a caring environment which nurtures pupils' concern for their work, other people and the community. Much of the school's work effectively contributes to the development of individual pupils and encourages them to become responsible members of society. The headteacher fosters a strong spirit of dedication and professional commitment amongst the staff and effectively promotes the development of initiative and creativity throughout the school.

The positive ethos which this leadership promotes is reflected in the work of the school.

The quality of teaching is good overall and is a significant strength of the school. It makes an important contribution to the maintenance of a positive ethos in the school.

The school has considerable success in promoting the personal development of its pupils. There is a strong community ethos.

Teachers have high expectations of pupil behaviour and adhere consistently to the school's code of conduct. Pupils are aware of the standards of behaviour expected of them and respond positively. The school successfully creates an ethos which encourages self-discipline. The school functions as a very orderly community.

OFSTED INSPECTION REPORT, 1997

Chart 38 The school's ethos

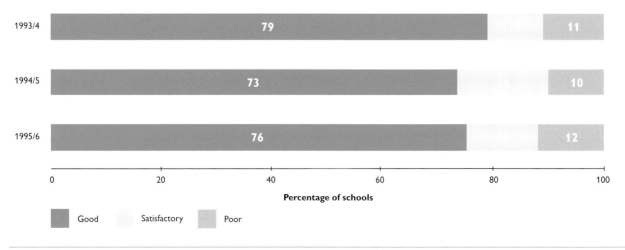

	Good	Satisfactory	Poor
1993/4	79		11
1994/5	73		10
1995/6	76		12

Percentage of schools

4.2 Spiritual, moral, social and cultural development

Assemblies are an important manifestation of the school's ethos and have the potential to make a significant contribution to pupils' spiritual, moral, social and cultural development (for the contribution of the curriculum to these elements, see 6.5, pages 111–115).

The 1996 Education Act (repeating former legislation in the 1988 Act) requires that "all pupils shall on each day take part in a collective act of worship" (6.1) which, subject to other provisions, "shall be wholly or mainly of a broadly Christian character". The OFSTED Inspection Framework directs inspectors to look for provision of spiritual development particularly in collective worship, and to ask the question: "Does the school provide its pupils with knowledge and insight into values and religious beliefs and enable them to reflect on experiences in a way which develops their self-knowledge and spiritual awareness?"

Over the first cycle of inspection, in commenting on spiritual development, reports increasingly

emphasised schools' failure to fulfil statutory requirements for a collective act of worship. Approaching half of schools are judged poor at fostering spiritual development, and a declining number, around one-third in 1995/6, are judged good (Chart 40). Provision in two-thirds of voluntary aided schools is good, largely matching the quality of their provision for collective acts of worship.

Where collective worship makes an important contribution to spiritual development, it is well planned across the year and involves pupils in both planning and presentation, taking account of the school's aims, the curriculum and major festivals and events, but with an element of flexibility to allow the school to respond to important current issues, such as the Dunblane massacre. Additionally, where a Christian perspective is balanced with attention to other beliefs, pupils are able to offer their own prayers and express their spiritual thinking, and those leading worship can take account of the differing beliefs and non-belief of pupils and teachers, thus minimising occurrences of withdrawal. At best, form tutors are encouraged to follow up ideas presented during the act of worship.

Cramlington School, Northumberland, used the flexibility allowed by the 1988 Act to provide an imaginative programme for collective worship. A guidance document on collective worship was produced for members of staff. These guidelines provide for two year-group acts of worship, one "video assembly" and two "thought for the day" class sessions each week. The guidelines set out the legal requirement and include a paper on spiritual and moral development. They emphasise the

Chart 39 Percentage of schools with evidence of non-compliance in collective worship

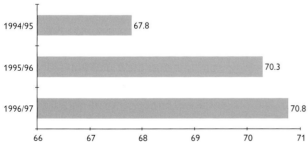

Year	Value
1994/95	67.8
1995/96	70.3
1996/97	70.8

Chart 40 Pupils' spiritual development 1993-1996

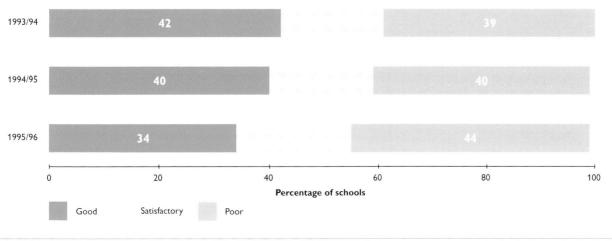

Year	Good	Satisfactory	Poor
1993/94	42		39
1994/95	40		40
1995/96	34		44

Percentage of schools

Good   Satisfactory   Poor

*importance of reflecting the school's stated
values, the need to be "broadly Christian" and
the importance of a time for quiet reflection or
prayer. In spite of the diversity of viewpoints
and beliefs among staff, most are now prepared
to take a leading role. Pupils also participate.
The guidance includes a helpful list of
resources and sets out the themes for collective
worship (called assemblies) for the next year.
Each half term has a theme with a strong
spiritual or moral association. These include
"new beginnings, new year"; "good versus evil -
light, hope, thank you" and "temptations -
talents and honesty". The assemblies in tutor
groups, often a weakness in other schools, are
taken seriously here. The "video assemblies"
are produced by pupils with the help of the
drama department. Each is on a spiritual or
moral theme and includes written "follow-up"
guidelines for tutors and students. The video is
broadcast to all tutor groups. Similarly the
"thought for the day" is usually led by a form
tutor and is generally taken seriously by pupils.
The "thoughts" vary in their explicit religious
content, but most include a clear point of
spiritual or moral interest for further reflection.
For example, in the week following armistice
day, a member of the history department led a
short reflection on the lessons to be learnt from
war.*

HMI INSPECTION, 1997

Some schools, particularly church schools, go
further than this in providing for pupils' spiritual
development. For example, Roman Catholic
schools are increasingly appointing ordained or lay
chaplains whose role combines spiritual guidance

and pastoral care. A few LEA maintained schools
have also appointed non-denominational
chaplains. Another practice found mainly in
church schools is the use of a retreat centre for
year groups or tutor groups to take part in
residential activities intended to give opportunities
for reflection and building relationships. For
example, **Notre Dame High School in Norwich**
provides a week-end retreat for Year 13 pupils.
The retreat is "reflective" rather than explicitly
religious and is attended by both believers and
non-believers.

In general, however, spiritual development, and in
particular the requirement for a collective act of
worship, has been ignored by many schools.
Where it is observed, in most secondary schools
collective worship is necessarily fragmentary,
consisting of regular meetings of sub-groups of the
school such as year groups, with much done in
tutor groups. With the exception of church schools,
it is rare for sixth-form students to be expected to
attend daily acts of worship of any kind. Some
schools which have well-planned assemblies
celebrating the shared values of the school and
giving time for quiet contemplation, so contributing
to spiritual development, are still judged to have
fallen short of the requirements that they should
be 'wholly or mainly of a broadly Christian
character'.

This very widespread non-compliance raises
questions about the Act and its interpretation, and
in particular whether schools in a broadly secular
society can or should bring their pupils together in
order to engage in worship. For Roman Catholic,
Church of England and other denominational
schools the answer is clear in principle. For most

Chart 41 Pupils' moral, social and cultural development 1993-1996 (average)

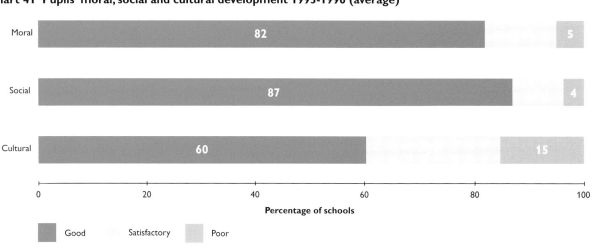

LEA and grant maintained schools, however, the notion of worship, and indeed that of prayer, can be problematic at both an institutional and a personal level.

The vast majority of schools make a positive contribution to pupils' moral development.

St. Benet Biscop School in Northumberland bases its moral code on explicit Christian values. Like many Roman Catholic schools it illustrates the interconnectedness of spiritual and moral development, religious beliefs providing the criteria for establishing moral values. The school emphasises the importance of "living" the values, and this is made clear to prospective parents and teachers. Appointments of staff take into account their willingness to be pro-active in promoting the school's values. The school emphasises human dignity, responsibility and self-direction. There are no bells and no prohibited areas during break and lunch-times. Shouting by pupils and teachers is frowned on. The school mission statement is prominent around the building and is known and understood by the pupils. Behaviour is exemplary and when misdemeanours occur, pupils are encouraged to think through the implications for themselves and find ways of making amends. This emphasis on personal morality within a system of corporate values is as fundamental to school life as is academic achievement, and indeed the two are seen as complementary by both pupils and staff. Exclusions are rare, and when they are unavoidable cause genuine anguish to the head and his staff.

HMI INSPECTION, 1997

In only a small minority of schools is provision for pupils' moral development judged to be unsatisfactory. There has, however, been an erratic but possibly significant fall over the four years of the inspection cycle in the proportion of schools where moral development is good, and this could be linked with a similar trend with respect to behaviour.

Schools making good provision for pupils' moral development generally include in their prospectuses clear statements of the moral values they seek to promote. These typically include honesty, fairness, consideration for others and

respect. Staff and pupils recognise that they have a direct responsibility for one another; pupils have a practical grasp of the difference between right and wrong. Good relationships and adherence to the rules which underpin the values of the school are recognised as a precondition for moral development and school effectiveness. Staff treat pupils with respect and set a tone which enables pupils to exercise responsibility. Weaknesses occur when there is a lack of commitment to agreed moral values among the staff. Pupils are quick to recognise inconsistencies among the staff in applying the school's moral code and this inevitably weakens the thrust of the school's message.

Most schools make good provision for pupils' social development, regarded broadly as learning to work and relate well with others and contribute to the life of the community. Pupils are encouraged to contribute not only to the life of the school, for example, by participating in team games and after-school activities such as the orchestra or chess club, but also to local community life. For example, they are involved in events such as the school band playing for services in local churches, carrying out a clean-up of the local environment, or providing weekly lunches for senior citizens. Such a range of involvement was seen at **Etone Community School, Nuneaton.**

The school provides a firm basis for social development and has clear policies which relate to social attitudes and behaviour. Charities are supported, and pupils take an active part in organizing fundraising events. They have just raised £1,000 for cancer relief in a 'readathon', and organized a show in aid of 'children in need', at their own initiative and at short notice. The school provides a good range of social activities and opportunities for leadership. There is a prefect system, which gives senior pupils an experience of responsibility; the Duke of Edinburgh's Award Scheme for older pupils; the house system with its competitions and sports; the very popular daily youth club run by trained workers during the lunch break; and the commendation system with its encouragement of good work and conduct.

OFSTED INSPECTION REPORT, 1996

An important means by which schools foster pupils' social development is by providing opportunities for them to hold positions of responsibility. At best, these are many and varied to allow the maximum number of pupils an opportunity to be involved. They include classroom monitors, librarians, sports captains, house captains and prefects, 'scavengers' who keep the school and grounds tidy and free from litter; and those who help to run the school tuck shop or school bank. In some schools all pupils have opportunities to handle administrative duties, beginning in Year 7 and increasing in responsibility as pupils become older. Many schools now have elected school councils. These are most effective when members are allowed to effect real changes and improvements, as at **Turton High School, Bolton.**

Pupils take an active and responsible role in school decision-making through the School Council. Their suggestions are taken seriously by the school and this in turn increases pupils' co-operation. During the week of inspection delegates from each form group were discussing the best way to use the school's overstretched accommodation as social and quiet areas during the lunch-times. The council is chaired by sixth-form students and only a minimum of influence on its decisions is exerted by staff.

OFSTED INSPECTION REPORT, 1997

As at **Penair School, Truro**, pupils are willing to contribute to lessons and the life of the school, and, where possible, to take some responsibility.

Pupils have a sense of fun as well as taking responsibilities seriously. IT monitors across all years have special responsibility for the IT room. They take responsibility for the area and help other pupils to develop competence. The prefect system gives experience of service and responsibility. The school council is another opportunity for pupils to develop responsibility. Two pupils represent each year; the council has a planned agenda and invites visitors to the committee from the staff

and from the local community. The meeting is responsibly chaired and serviced by pupils. They decide on the spending of the budget, arrange charity events and aim to take the message of the school to the community. In some subjects pupils have responsibility for their own assessment, there is a paired reading scheme, a 'buddy scheme' to support the new entry and many are involved in community work through the Duke of Edinburgh's Award Scheme.

OFSTED INSPECTION REPORT, 1997

Some schools give sixth formers the opportunity to undertake particular responsibilities in helping younger pupils, either in settling in or more specifically with their mathematics, reading and writing or music practice, as well as in other aspects of the life of the school. This is exemplified at **St Peter's School, Solihull.**

Pupils' social development is strongly encouraged through many aspects of the school's life...In the sixth form, many students are trained for the paired reading scheme, through which they support pupils in the main school, and there are opportunities for community service, the organisation of the school bank, coaching in sport or as members of the school council.

OFSTED INSPECTION REPORT, 1996

Few schools make poor provision for social development, but weaknesses include insufficient provision for pupils to work together and uneven distribution of responsibilities, with too few pupils, especially younger pupils, having opportunities to take responsibility.

Over half of secondary schools make good provision for pupils' cultural development, but in about one school in six provision is unsatisfactory. Where cultural development is good, pupils gain an understanding of British and other cultures including values and beliefs, traditions, literature and arts. Provision is unsatisfactory where schools have given little thought to cultural development, or where there is an imbalance between attention to the cultural traditions of the United Kingdom, the other cultures that make up our diverse modern British society, and other European and world cultures.

Some schools are successful in providing opportunities for pupils to understand and appreciate the diversity of beliefs, traditions and cultures through assemblies and special events. **Deptford Green School in Lewisham** is particularly successful in these respects.

The school's approach underlines the diversity of cultural traditions represented in the school and the value attached to these by the celebration of religious festivals and special events such as a Black history week... Visits to theatres and art galleries, foreign exchange visits, school concerts and drama productions are regular features of school life. Additionally, numerous opportunities to become involved in artistic activities, sometimes outside the school, such as South Bank music projects or working with artists in residence, extend pupils' cultural experiences. Furthermore, a staff appointments policy and practice has resulted in a well-balanced group of teachers and support staff representing good role models from a wide range of cultural backgrounds.

OFSTED INSPECTION REPORT, 1996

Overall, however, there is a need for further debate on what constitutes cultural development and how schools can provide for it more effectively.

4.3 Pupils' attitudes to learning

Clearly, pupils who share in the positive ethos of the school, who are well motivated and who understand that the school strives for their benefit, make more rapid progress and ultimately attain more highly. Additionally, having contributed positively to the life of the school, they are more likely to leave school as young citizens able to make a considered and beneficial contribution to their community and society at large.

Chart 42 Pupils' attitudes to learning, Key Stages 3 & 4

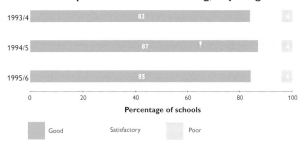

In the majority of schools the attitudes of most pupils are positive and in one school in three they are very good. For example, inspectors found a very strong link between attitudes and learning at **Brine Leas School, Cheshire**.

Generally pupils' attitudes to their learning are positive, as are their relationships with each other and with their teachers. They show enthusiasm, enjoyment in learning and a willingness to work hard. Their response to challenges and difficult tasks is purposeful and they can concentrate well, persevering with determination and making good use of their time even when interest in their work is beginning to fade. A consistent feature of lessons in all year groups is the readiness with which the pupils help one another. As a consequence they work particularly well in pairs and in a variety of larger groups and teams. They are equally competent when occupied with individual tasks and organise their own work well. Pupils are generally well motivated and show curiosity and interest in their work. They are responsible, co-operative and well-behaved learners.In many lessons pupils skilfully communicate their ideas and information and make effective use of observation and information-seeking skills. Many subjects offer good opportunities to look for patterns and to develop deeper understanding, for example in English, modern languages, geography and history where they have to find out information and give explanations. In a wide range of subjects they make interesting and perceptive comments, show confidence in the use of specialist vocabulary and speak with fluency and accuracy in modern foreign languages. They show flair when they communicate ideas and interpretations as in drama, physical education and personal and social education. In science, technology and art pupils demonstrated good practical ability, making thoughtful observations, speculating and testing their ideas and evaluating the outcomes of their investigations. Pupils showed themselves to be capable of evaluating their own work in a wide range of lessons including physical education, drama, English, technology, art and French.

OFSTED INSPECTION REPORT, 1994

Most pupils have good relationships with peers and with teachers, respect the values and beliefs of others, and understand the consequences of their actions for themselves and others.

Chart 43 Response by Year Group, all lessons 1996/97

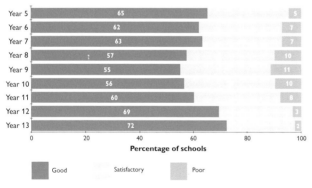

Percentage of schools

Good   Satisfactory   Poor

4.4 Pupils' behaviour

Pupils' behaviour in the large majority of schools is good. However, a more detailed analysis shows that the proportion of schools where behaviour was judged to be very good fell from two-thirds to one-third between 1993 and 1997. The number of schools where behaviour was judged to be unsatisfactory or poor remained constant at one in twenty. Typical of the schools where behaviour is very good is **Chatham South School, Kent.**

Pupils' behaviour in almost all lessons and around the school is very good. The school functions as an orderly community, where pupils understand what is expected of them and demonstrate a high level of self-discipline. The quality of relationships within the school is very good, with the school providing a caring environment in which pupils are polite and friendly. Pupils' behaviour and attentiveness make a very positive contribution to the quality of learning and the quality of life in the school. The school's success in developing every pupil's sense of belonging and avoiding disaffection, even among children who enter the school with a history of behavioural difficulties, is an outstanding feature and an important strength of the school.

OFSTED INSPECTION REPORT 1996

In the great majority of schools teachers attempt to manage pupils fairly, staff and pupils respect each other, and most individual pupils feel secure and well supported. In a minority of schools, sporadic low-level disruption continues despite the efforts of teachers. As a result, pupils' attainment is low and their progress curtailed. In a small number of schools, the management of behaviour occupies an inordinate amount of time, and in some lessons and parts of the school teachers are not in sufficient control. In a very small number of cases individuals and groups of pupils display very antisocial and sometimes violent behaviour, often predominantly influenced from outside the school.

It is, nevertheless, a long-standing problem for many schools that a small number of badly behaved pupils can cause a large amount of

Chart 44 The behaviour of pupils

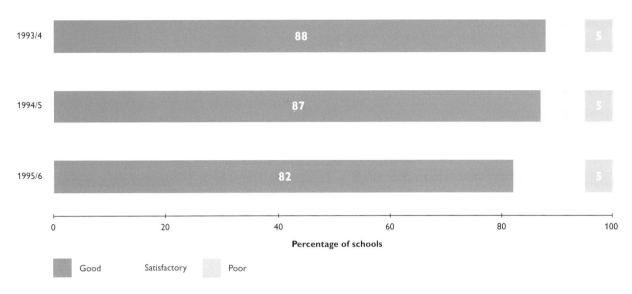

Percentage of schools

Good   Satisfactory   Poor

disruption that threatens the progress not only of the pupils concerned but of all other pupils with whom they are taught. Most poor behaviour takes place in or immediately around the classroom, involving disputes with other pupils and bullying, disruption of lessons, persistent failure to obey school rules and confrontation with teachers, sometimes with verbal abuse and occasionally with physical violence. Many of these incidents could neither be anticipated nor avoided, and occur despite every effort at the level of the school and individual teacher. In some cases, however, incidents occur where teachers do not manage or teach classes effectively, and where the resulting strained relationships spill into other lessons. A minority of incidents occur around the school at break and lunch-times, and are often concerned with disagreements between pupils, at worst in the form of intimidation or bullying and occasionally criminal offences, usually related to theft or substance abuse.

Some groups of pupils are more likely to behave poorly than others. For example, schools receive some pupils in Year 7 who are already influenced by an anti-education culture which includes 'learned bad behaviour' derived from home or from association with older peers. This can openly discourage pupils, predominantly boys, from actively engaging in the learning process. Schools serving disadvantaged areas are particularly likely to suffer from such pressures. Problems are also posed for schools which receive disaffected pupils excluded from other schools or pupils transferred

on the advice of their previous school to leave voluntarily or face exclusion. Both of these groups of pupils can unsettle schools, even those which have a successful track record in managing 'their own' pupils. The effect of some of these pupils on schools already under pressure is of real concern. In some schools, up to three-quarters of all exclusions are of pupils who have previously been excluded from other schools.

The lack of skills in literacy which some pupils bring with them can also have an important impact on their attitudes and behaviour. Boys of below average ability but ineligible for SEN support, who have difficulty in successfully accessing the reading content of many subjects of the curriculum, are particularly likely to misbehave. Some of these pupils choose to disguise their learning weaknesses by disrupting lessons. Schools which monitor incidents of poor or inappropriate behaviour to identify patterns and trends often find that modern foreign languages and science lessons are areas of particular concern.

Additionally, a particular cause of concern is the overall increase in exclusions of minority ethnic pupils, particularly African-Caribbean boys and boys of dual heritage, which together constitute 50% of all minority ethnic exclusions and 24% of all incidents of exclusion. Although the behaviour of Traveller children is often good, a disproportionate number of this group, too, are excluded.

4.5 The management of pupils' behaviour

All schools have behaviour policies and an increasing number have developed codes of behaviour that have been negotiated with pupils, parents, teachers and other adults in the school and governing bodies.

At **South Camden Community School,** the behaviour policy includes aims, objectives, responsibilities of staff, exclusions criteria, and strategies for promoting high standards of behaviour. These address matters such as ethos, differentiation, motivation, relevance, and the promotion of pupils' self-esteem. The policy is encapsulated in the Classroom Code:

Teachers

- set tasks clearly

- be aware of pupils' needs

- involve all pupils in lessons

- prepare a variety of tasks to suit everyone

- praise efforts and achievements

Pupils

- ask for help

- take responsibility for your own behaviour

- pay attention to instructions

- be well prepared for lessons

- finish homework on time

- do not name call or cuss

Pupils and teachers

- value each others' languages

- arrive at lessons on time

- treat each other with respect

- keep classrooms safe, calm places for working

- keep good order and set high standards of behaviour

- listen to others' views

SOUTH CAMDEN COMMUNITY SCHOOL
CLASSROOM CODE

The inspection report recognises the effectiveness of this code in the daily life of the school.

Behaviour around the school is good; students are courteous towards each other and towards adults. Students show consideration and respect for others, for their beliefs and values, and for property and equipment. This helps to create an orderly and safe environment which is of particular benefit to the small number of physically disabled students, enabling them to participate safely in the daily life of the school.

OFSTED INSPECTION REPORT, 1996

The quality of these behaviour policies and the extent to which they are rigorously applied can have a significant impact. Often, and increasingly in the last five years, schools have adopted a positive approach to behaviour management, placing greater emphasis on rewards such as certificates of merit and access to privileges and accompanied by structured sanctions so that pupils are aware of the consequences of any bad behaviour.

However, where an approach is applied too mechanistically, or where some teachers have not fully grasped the implications of the structured sanctions, there is a tendency for the hierarchy of sanctions to dominate. Additionally, problems occur where behaviour policies are not spelled out for each new intake, and where staff take for granted pupils' understanding of a list of rules and the consequences of not following them.

As noted above, schools in certain circumstances have more pupils who behave poorly than others. Equally, some schools are more effective than others in dealing with such difficulties. For example, comparisons of schools in disadvantaged areas show that pupils in schools sharing the same catchment and with the same ability profile can behave very differently, often reflecting differences in other aspects of the schools' performance such as overall attainment. Where such schools articulate their value system and all staff work together to set an example to pupils, this has a positive effect on their behaviour. At best, for example, information gathered by pastoral staff concerning behaviour and motivation is shared with heads of department who in turn use it to inform lesson planning or to stimulate a review of teaching and classroom management. In these circumstances pupils, despite many having learning difficulties compounded by social disadvantage, are motivated to achieve.

Some schools have particular difficulty in dealing effectively with misbehaviour amongst pupils from minority ethnic groups. Little relevant staff development has been undertaken by schools serving mixed racial areas in recent years. Increasingly, however, schools, LEA elected members and community groups are giving the issue higher priority, linking concerns about behaviour to those about underachievement by minority ethnic groups. An example of such an approach to behaviour management was noted by inspectors at **Leytonstone School, Waltham Forest.**

Expectations about standards of behaviour are clear and consistently reinforced. The well-established systems of reward and praise are having a positive effect and are supported by the parents. Poor behaviour is dealt with effectively and recorded on incident referral forms. There is appropriate emphasis on helping pupils identify and log strategies for improvement. Parents are confident that the school sets good standards of behaviour and that any racism will be dealt with effectively. Incidents of bullying and racism, however minor, are taken seriously and strategies are being developed to support pupils. Parents are encouraged to monitor their child's effort and behaviour through the school diary. The proper procedures for exclusions are observed. These are monitored and reported fully to the governors. The high proportion of pupils excluded who are of ethnic minority origin is of concern. Numbers are reducing and the use of other strategies, including community service, is positive.

OFSTED INSPECTION REPORT, 1994

Since that time the school has taken a number of steps.

Data was analysed carefully to identify patterns of poor behaviour, and the school consciously moved towards a system which emphasised rewards rather than sanctions and targeted specific action at specific groups of pupils. The school has for some years used an 'On-Call' system for dealing with poor behaviour. Teachers needing help with a pupil page the senior management team member on duty, who attends, writes the name of the pupil and the misdemeanour on the 'On-Call' register, and takes appropriate temporary action. The data from these registers is analysed by gender, ethnicity, subject, teacher, day and time of event. Call-out data is used to inform discussion with parents, teachers and heads of department. The school has attempted to emphasise rewards and publishes a weekly 'magazine' which mentions classes and individuals who have done particularly good work. The school has also initiated projects specifically to tackle underachievement and the poor behaviour of particular groups of pupils.

HMI INSPECTION, 1996

In order to support such effective strategies, managing pupils' behaviour in the classroom should be a priority for in-service training. Many teachers lack a sufficient understanding of how young people develop socially and intellectually. Some teachers, for example, fail to realise sufficiently that children's behaviour is not that of adults, that to take on responsibility children have to be trained in taking it, and that inevitably there will be times when they fail. Many teachers also have difficulty in understanding the cultural and sub-cultural issues that many pupils bring to schools, and the implications of these for teaching and learning.

The majority of schools are effective in making contact with parents where there is concern over their children's behaviour. In most cases schools are sensitive to the concerns of parents and their anxieties. Where they feel that parents are supportive, even where the parental support is ineffective, schools are more likely to be sympathetic to the pupils and their family circumstances and temper their approach accordingly. Where parents are aggressive and uncooperative, schools move more quickly to exercising severe sanctions including exclusion. Some schools are more effective than others at harnessing the goodwill and support of parents, and indeed at providing parents with additional authority.

At St Margaret's Boys' School, Liverpool, a system called 'Headteacher's Review' is used by the senior management team to support both pupils and parents where boys are in difficulty in school. The parents and pupil are seen by the headteacher, where the situation is explained and agreement is reached on targets to be achieved for a two-week period. The targets are not just academic and behavioural, they can also be set for the home, for example, with the school supporting a parent in insisting that a child is at home by a given time. Parents state that this strategy has been beneficial in assisting their management of their children, and the school is aware that it is a critical mechanism for keeping the child in school and thus avoiding the consequences of using the ultimate sanction of exclusion. The strategy does not work for every pupil or every parent. However, a large number of parents who have been through the process are positive about its benefits.

HMI INSPECTION, 1997

Exclusion of pupils

There has been widespread and sometimes heated public debate surrounding the issue of the exclusion of pupils from schools: this centres on the extent and the effectiveness of exclusion as a sanction, and on the wider consequences for individuals and the community at large. The numbers of exclusions, both fixed-term and permanent, have risen in recent years but the lack of reliable statistics makes it impossible to quantify the precise scale of this increase. Permanent exclusion is a very serious matter, frequently marking the end of full-time schooling and too often leaving the young person vulnerable to the temptations of crime.

Some schools, often in quite disadvantaged circumstances, succeed in restricting the numbers of exclusions to very low levels. Others, however, exclude large numbers of pupils. In some cases an increase in numbers of exclusions can be attributed to the application of new stratified codes of conduct in which exclusion is a 'fixed penalty' on a sliding scale: whereas in the past, for

example, incidents of fighting were dealt with by pastoral staff as arbitrators and conciliators, many recently adopted behaviour codes stipulate temporary exclusion as the punishment for fighting. Some schools exclude over-hastily, and in so doing put the excluded pupils further at risk. On the other hand, there are also some schools which on occasion fail to use exclusion as a punishment when it might be beneficial to all parties concerned if they did so.

Few pupils are excluded for single major offences; most exclusions are for an accumulation of incidents over a long period of time and when other disciplinary procedures appear not to be having an effect. Of all pupils excluded for up to three days, six out of ten do not re-offend in the following twelve months, an indication that such short-term exclusion is often an effective punishment.

A matter of great concern is the disproportionate number of exclusions which can be linked to fragile relationships between some teachers and pupils from minority ethnic groups, and particularly African-Caribbean boys. Evidence from schools suggests that three-quarters of the pupils excluded from this ethnic group are of average to above-average ability, but are seriously underperforming academically. This is in sharp contrast to their white peers who are excluded, three-quarters of whom are of below-average ability. Frequently the incident leading to exclusion involves confrontation in which black boys or girls challenge the teacher. Often this stems from a perception of injustice, and sometimes racism is inferred by the pupil. Similar trends are beginning to appear with some Asian heritage groups, particularly Pakistani and Bangladeshi boys. They

Chart 45 Permanent exclusions 1994/95/96

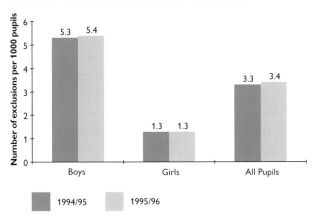

too are beginning to seriously challenge some staff whom they perceive to be racist. Even in girls' schools, where generally incidents of disruption are low, black and some Asian heritage girls are becoming more difficult for the schools to manage. All the evidence suggests that the attitudes and expectations of staff, together with the perceptions and attitudes of some pupils, can sometimes lead to an explosive situation that cuts across gender lines. There is an urgent need for schools to monitor more carefully achievement levels and incidents of poor behaviour by different ethnic groups to help secure equality of opportunity and treatment. Related staff development is also a priority for many schools.

External agencies such as the Education Welfare Service and Educational Psychological Service work hard to support schools but, where faced by limited resources, find it difficult to meet both the demands from schools and their other statutory duties. The impact of funding cuts on Child Guidance Services over the last four years is beginning to have a serious impact on schools' ability to manage certain children, and more children now find themselves out of mainstream school and in alternative provision, which is more expensive to provide than maintaining a pupil in full time mainstream provision.

Drug-related incidents

One cause of exclusion is the involvement of pupils in drug-related incidents - mainly alcohol, tobacco and solvent misuse rather than illegal drugs. Three-quarters of secondary schools have responded to the DfEE Circular 4/95, Drug Education in Schools, by writing policies for dealing with drug-related incidents or by reviewing their existing guidelines. In the remaining quarter of schools and in some others where there is insufficient detail in the policy statements, there is often confusion as to how best to deal with drug-related incidents. For example, in some schools there is uncertainty about when and how to involve pastoral staff, parents, the senior management team and outside agencies in dealing with particular incidents. Such lack of a clear policy leads to a minority of schools simply invoking their disciplinary procedures which in turn can lead to their moving too quickly to exclusion. In these cases schools fail to consider carefully enough the educational and social development of the pupil concerned and the

impact of the exclusion on the pupil as well as on others. Exclusion can place the pupil at risk of further exposure to drugs. In the majority of schools, isolation of the pupil or temporary exclusion provide a breathing space while the school, in consultation with others, decides on the most appropriate course of action. Generally schools are using permanent exclusion only in cases of repeated possession of drugs or for instances of drug dealing.

While the overall level of exclusions has increased in the last four years there has been no significant reported increase in the number relating to drug misuse. However, this may disguise the true picture. There is evidence that schools do not always record the involvement of drugs in incidents where pupils have been excluded for disruptive behaviour. For example, in a small number of cases, violent behaviour, the recorded reason for exclusion, is associated with the consumption of alcohol.

Some schools, mainly but not exclusively serving inner-city areas, work hard to keep drugs, solvents and alcohol out of the school.

In an inner-city secondary school in Birmingham, a group of mainly Year 9 pupils was involved in glue sniffing. The material for this had been supplied by a local dealer: the police were informed and the dealing stopped. The pupils involved were identified, and to ensure their safety, isolated from their lessons and kept in constant contact with a member of staff. They were then interviewed by their tutor/head of year and their parents were involved at an appropriate stage. At all times the school aimed to be supportive rather than punitive and at no time was any pupil excluded. For each of the pupils involved, the school, parents, and pupils themselves devised a strategy for coping with the problem. In some cases this involved pupils being delivered to the school by parents on their way to work and being collected at the end of the day. Throughout the school day they were offered supervision and purposeful activities. Overall the policy was very effective in practice and enabled all the pupils concerned to return to their normal work and avoid further involvement in substance abuse.

HMI INSPECTION, 1996

For schools on large campuses with several entrances this can be very difficult, but in general they are vigilant in supervising and ensuring the welfare of the young people in their care, with some examples of particularly good practice.

4.6 Pupils' attendance

Many schools, including schools in areas of disadvantage, maintain good attendance, as is the case at **Cardinal Pole School, Hackney.**

High standards of attendance and punctuality make a positive contribution to pupils' progress and attainment. Clear expectations, consistent standards, prompt action and regular monitoring have achieved a good record of attendance and punctuality. Registration takes place at the beginning of the morning and afternoon sessions and attendance is monitored throughout the day. Sixth-form students are required to register in the morning and remain in school for lessons and supervised independent study, but independent study time can be spent off site in the afternoon. There is no post-registration truancy. Parents are expected to notify the school promptly if pupils are absent and if they do not the school contacts them promptly. On return to school pupils must provide a note from parent/carer giving an explanation for absence. Regular team meetings are held to monitor any patterns of absence and identify pupils who have attendance problems. These pupils can be helped with a variety of strategies including individual attendance records and regular meetings with the support team. The school's policy on attendance and punctuality is clearly set out for pupils and parents alike and is backed by a system of sanctions and rewards. Most of the pupils are prompt for lessons, despite the crowded stairs and corridors, enabling the school day to proceed in an orderly and efficient way. Pupils who are absent for any length of time are well supported by the school on their return.

OFSTED INSPECTION REPORT, 1996

A small proportion of young people have a poor record of attendance which can be closely linked to their poor attitudes towards learning and poor behaviour. Such pupils are the most likely to be excluded or to exclude themselves by persistent non-attendance. Additionally, particularly in inner-urban and some rural schools, significant numbers of pupils whose attitudes are generally satisfactory lose a portion of their education because of the willingness of parents to take them out of school for their own reasons, such as shopping expeditions or childminding, and to condone their child's absence for trivial reasons. Increasingly over recent years, parents across the socio-economic spectrum have begun to take pupils out of school during term-time so that the family can enjoy a cheaper holiday. Asian heritage pupils' attendance is generally good, but long absences due to visits to the parents' or grandparents' homeland can have a detrimental impact on achievement.

Chart 46 Percentage of half days missed owing to absence 1994-97

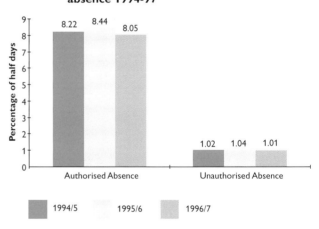

Pupils with poor literacy skills and a negative attitude to learning tend to have erratic patterns of attendance, which compound their difficulties as few schools have effective mechanisms to support pupils in catching up on lessons missed. Erratic attendance can eventually lead to prolonged non-attendance. Where it has become firmly established by the end of Key Stage 3 it can result in pupils opting out of school altogether in Key Stage 4 as they become more and more aware of the gaps in their learning and fail to meet the work demands of GCSE courses. There is a strong link between disadvantage and poor attendance. For example, parental unemployment can affect attendance. Also, schools serving disadvantaged

Chart 47 The overall attendance of pupils

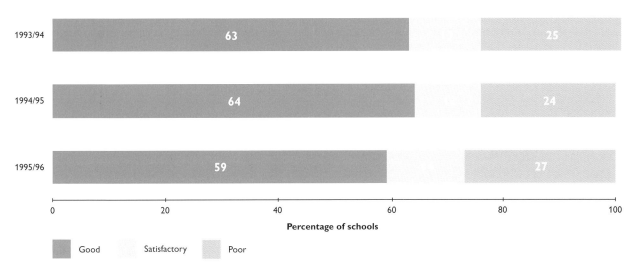

Percentage of schools

Good   Satisfactory   Poor

areas have a higher proportion of pupils who are the first people to get up in the household; quite often they are also responsible for getting younger brothers and sisters up and off to school. They also have to take a strong lead in the care of younger children and often are expected to act as friend and companion to adults who do not find coping easy. Many of these children, because of their past history of poor attendance, are below average attainers and have serious gaps in their learning, and the ability of schools to deal with their learning needs is limited in terms of time and resources.

Faced with such difficulties, some schools struggle to reach a 90 per cent attendance level (Chart 47). Many of these schools have attempted to apply a range of strategies to try to get pupils to attend school and remain there through the school day. However, even when supported by effective and efficient Education Welfare Services, some of these schools fail to make consistent improvement. In some LEAs parents have been taken to court, but with varying degrees of success. Where schools have been more successful in raising attendance, they have generally gone beyond looking at systems and have reconsidered fundamental issues, such as access to a relevant curriculum, which will attract pupils to school and hold them there.

4.7 Pastoral support and guidance of pupils

The pastoral programme and, especially, the role of the tutor have the potential to play a crucial part in balancing academic with pastoral

monitoring and guidance as a central feature of overall school policy. In most schools the quality of pastoral leadership is good. Heads of year, heads of house, or more occasionally heads of key stage, work hard to ensure that they know all the pupils in their care well.

At the **Rydon Community School, West Sussex,** this works through a year system.

The school provides good educational support and personal guidance for its pupils, including those with learning difficulties. It has developed good policies and procedures and takes effective actions to ensure pupils' academic, welfare, and health and safety needs are fully met. The roles of all staff involved in pastoral work are well-defined, understood and practised. The pastoral team is ably led by a member of the senior management team who has responsibility for special educational needs and pupil learning. This integration of responsibilities ensures that both pastoral and academic matters receive equal attention, and provides a coherent means of monitoring and supporting all aspects of pupils' development. Both pupils and parents value the care, sensitivity and patience shown by the pastoral team and form tutors. There is effective communication between heads of year and form tutors which is complemented by regular, well-managed and recorded team meetings.

OFSTED INSPECTION REPORT, 1997

At **Philip Morant School, Colchester,** a house system is preferred.

> *The school has clear and effective systems and structures in place to promote pupils' welfare and to support good learning. The form tutor has the major responsibility for the oversight of pupils' academic progress, as well as their personal well-being. Academic progress is assessed termly and is very closely monitored. The tutor functions within a well developed house system. The school has regularly reviewed the nature of the house system and consulted widely about its effectiveness. These reviews have always revealed enthusiastic support for the system and produced improvements. Commonality of practice is achieved through the very regular meetings of the heads of house, chaired by the Head or Deputy Head (pupil services). Within this general agreed ethos, however, appropriate different initiatives and activities flourish.*
>
> *OFSTED INSPECTION REPORT, 1996*

In a significant number of schools, the pastoral head's role has been extended to embrace a more explicit oversight of pupils' academic progress. By contrast, however, there has generally been a diminution over the last five years in the time available for these duties. Non-teaching time for pastoral purposes can be as little as 70 minutes per week over and above that allocated to all staff for lesson preparation and marking, for oversight of a group of pupils typically ranging from 150 to 250 pupils. Additionally, few school timetablers ensure that key pastoral staff are allocated non-contact time, other than registration time, at the beginning of each day when it is most needed.

The time available to pastoral heads can be further eroded when classroom teachers refer pupils directly to them rather than the form tutor in order to deal with minor issues. This, coupled with the significant amount of time that pastoral heads spend with a relatively small group of pupils whose attitudes and behaviour require more consistent and sustained input from staff, means that their broader role cannot be effectively discharged. In particular they often find it more

and more difficult to allocate time to counsel and support some pupils. Furthermore, by becoming locked into a policing role, pastoral heads find it more difficult to fully develop their role of overseeing pupils' academic as well as social development.

The role of the tutor is potentially complex, requiring involvement as mediator, friend, parent, counsellor, confidante and academic mentor. In nearly six out of ten schools tutors perform their duties well, but in nearly one in eight they are unsatisfactory. Where tutoring is good, pupils develop a sense of group identity and loyalty to each other and the school. There is strong evidence to suggest that positive leadership from the tutor focuses pupils on learning and achievement, encourages them to participate in a wide range of school and community activities, and develops their sense of self-worth. In the majority of schools pupils feel well supported in terms of advice and guidance, and most pupils feel that there is at least one member of staff to whom they can turn if they have any concerns. In the more effective schools, the tutor is actively engaged with the pupils in setting targets for each year and in ensuring that the support is provided to meet them. Depending upon the extent of the role of the tutor and the content of the tutorial periods, schools have explored other ways of providing for the close monitoring of academic progress, as at **Shenley Court School, Birmingham.**

> *Pupils are attached in small groups to an academic tutor in Year 7. All staff are involved in this programme. Pupils meet with their tutors at increasingly frequent rates as they progress up the school. Individual tutorial sessions are held after school for 25 minutes. The content of sessions is planned by a senior member of staff, and results in pupils drawing up their individual action plans in consultation with their academic tutor and subject teachers. The scheme has proved successful and popular with staff and pupils.*
>
> *OFSTED INSPECTION REPORT, 1994*

Some teachers give minimal attention to their role as a tutor, going little further than the completion of mandatory tasks such as registration. Where the quality of tutoring is less than satisfactory, pupils' sense of identity and commitment to the school can be adversely affected. As a consequence, they become more difficult to manage, and this has a negative impact on classroom performance across the curriculum.

A responsibility of teachers as tutors in many schools is to assist pupils in the completion of their Records of Achievement (RoA). RoAs exist in the majority of schools, sometimes throughout the school from Year 7 but more frequently in Key Stage 4 and beyond - often leading to the issue of the National Record of Achievement to school leavers. In most schools, there are positive effects in terms of dialogue between pupils, tutors and subject teachers. In the best practice, RoAs provide a vehicle for the development of pupil self-evaluation and for target-setting in both subject and pastoral contexts throughout the school. Such schools demonstrate the potential of RoAs to support the improvement of standards of work. However, in a significant number of schools the status of the RoA is low, often because of a perception that it is not held in high esteem by future trainers or employers.

Management of sixth forms is most successful when the head of sixth form is a member of the school's senior management team, with suitably delegated authority, and is supported by a team of sixth-form tutors who themselves have clearly defined roles. In a minority of schools, however, there are examples of overlapping responsibilities between a deputy headteacher and the head of sixth form, and between the head of sixth form and sixth-form tutors, which leads to inefficient and ineffective procedures. In some schools information on, for example, value-added analysis of examination results is made available to heads of department for departmental purposes, but not to sixth-form tutors for advising and supporting students.

Some schools have recently begun to develop more sophisticated monitoring and review procedures for tracking individual students' progress in their sixth forms. As part of this process, tutors and subject teachers use baselines and value-added data to set future targets, and mock examination

results are sometimes evaluated in the same way. Few schools, however, systematically assess and record students' wider achievements and development. Records of Achievement, for example, are rarely extended into the sixth form. Guidance is most highly valued by students when it is part of timetabled contact time and has a clear purpose. Students respond well when the school's assessment system provides clear feedback on progress and the opportunity to discuss subject-specific and overall progress with staff.

Many schools provide induction programmes for new entrants to the sixth form, often including a residential element. This is generally well received by the students and is helpful in enabling them to adjust to the demands of sixth-form life.

4.8 Links with parents

The arrangements made by schools to link with parents are effective in most schools, but more so in schools in favoured socio-economic contexts than those in areas of social disadvantage. Schools which are effective have established policies, communicate with parents frequently and in clear language, and sustain an expectation amongst parents that they will be informed about issues relevant to their child's education and that their opinions are valued. Additionally, such schools provide a welcoming environment for parents who wish to visit the school, particularly where the subject of the visit is a matter of concern relating to their child.

Chart 48 Links with parents

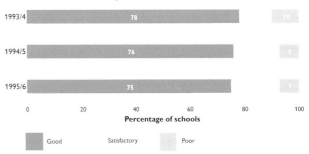

An increasing number of schools have introduced home-school contracts that formalise the expectations of all the parties involved in the education of the child. At the **Hewett School,**

Norfolk, for example, links with parents are set out in a 'Contract of Educational Partnership' to be signed by pupil, parents and the school.

Parents and students have the right to expect from the school:

- A safe, well-ordered, and caring environment in the school, appropriate for the age and needs of the individual student.

- Challenging programmes of teaching, learning and guidance, appropriate for the age and needs of the student.

- Early warnings of any problems associated with school work, relationships or discipline.

- Accessible channels to express their views on wider school issues.

- Clear aims and objectives relating to all courses of study.

- Accurate and helpful information about each student's efforts, progress and achievement.

- Opportunity and encouragement to take part in a variety of school activities.

Above all, it is the school's responsibility to demonstrate that each student is valued as an individual and that every effort is made to meet his or her needs.

The school will expect from Parents who have chosen to send their son or daughter to Hewett:

- Support for the code of conduct and discipline necessary to ensure the smooth working of the school.

- Support in encouraging and sustaining the efforts and achievements of their son or daughter.

- Participation in regular scheduled discussions on the student's effort, progress and achievement.

- A willingness to make full use of the established channels of communication.

- Early contact with the school to discuss any matters which might have a bearing on the student's progress, happiness or behaviour.

- The assurance of regular and punctual attendance by their son or daughter, correctly dressed and equipped for effective school work.

Above all, Parents' support for the work of their son or daughter and his/her teachers is vital for the student's success.

The 1994 OFSTED report on **Hewett School** said:

The school has good links with parents, industry and the community. It endeavours to ensure that those links are not only social but also contribute to pupils' learning. Parents particularly value the help offered them through meetings, the Parents' Clinic and through the school's professionally presented documentation. This provision enables them to support their children when they first enter the school and at the various stages when educational choices have to be made.

OFSTED INSPECTION REPORT, 1994

Weak links with parents can arise where the school has a low expectation of their involvement, and where communication with them is not seen as a priority and little guidance is given to parents on how they might be more involved in supporting their child's work. This is reflected in parents' poor attendance at meetings and lack of support for other school activities. On the other hand, some parents undermine the work of the school by being singularly uncooperative in supporting basic rules or in enforcing requirements such as the completion of homework.

Reports to parents on pupils' progress

A major responsibility of all teachers is to report to parents on individual pupils' progress and attainment at regular intervals. Most schools' assessment policies make reference to reporting to parents, although many of these do not sufficiently emphasise statutory requirements, particularly to report on weaknesses as well as strengths in pupils' progress and attainment.

Over the period of this review, annual reports to parents have shown some improvement as schools have increasingly moved towards meeting the statutory requirements. However, in the overall effectiveness of schools' reporting about pupils' progress, inspectors have found no improvement. Parents are usually appreciative of the information received through reports and the considerable time spent by teachers in preparing them. Most reports allow sufficient space for subject teacher comment, with a covering sheet for general comment from form tutors, pastoral heads or the

Chart 49 Reporting about the progress of pupils, Key Stages 3 & 4

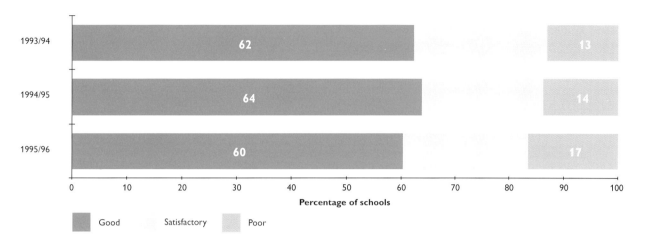

headteacher. Most schools provide quantified and verbal information, and almost all schools provide end-of-key stage results data as required statutorily. Some schools are considering the inclusion of some form of individual targets in reports. It remains to be seen if such targets are effective and well used in raising standards and whether the considerable time spent on target setting activity is a good investment. Some schools also give information about each course being followed and allow for the inclusion of pupil self-assessments of their progress and attainment.

In a significant minority of schools, there is, however, still a range of weaknesses in reports prepared by teachers. Quite commonly, inconsistent formats are used across subjects and these can confuse pupils and parents. Many subject teachers write more about effort and attitude than actual attainment and progress. In some schools, reports are internally inconsistent, for example between quantified data, such as marks or grades, and teachers' comments, or between teachers' comments and pupils' comments.

The major weakness of reports in many schools remains their failure to reveal the weaknesses in pupils' progress and attainment, or the subject-specific targets which pupils need to address. In many schools, reports in at least some subjects are too complimentary - providing parents only with details of what the pupils can do rather than areas which they still need to address.

A majority of schools provide, in addition to the statutorily required annual reports and a parents' evening at which their children's progress can be

discussed, at least one interim report. This is usually a single sheet providing quantified information in the form of grades or marks. The good intent and potential of this increasingly common practice is not fully realised because most schools report mainly or only on pupils' effort at this stage, with little or no evidence of progress and attainment.

In most schools, reports are checked by a senior member of staff - commonly the headteacher, deputy or a pastoral head, to provide a measure of quality control. However, too often monitoring picks up only omissions or errors in spelling, and does not address the range of weaknesses to which reference is made above.

5
TEACHING

Good teaching is the key to high standards of achievement and it is encouraging that in 1996-7 overall half of lessons in Key Stage 3 and slightly more in Key Stage 4 were well taught (Chart 50). Although teaching was broadly satisfactory in a further three out of eight lessons, it was poor in about one lesson in eight. As Chart 51 shows, there is considerable variation among subjects in the quality of their teaching and the extent of improvement in Key Stage 4. (The trend for each subject over the first three years of the cycle is shown in separate subject sections, below). Overall, therefore, there clearly remains considerable scope for further improvement.

5.1 Specialist teaching

Subject knowledge

In the great majority of schools, nine schools out of ten, most teachers in both Key Stages 3 and 4 have a good command of the subject they teach. In each key stage, subject knowledge is now generally poor in only one school in fifty. Although the amount of teaching where subject knowledge is inadequate is small overall, it can have a significant impact on particular pupils who may experience this poor teaching for a whole year or more.

Staff involved in teaching GCE AS and A-level

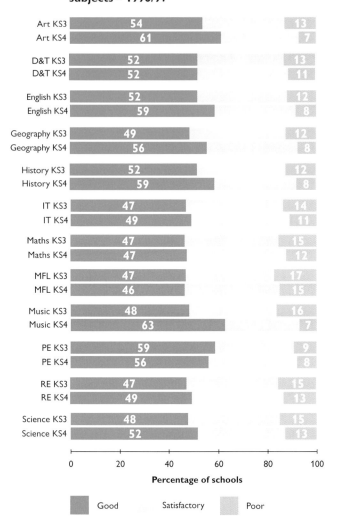

Chart 51 Quality of teaching lessons at KS3 & KS4 by subjects – 1996/97

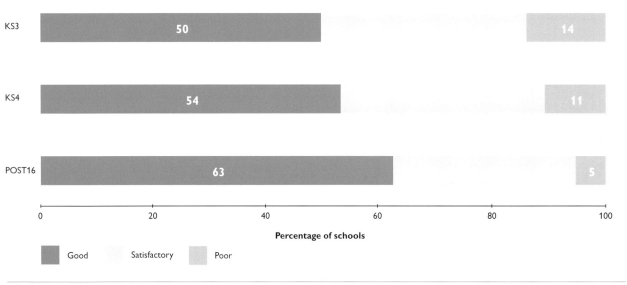

Chart 50 Quality of teaching by key stage 1996/97

courses almost invariably have the necessary subject expertise. Even when schools have a shortage of specialists in a particular subject, such as physics, A-level courses are generally given priority in the deployment of teachers. In GNVQ courses staff expertise is generally satisfactory in areas such as art and design and business studies. However, in vocational areas such as health and social care and leisure and tourism, new courses which cut across subject boundaries, staff expertise is usually less satisfactory.

Chart 52 Teachers' command of the subject

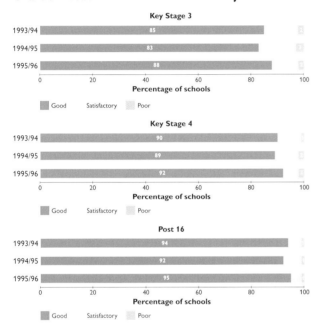

When teachers are thoroughly in command of their subject, they are able to adapt their teaching to the responses of the pupils, to use alternative and more imaginative ways of explaining, and to make connections both between aspects of their subject and with the pupils' wider experience, so capturing their attention and interest. The teacher's ability to answer pupils' spontaneous questions is an important factor in generating enthusiasm for the subject. Aware of the aims and expected outcomes of teaching their subject, they are able to set appropriate priorities in their planning, take short cuts if necessary and assess whether the essential aspects of a topic have been mastered. Teachers with a good understanding of how pupils learn their subject sequence work in the most effective way, build up pupils' knowledge, skills and understanding progressively, ensure that earlier learning is adequate to support later demands and encourage pupils to apply what they have learnt in new situations.

Good subject knowledge is an essential, but not a sufficient condition for good teaching. There are some teachers who have excellent academic qualifications but are relatively ineffective because they have not identified how pupils' understanding of the subject develops nor found appropriate ways in which this can be assessed. Teachers sometimes fail to recognise the common misunderstandings that pupils may have. In mathematics, for example, some teachers fail to recognise that many of the errors made by a pupil arise from a lack of understanding of fundamental principles, such as place value in number work.

There are thus two important facets to teachers' specialist subject knowledge. First, teachers need a secure knowledge of their subject and in particular the precise content of the National Curriculum and of the public examination syllabuses they are required to teach.

In a Year 10 GCSE art lesson, pupils were given the task of painting a still-life group of fruit, bottles and boxes, and were asked to emphasise the effects of light and shade. They experimented with moveable lamps and a spotlight to create dramatic lighting for the still-life. The teacher demonstrated how light and shade could be painted, and showed a series of still-life paintings by well-known artists which emphasised the effects of directional lighting. These were discussed and analysed by the pupils. The teacher's practical skills and her extensive knowledge of the techniques used by the artists gave the pupils a head start when they began their own still-life paintings.

HMI INSPECTION, 1996

Second, teachers must have a command of the pedagogical skills necessary to make the subject understandable to the pupils. This will include an awareness of the common difficulties that pupils encounter.

A teacher in a girls' secondary modern school had given much thought to how pupils might be helped in the arduous but necessary business of learning French verb forms; in this Year 9 lesson, they were tackling the perfect tense of irregular verbs. The teacher recognised that memory might be better assisted by a more 'visible' classification than the traditional one:

irregular verbs were thus called "les verbes bruns", and printed in brown on the teaching aids used. She acknowledged that explicit grammar practice, though essential, can be arid: drills were ingeniously designed to involve also more communicative use of the language in giving directions - useful recycling of previously learnt material. This teacher refused to compromise the firmly established use of the target language at all times, but recognised the particular need for non-linguistic support in dealing with 'abstract' grammar : she made much use of carefully prepared overhead transparencies and other visuals to aid comprehension and 'illustrate' patterns. After half an hour of intensive whole-class practice, recognising that pupils needed to continue practising but in a different mode, the teacher moved them to combined skill work using computers, which they clearly enjoyed. Knowing, however, that when pupils work independently they are more likely to lapse into English, she had taught them the necessary IT terms in French and established that maintaining the use of the target language to the limit of their knowledge was equally as important as the drill exercises themselves. Motivation was acknowledged as paramount in successful foreign language learning: those who showed particular initiative in speaking - for example, in pointing out an oversight in one exercise - were publicly praised; any backsliding in routine exchanges between pupils was gently admonished. Thus, in addition to an excellent command of French, the teacher showed understanding of how difficult aspects of learning could be eased and made more appealing, how pupils' attentive practice could be maximised, and how essential features of appropriate 'language learning behaviour' could be ensured.

HMI INSPECTION, 1997

The match of staffing to the curriculum

On the whole, schools are sufficiently well staffed to be able to meet the demands of most subjects of the National Curriculum, and the overall availability of suitably qualified teachers is good or better in nine out of ten schools (Chart 53). In one in three schools, however, the match is unsatisfactory in one or more subjects. A small but significant number of schools (about one in 20)

experience difficulties in achieving an adequate match of subject taught and initial qualification to such an extent that this depresses the standards achieved across a range of subjects.

Many schools, particularly but not exclusively in disadvantaged areas, experience significant problems in recruiting and retaining appropriately qualified teachers in a number of curriculum areas. There have been long-standing staffing difficulties in relation to IT and RE. In certain subjects, including mathematics, the physical sciences and modern foreign languages, the teaching profession has consistently failed to attract newly qualified graduates in sufficient numbers. It is clear from the persistent shortage of subject expertise in important areas of the curriculum that the flexibility of schools to offer additional allowances to recruit and retain specialist teachers has not provided an adequate solution to the problem.

There are large numbers of schools where the overall 'match' in subjects is barely satisfactory, and some non-specialist teaching is required. For example, this affects design and technology teaching in one-third of schools and English, mathematics and music teaching in over one-quarter. Other subjects affected in a significant minority of schools include RE, IT, modern foreign languages, geography, PE and art. In middle schools, the shortage of suitably qualified mathematics teachers often has an adverse effect upon the teaching of this key subject. Shortages of teachers in some subjects force other teachers to teach two or three subjects, occasionally even more, and often non-specialists are placed with lower ability groups and lower age classes.

In a number of subjects, teachers are commonly required to teach all aspects of the National Curriculum Order although their own initial qualification may correspond to it only in part. Thus, for example, science teachers whose degree is in biology are often required also to teach both the physics and the chemistry elements of the National Curriculum Programme of Study for science. The situation is similar in design and technology. In modern foreign languages, as a consequence both of a general shortage of linguists and of the fact that most schools now offer alternative first foreign languages, teachers are increasingly required to teach a language in which they have only a minor qualification and in which

Chart 53 The availability of suitably qualified teachers

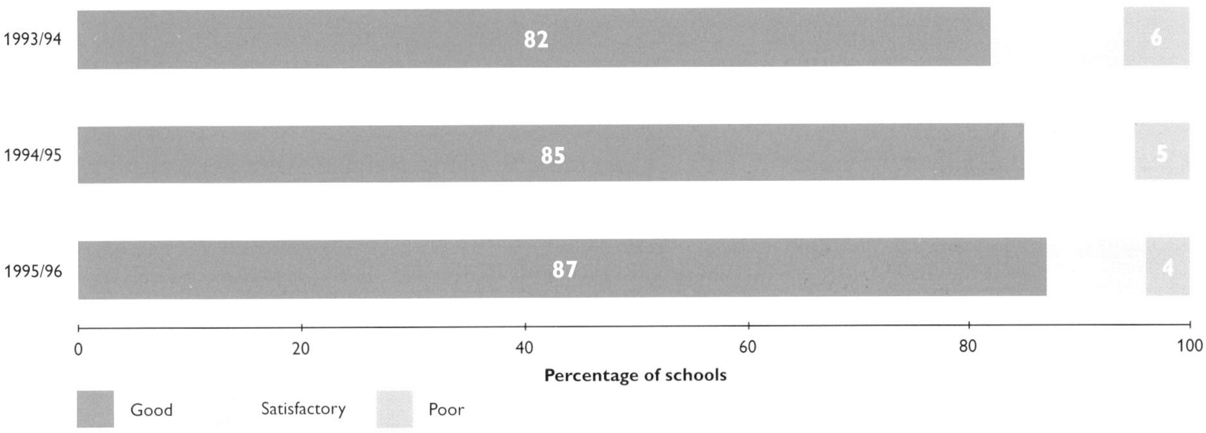

1993/94	82	6
1994/95	85	5
1995/96	87	4

0   20   40   60   80   100

Percentage of schools

Good   Satisfactory   Poor

their fluency may be limited. Such weaknesses in the subject knowledge of specialist teachers can also constitute a significant, though hidden, problem of 'match'.

Those schools which are effective in minimising the impact of unavoidable non-specialist teaching or high staff turnover provide teachers with good support in a number of ways. These include an effective induction programme, comprehensive schemes of work, and systematic monitoring of teaching which both enables effective diagnosis of the development needs of staff and facilitates effective deployment. The efficient use of teaching staff is achieved in at least nine out of ten schools, but in one in ten schools better timetabling would improve the deployment of available specialist teachers and reduce significantly the proportion of non-specialist teaching which occurs.

The ability of schools to provide curriculum breadth and balance and to give pupils an appropriate range of choice in Key Stage 4 and post-16 is dependent not only on the existing expertise of the staff, but also on their ability to respond to changing needs and on the success of senior management in providing suitable staff development opportunities. For example, small schools often experience difficulties in responding to changing demands because of the more limited

flexibility offered by a smaller number of teachers. Conversely, larger secondary schools generally have a larger and more diverse pool of staff expertise to draw upon.

Specialist teaching is an important issue in planning for the teaching of key skills in GNVQ courses. Satisfactory to good standards of achievement in the three key skills usually occurs in those schools where specialist English, mathematics and IT teachers form an integral part of the GNVQ team. These specialists are most effective when contributing fully to the planning, teaching and assessment of the courses. Their involvement usually has an important impact on the depth and breadth of key skills coverage, and on the rigour of key skills assessment. The lack of IT specialist teaching usually means that students develop too narrow a range of IT skills. Where mathematics specialists are not involved, the Application of Number unit is often covered at a fairly superficial level, and opportunities to exploit numerical methods are missed. Vocational staff who take responsibility for the key skills themselves, whilst acknowledging difficulties in coping with the application of number, and sometimes with IT, usually feel quite confident in dealing with communication; this confidence, however, is not always justified, particularly in relation to the rigour of their assessment.

Over the period of this review there has been a steady increase in the level and quality of support staff in many secondary schools. Increasingly, support staff are well qualified and many undertake professional development to enhance further the already valuable contribution they make. In all schools support staff enable headteachers and teachers to fulfil their

Chart 54 The deployment of non-teaching staff

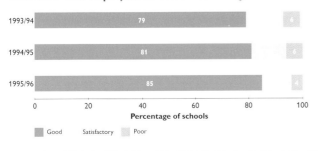

1993/94	79	6
1994/95	81	6
1995/96	85	4

0   20   40   60   80   100

Percentage of schools

Good   Satisfactory   Poor

professional roles more effectively and efficiently and important aspects of teaching and learning would be curtailed without their help. The deployment of non-teaching staff, already good overall, shows steady development and improvement. The level and quality of support by classroom assistants and non-teaching staff is good in most subjects, as is that of technical support staff in science. However, there is a lack of suitable technical expertise in many schools to support IT; this makes inappropriate demands upon IT teachers and detracts from their teaching. Technical support for design and technology is good in two in five schools, but poor in one in five.

5.2 Lesson planning, classroom organisation and teaching methods

In Key Stages 3 and 4, the overall quality of lessons improved from 1993 to 1996. In Key Stage 3, the lesson content and the suitability of learning activities were good in nearly seven out of ten schools in 1995/96, compared with nearly six out of ten in 1993/94; in Key Stage 4, the respective proportions were over seven out of ten, compared with just over six out of ten. The proportion where they were poor fell slightly in both key stages. The effectiveness of lesson content and activities in A-level classes remained good or very good in over eight out of ten schools throughout this period. From 1996 inspectors were required to judge how well teachers 'employ methods and organisational strategies which match curricular objectives and the needs of all pupils'. Teachers' methods and organisation were found to be good in about five out of ten of schools in both Key Stages 3 and 4 and in six out of ten post-16. They were poor in about one in ten schools in both key stages but only in one in thirty post-16.

Planning

Curriculum planning and the preparation of lesson plans help teachers to focus their work, with clear goals and sensible strategies for achieving them. Effective plans for single lessons and series of lessons complement and amplify the departmental scheme of work (see page 103). Teachers' lesson objectives have steadily improved at all secondary stages. Dramatic improvements in the quality of teaching have occurred in some schools where

teachers have increased the detail of planning and particularly where the teaching has then been evaluated by classroom observation.

Good lesson planning translates school policies and subject guidance into informed classroom practice; it identifies learning objectives, making provision for the different learning needs of pupils; and specifies the activities to be pursued in the lesson, the use of time, the resources, any assessment opportunity and any link to cross curricular themes and spiritual, moral social and cultural development.

Year 11 pupils taking textiles GCSE have a term to complete a major project. Objectives are clear and are shared with pupils. At the beginning of the term, the teacher had explained the assessment requirements and provided a planning sheet with suggested deadlines for stages of the work. Pupils have one 2 1/2 hour lesson a week. Pupils of all abilities work hard to make maximum use of the time available. They make good progress, particularly in their practical skills, decision making and problem solving. A significant factor is that they know what they have to do and when they have to complete the various parts of their work, if they are to remain on target. They also know that the teacher is monitoring their progress.

HMI INSPECTION, 1997

Clear objectives for lessons are important; poor lesson planning details only the content to be covered, and does not specify what pupils are to

Chart 55 Objectives for lessons

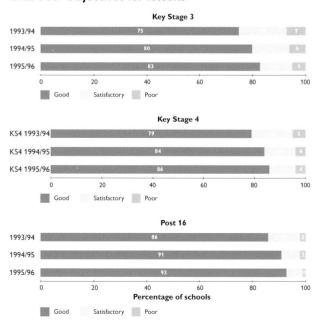

Percentage of schools

gain by being taught it. For example, a history lesson on the trade in slaves may be intended to make a major contribution to pupils' spiritual, moral, social and cultural education, but this needs to be explicit in the planning if it is not to be lost, or at best remain implicit, within the narrative.

In the very large majority of sixth-form lessons teaching and learning objectives are appropriate, relating directly to syllabus or assessment requirements. In the best A-level practice these objectives are clearly articulated and shared with the students, who are provided with a clear overview of the whole course and schedules for completion of their work. In most GNVQ work, well-written assignments set out precisely what the student is expected to achieve in relation to the vocational specifications; however, they are often insufficiently specific about what is expected in the key skills.

Where GNVQ assignments have been well planned the students have, as a consequence, been engaged in a variety of activities, often taking them out of the school to meet staff in local businesses, industry and services and to collect relevant illustrative material and information. However, the planning of this aspect of work is less than satisfactory in approximately one-fifth of schools.

Exposition and questioning

In general there has been an improvement in teachers' choice of lesson content and the tasks which pupils undertake in both Key Stages 3 and 4 and post-16.

Chart 56 Lesson content and activities

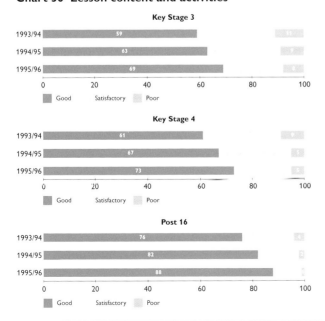

Key Stage 3

1993/94	59
1994/95	63
1995/96	69

0 20 40 60 80 100

■ Good   Satisfactory   Poor

Key Stage 4

1993/94	61
1994/95	67
1995/96	73

0 20 40 60 80 100

■ Good   Satisfactory   Poor

Post 16

1993/94	76
1994/95	82
1995/96	88

0 20 40 60 80 100

■ Good   Satisfactory   Poor

Often, however, one of the weaker elements of lessons is the introduction, revisiting and reinforcing material taught in the previous lesson or series of lessons, or making links with earlier work. HMCI's Annual Report for 1996/97 cites several subjects in which pupils' poor factual recall is a matter for concern, in particular mathematics but also science, history, geography and modern foreign languages; the wider point is also made that many pupils do not have the strategies to learn and recall key material, or the ability to use it in new contexts. Many effective lessons begin with a recap in the form of questioning or 'brainstorming', to find out what pupils already know about the topic, to reinforce material learned previously and as a sensible introduction to new work. Such procedures are very important, but are too often ignored in weaker lessons. In good mathematics lessons, for example, teachers often begin with rapid-fire questioning to sharpen pupils' mental mathematics. In a history lesson on the British Empire a few minutes were taken to recall the way in which the Romans treated the peoples that they conquered, thus making appropriate connections and developing pupils' understanding of the concept of 'Empire'.

Exposition is central to the art of teaching. It is often used effectively to introduce new material, to build on pupils' prior knowledge, to make links with other work and to establish principles which pupils can subsequently apply. In so doing, good teaching also stimulates interest and enthusiasm; many teachers do this well.

An introductory human geography lesson in Year 12 on the French region of Lorraine began with the teacher providing a stimulating account of the historical background to set the geographical context. The students were encouraged to think and reflect about the information provided for them on a set of helpful data sheets, and effective use was made of the overhead projector for maps and diagrams.

HMI INSPECTION, 1997

There is normally less formal exposition in GNVQ than in GCE A-level lessons, because of the different requirements of the courses. However, GNVQ teachers are increasingly appreciating the need for more direct input when new topics are introduced, to ensure that students have the necessary knowledge and understanding to deal effectively with their assignments.

Good exposition is sometimes enriched by the teacher acting out or demonstrating the idea or skills being presented.

In a Year 10 English lesson with a lower set the teacher's objective was to revisit work on listening and responding and the use of words and body language, before undertaking an assessment of pupils' oral skills. In an outstanding plenary the teacher demonstrated and used role play to show the difference between language which works and that which does not. Ideas were assembled on the board. The pace of work was well measured, giving pupils time to develop their understanding and to practice before formally responding to the task in role. Pupils spoke with confidence and attainment was good.

HMI INSPECTION, 1996

Demonstrations can play a valuable part in science lessons by enabling teachers to focus on particular practical techniques, illustrate or introduce new principles, or show pupils experiments which they could not for reasons of safety or resources do themselves. Pupils are less likely than in class practical to be distracted by the need to follow instructions or arrive successfully at a prescribed endpoint; interaction between the teacher and pupils can be carefully structured. This does not, however, mean that demonstration activity need be 'closed' and pupils certainly need not be passive observers.

In order to provide a dramatic illustration of 'competition' in chemical reactions a Year 9 teacher demonstrated the 'thermit reaction'. This was preceded by a discussion of the reactivity series; pupils were asked to predict what the products of the reaction might be. Safety precautions were also discussed and, following the demonstration, the teacher explained how the reaction could be used in an industrial setting. Throughout the lesson opportunities were taken to reinforce ideas about a 'league table' of reactivity and prepare pupils for their own investigatory practical work.

HMI INSPECTION, 1996

A minority of teachers enhance the quality of their exposition by the use of computers.

In a mathematics lesson on binomial probabilities, ideas were introduced by means of simple practical demonstration, the basic theory was developed, with the students themselves being skilfully encouraged to take the lead, and then computer software was used to generate large quantities of simulated data, to see whether the theory fitted practical outcomes on a scale impossible to check otherwise in the classroom.

HMI INSPECTION, 1997

Many teachers use questioning well. Effective questioning checks that pupils have understood; prompts them to think further; brings any misunderstanding out into the open; keeps pupils attentive; and gives them the opportunity to demonstrate their understanding. It offers pupils the opportunity to ask their own questions without fear of censure or ridicule. Once pupils have the confidence to put questions and volunteer comment, effective questioning by the teacher helps them to refine their enquiry or justify their opinion. In this way pupils learn to ask the right questions as well as to give the right answers.

Although the fundamentals of teaching – exposition, demonstration and questioning – are generally satisfactory, there are common failings which weaken the impact of too many lessons. Over-long exposition makes too many demands on the concentration span of some pupils while poorly structured exposition conceals rather than illuminates. Demonstrations work poorly where pupils do not have a clear view or where pupils are simply passive observers. Where questioning is poor it may over-rehearse well-known material, focus on a limited group of pupils, close pupils down with questions which only allow a limited response, or fail to build on the answers pupils have given with further questions to correct or amplify. Too often teachers seem scared of silence, so that they fail to allow pupils sufficient time to think and muster a response. Sometimes they are undemanding or over-sensitive to pupils' feelings, accepting a wrong or partial answer rather than pressing the pupil to reflect and refine or go a stage further. Over-directive teaching limits pupils' independence in posing their own questions.

Setting appropriate tasks

If pupils are to gain secure knowledge and understanding they need opportunities to discuss, to consolidate, explore and expand on what they have learnt from the teacher's introduction. Well-managed, teacher-led discussions are an essential preparation for more independent group discussion. Whole-class discussions have the advantage that the teacher can ensure pupils stay on track, as well as playing a vital role in challenging pupils' thinking, posing hypotheses, playing devil's advocate and drawing pupils on to recognise the implications of their suggestions or to refine the quality of their expression.

The teacher retains a vital role when pupils move on to group discussions. In the best of these, teachers make sure that pupils understand the ground rules, for example that a group leader or spokesperson must be chosen and that all must take turns in speaking. They give the groups a limited number of clear points to discuss, and during the discussion they circulate to check that this agenda is being followed and that all participate and, by judicious questions or suggestions, nudge the discussion to a higher level.

In a Year 8 mixed ability history class pupils were investigating the impact of the Second World War on civilians. After a stimulating opening pupils moved into groups stipulated by the teacher. Five groups worked on different aspects of the impact of war. The lowest ability group completed worksheets with questions based on photographic and textual evidence. The upper ability group used documents requiring close reading for understanding and the making of inferences. Other groups worked on material of intermediate demand. Pupils in groups worked together collaboratively for the first half of the lesson. They were then regrouped into mixed ability groups. Each group member was required to report back to the others on their uniquely held information in order to contribute to a group display. All pupils had the opportunity to present and discuss their findings. This was a very well organised lesson, and the teacher was active in prompting all pupils, including some reluctant learners, to take a full part.

HMI INSPECTION, 1995

Pupils are set a wide range of written tasks across the curriculum. At best, written work provides pupils with time to think, to reflect, to refine and to practise. Pupils are often required to make notes, sometimes by copying from the board or receiving dictation. This might be for lack of resources or because it is an efficient way of conveying essential information or making a quick link between items. However, in some subjects, such as music, science and RE, it is over-used, fails to develop enduring knowledge or promote understanding and is a cause of demotivation. It militates particularly against pupils of below average attainment who often fail to make an accurate copy or to be aware of the substance of what they have written. Note-making is an important skill which is rarely explicitly taught. In order to promote high-quality notes, particularly in examination courses, teachers need to check the quality of pupils' notes periodically, make constructive comment and demand remediation where necessary. Often notes receive only cursory attention from the teacher.

A common failing of the writing required of pupils in subjects such as science, history, geography and RE is that it consists of closed questions which only require lifting from the text or develop only lower-level skills of comprehension, selection and response. The exhortation by teachers that pupils should 'respond in their own words' is frequently an admission of the limitations of the task, that is the culling of material. Setting appropriately demanding written tasks is a key to the development of higher-level skills and understanding, and is the subject of further discussion in sections 2.5 and 7.1.

Pupils' learning is not, of course, limited to acquiring knowledge through language; they also learn by carrying out practical operations. They may work individually or in groups, but essentially the same features of good teaching obtain as for language-based tasks. In music there has been an encouraging increase in practical activity, and in particular an improvement in the way teachers teach pupils how to compose. In too many design and technology classes, on the other hand, over-teaching of designing and making, step by step, leaves pupils without the ability to see how their work will develop through to completion, and an inability to transfer their skills.

The role of the teacher in several subject areas in developing and supporting the skills of investigation and problem-solving has to be carefully planned. Some teachers help pupils to acquire the necessary knowledge and skills, but fail to give them sufficient scope to research or to confront real problems, or to apply their knowledge and skills in further enquiry. By the same token some teachers set pupils to work on 'investigations' when they have not been given sufficient practice in the basics. Pupils need to be given guidance in research skills and in analysing a problem to identify how basic skills are to be applied to it. This is helped by clearly stated objectives; by encouraging pupils to develop hypotheses, to reason and justify; and by establishing clear success criteria including a framework for recording. During the process of investigation and problem-solving, effective teachers intervene to keep pupils on track, to stimulate new avenues of enquiry, to break tasks down where necessary, and to maintain the momentum of the lesson. There is increasing good practice in all of these respects. In science, for example, teachers are increasingly confident in teaching pupils how to carry out practical investigations and in establishing the right conditions for them to practise their skills. In geography, the quality of fieldwork investigations continues to be a strong feature of pupils' work. Much good A-level work involves problem-solving.

In a Year 12 Advanced-level English language class, students analysed syntax, grammar, spelling and punctuation in an old English text with modern translation, to investigate how much change there has been since the time of Chaucer. This was a very challenging task, supported by pre-prepared guidance on the board to reinforce previous learning, and excellent one-to-one teaching which prompted the students to greater depth and closer analysis of language.

HMI INSPECTION, 1997

Much of the work done by students in GNVQ requires them to carry out assignments designed by teachers. The majority of assignments make appropriate demands on students in terms of relevant knowledge, skills and understanding, and meet the requirements of the GNVQ specifications. These assignments are based on realistic and interesting vocational applications, usually involving some practical experience. For example, Advanced art and design students in one school took complete responsibility for stage sets and costume designs for the school production of Macbeth, as part of their course requirements. Assignments in a number of schools in both leisure and tourism and business courses make effective use of work placements, for example in department stores and holiday centres, to provide realistic firsthand material for the study of customer care. However, in approximately one in five of courses observed during the academic year 1995/96, assignments were poorly planned, uninteresting and lacking in application and challenge. Too little attention was given to ensuring that students had a grasp of key knowledge and understanding and too much attention was given to compliance with a narrow interpretation of the GNVQ specifications. Resulting work was often dry and theoretical, sometimes including material directly copied from other sources.

5.3 Teachers' expectations of pupils' achievement

Teachers' expectations of what pupils can achieve are good or very good in just over half of schools in Key Stage 3 and just over three schools in five in Key Stage 4. They are poor in almost one school in six in Key Stage 3 and in about one in seven in Key Stage 4. Post-16, expectations are good or very good in over four schools in five; they are very rarely poor.

In a middle set Year 10 science lesson teacher and pupils shared high expectations. In the first part of the lesson marked test papers were returned to pupils and the teacher's dissatisfaction was reflected in the close attention which pupils gave to making corrections, answering and asking questions during this process. Pupils responded positively to criticism in the knowledge that the test had challenged them to the utmost. The lesson proceeded briskly using well-chosen video clip to introduce new material. Good use was made of the hold button to allow further comment and questioning in matters of detail. Overall the rigorous teaching promoted very positive response and promoted rapid progress.

HMI INSPECTION, 1997

High expectations are reflected in the challenge and pace of lessons and the motivation of pupils, which have shown steady improvement and are judged good or very good overall in the majority of schools, and rather better in Key Stage 4 than in Key Stage 3. Over the inspection cycle there was a decline in the proportion of schools where these features were poor. The challenge and pace of work in GCE A-level subjects was also judged to be good or very good in an increasingly high proportion of schools, reaching eight out of ten in 1996. In only a small proportion, one in twenty-five, was there insufficient challenge or too slow a pace to the work.

The pace of lessons

Where the pace of a lesson is good, there is a prompt start; the purpose of the lesson and instructions are clear; pupils have just enough time to gain the necessary knowledge, understanding or skill but without the point becoming laboured, and once set a task, they have time to finish it to an appropriate standard.

In a Year 10 English lesson using an examination board's anthology, pupils studied three poems and responded to questioning on their content, meaning and the poet's technique. The lesson was very efficient with a brisk introduction providing clear instructions rapidly followed by well-managed group work, which was productively used by pupils to explore the poems and respond to the set tasks. The clear requirement to complete group discussion in time for a plenary session forced the pace. Pupils engaged fully and animatedly in discussion, working well in groups with minimal supervision. Excellent questioning in the plenary session challenged most pupils individually, and supported a deepening understanding of the poetry as well as developing pupils' specialist vocabulary.

HMI INSPECTION, 1997

Much lesson time is wasted either because the pace is too slow, the chosen teaching method is inappropriate, or simply because the full period of the lesson is not well used. In such lessons, for

Chart 57 Teachers' expectations of pupils

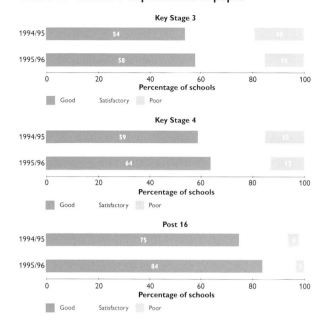

Chart 58 Challenge, pace and motivation in lessons

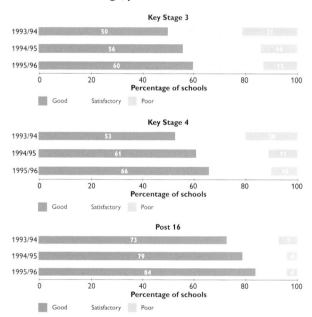

example, pupils are given far too much time for limited activities with no clear deadline, often described misleadingly as 'working at their own pace'; exposition is too long, so that pupils lose concentration; or the start of the lesson is indecisive and the teacher does not hold pupils on task until the termination of the lesson. Good teachers are sensitive to the progress that pupils are making and adjust the pace accordingly.

In a Year 8 lower set French class, pupils were talking about their bedroom in the target language, then drafting a description in writing. The teacher's enthusiasm transmitted itself to the pupils to the extent that she needed to slow down this part of the lesson to ensure that all pupils were given a chance to speak formally and to fully master the language structures. Pupils were more reluctant to undertake written work, but clear instructions, close support and the regular drawing of attention to individual pupils' writing as an immediate acknowledgement of work done to the expected standard helped to maintain a brisk pace.

HMI INSPECTION, 1997

Challenging all pupils: the use of ability grouping

Teachers experience considerable difficulty in matching work to the needs of individual pupils and especially in challenging pupils of differing ability within the same class. As a consequence there is significant, undue variation in the progress of pupils in different parts of the ability range in two schools in five. The nature of the problem varies from school to school, and in many it is more evident in one key stage than in the other, or it occurs only in certain subjects rather than being a consistent problem across the curriculum. Where there is a problem, it is most often identified at the extremes of the range: sometimes it is low-attaining pupils who are making insufficient progress, but in a large number of cases it is the high-attaining, more able pupils who are failing to reach the standards of which they are capable. Overall, the evidence suggests that pupils with special educational needs make unsatisfactory progress in one school in ten and that provision for, and progress by, higher-attaining pupils is weak in about three schools in ten.

The great majority of schools adopt mixed ability grouping in particular year groups or subjects, sometimes through necessity because of the small size of the cohort; or because it is seen to be educationally effective; or because it is used to avoid the clustering of particular groups of pupils, often boys, into potentially disruptive groups. Most schools also use some setting, organising pupils in a year population into teaching groups for a particular subject, on the basis of prior attainment and/or perceived aptitude in that subject. In schools that set, pupils are grouped differently for the different 'setted' subjects. Many schools prefer to use banding, dividing the pupils in a year into several populations, typically upper, middle and

lower, on the basis of perceived general ability or overall attainment and then organising teaching groups within - and not across - these bands. There may also be some setting for certain subjects within a band, though it will usually be less extensive: form groups are more often used as subject teaching groups. In the tiny minority of schools with streaming, pupils usually study all their subjects in the same groupings which are formed on the basis of overall attainment. Setting, banding or streaming provide a narrower range of attainment within any teaching group, but no group will be entirely homogenous and teachers need to take account of this in planning their teaching.

The extent to which ability grouping is adopted for different subjects is very variable. Some form of grouping by ability is very common in Key Stage 3 for mathematics and modern foreign languages, but rare in PSE. There is setting and mixed grouping in roughly equal proportions in English, science, history and geography. Four-fifths of classes in information technology, design and technology, art and PE are mixed-ability, and rather less than this in music and RE. In Year 7, in all subjects except mathematics, where half of classes are setted, mixed-ability grouping generally prevails. Setting then becomes increasingly common in Years 8 and 9.

In Key Stage 4, the trend to setting established in Key Stage 3 becomes more marked in some subjects: by this stage, only one-twentieth of mathematics classes and one-tenth of science classes are taught in mixed ability groups, and ability grouping is used in two-thirds or more of lessons in English. In part, this reflects the schools' response to tiering arrangements in the GCSE. In some subjects, however, mixed ability groups are used in Key Stage 4 as a consequence of the small numbers opting for these subjects in particular option pools rather than through any disinclination to set the pupils.

The overall trend in grouping across the four years of the inspection cycle has been towards an increased amount of setting, and in large part this is associated with the pressure for higher standards. Some schools are managing the Key Stage 4 option arrangements more carefully in order to maximise the scope for ability grouping, for example, by careful placement of those subjects which tend to attract pupils of particular abilities. Schools in Special Measures often give serious consideration to the way in which pupils are grouped as part of their strategy towards school improvement. However, setting is not in itself a guarantee that work will be well matched to the range of ability in the class. Setting can be helpful to teachers in more closely defining the limits of the ability range, but it is the quality of teaching itself which determines whether the form of grouping used by the school is effective. Inspection evidence about the relative effectiveness of teaching in ability-grouped and mixed-ability classes is complex. Broadly, pupils make slightly better progress overall in upper and lower setted groups than in middle setted groups and mixed ability groups.

While setting or streaming reduces the range of attainment in a class it does not necessarily result in a high degree of match of task and challenge. For example, grammar schools do not always provide well for their most able pupils or for those who, in their terms, are less able. Equally, teaching to bottom sets in comprehensive or modern schools often fails to address the particular requirements of a small number of pupils with special learning needs who are included in these groups or, in particular, lower ability pupils who are not on the special needs register and who do not therefore get additional support. As with mixed ability teaching, the teaching of setted groups often meets the needs of pupils of average ability for the group better than those of pupils at either end of the spectrum.

Challenging all pupils: teaching techniques and organisational strategies

Whatever form of grouping is used by the school, teachers should make sure that all pupils make good progress. In seeking to achieve this ideal, teachers use a range of techniques. At one extreme teachers attempt to provide different material and tasks so that pupils learn individually. This happens particularly in mathematics where pupils sometimes use computer-based systems or published schemes which take pupils along individual pathways. Such schemes have some merit, but equally there are serious drawbacks including the limited opportunities for whole class teaching and pupil discussion.

Some teachers successfully make use of two or three different tasks in a lesson in order to address

the needs of identified broad groups of pupils within the class. For example, in an RE lesson:

The upper ability pupils wrote an essay about Jesus' and St. Paul's attitude to women, and how they have influenced attitudes today. The middle ability were given a helpful grid on which were written the appropriate Biblical quotations. The pupils had to complete the grid explaining the meaning and relevance for today of the quotations. This task required less synthesis of material and assisted pupils by identifying the quotations to be used, whereas the upper ability group had to incorporate references to the text into their argument - a far more complex task. Lower ability pupils were given cloze exercises which made limited demands on their writing ability but which promoted understanding.

HMI INSPECTION 1997

More commonly, teachers pitch their teaching largely to the middle of the ability range in the class but provide some additional support for those who might otherwise struggle. Teachers frequently attempt to sustain these pupils by giving them more individual help in lessons - and therefore committing more time to them. While this often provides a measure of success, it leaves other pupils relatively neglected. Other teachers provide less able pupils with worksheet-based tasks while they concentrate on the main body of the class. These worksheets are often undemanding and fail to secure effective progress for these pupils.

More able pupils within teaching groups are less often explicitly catered for than the less able. Although provision for able pupils is satisfactory in the majority of schools, it is particularly good in only one school in ten and is weak in three in ten. Too often the tasks set for the whole class put a ceiling on what able pupils can achieve which is well below their capability. This occurs in subjects such as history, geography and especially RE. In such situations there is insufficient differentiation of learning tasks, lack of attention to higher order learning skills, lack of challenge and limited opportunity for enquiry. In some cases this leaves able pupils failing to use their good levels of knowledge to predict or speculate. Examples of such poor provision are found in schools of all types, including those with advantaged and disadvantaged intakes.

In schools which give due attention to the needs of able pupils provision is characterised by a background of high expectations and an emphasis on appropriately demanding work through, for example, extension tasks and specially targeted activities. Some teachers cater effectively for this group by providing analytical, investigative or problem-solving work which enables high fliers, having already mastered the basic knowledge and skills relevant to a topic, to follow their own lines of enquiry with some independence. Such work is often open-ended and provides opportunities for pupils to work to a high level.

In a Year 10 mixed ability history lesson pupils were working on the New Deal. In a good recap the teacher tested out understanding of concepts such as capitalism and laissez-faire, using questions stepped in difficulty. Pupils were then given an array of source material and worked in pairs to decide whether the New Deal was a success. A time limit was set to force the pace. Pupils worked at a range of levels, but all were able to contribute something to plenary discussion either in the form of description, evaluation or inference. Lower attaining pupils offered arguments for and against, while higher attainers weighted the evidence according to perceived reliability and utility in order to argue a reasoned response. The lesson provided a very solid basis for a substantial homework.

HMI INSPECTION, 1996

However, where this approach is less effective the tasks set for extension work repeat what has already been done, rather than actually taking the pupil further.

An increasing minority of schools have embarked on a range of strategies to improve provision for more able pupils. These include in-service training for teachers; revision of schemes of work; better monitoring of achievement and use of assessment information; and reviewing teaching methods. Overall, the schools that are making greatest progress are the ones which identify able pupils at an early stage and set clear and high expectations of the standards that such pupils should achieve. They also regularly monitor the achievements of these pupils to ensure that they are making appropriate progress.

5.4 Teaching pupils with special educational needs

The Code of Practice on the Identification and Assessment of Special Educational Needs has led to steady improvements in the way most schools manage SEN provision and the progress made by pupils has also improved. Schools have revised their SEN policies in line with the guidance in the Code, and have worked hard to identify and define pupils' learning and behaviour problems and write relevant Individual Education Plans (IEPs). The educational provision for pupils with statements of special educational need generally matches the requirements of the statement; but some statements are of poor quality and out of date or so general that schools find it difficult to use them to develop IEPs. A minority of schools have yet to come to grips with the full implications of the Code. In these cases the schools lack good leadership and management or do not recognise fully that they have pupils with special educational needs.

Chart 59 Progress of pupils with special educational needs

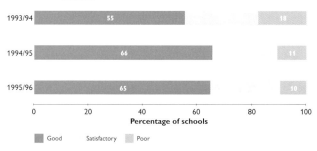

	Percentage of schools
1993/94	55 ... 18
1994/95	66 ... 11
1995/96	65 ... 10

■ Good Satisfactory ■ Poor

The Code has helped to create a growing awareness that all teachers, not just the Special Needs Co-ordinator (SENCO), have a significant responsibility for managing SEN. In many schools the status of the SENCO has been raised, they have a more important part to play in assessment and curriculum planning and in some schools they are members of the senior management team. At best, SENCOs have worked with subject teachers or special support assistants in producing IEPs; these lead to better targeted support and clearer justifications for referrals to outside agencies, particularly where the arrangements for regular review are incorporated into the school's overall arrangements for assessment, recording and reporting for all pupils.

*At **Archbishop Grimshaw School, Solihull**, the learning support department consists of a SENCO, one full-time and two part-time teachers, plus support staff for pupils with statements for moderate learning difficulties. The SENCO, with the support of senior managers, successfully promotes the involvement of all staff in meeting the needs of pupils with learning difficulties. All departments regularly allow time for discussion of SEN matters and the review of individual pupils' progress. There is also a programme of regular reviews between the learning support department and form tutors, resulting in a profile for discussion with parents. If parents are in agreement an individual education plan or group education plan is produced. There is also close liaison with external services such as the learning support team and with the two LEAs from which pupils are drawn, each of which has different funding arrangements.*

HMI INSPECTION, 1997

IEPs are most likely to be beneficial where they are well known to all subject teachers. It is unrealistic, however, to expect an IEP for each subject, and the effectiveness of the Plan will to a large extent depend on the degree to which departments and individual teachers are able to translate it into practice. In general, more could be done if subject teachers paid greater attention to IEPs. For example, some subject teachers set tasks which either are simply too difficult for such pupils or over-emphasise poorly conceived mechanical and repetitive tasks. Such limitations in the teaching effectively deny pupils opportunities to succeed. The best practice involves SENCOs in working collaboratively with subject departments and often leads to departments revising their schemes of work; this may involve the allocation of special needs team members to subjects, or the identification of a teacher from each department with specific responsibility for ensuring special educational needs are met within their subject. Where senior management has not made adequate provision of this sort, then the role and responsibilities of the SENCO can become unmanageable.

Schools have found that the day-to-day implementation of the Code has made great demands on them. Most have established the necessary administrative procedures, for example, for writing and reviewing an IEP for each pupil whose development gives cause for concern, and have established a register recording each pupil's level of need. The demands of these procedures have caused difficulties in some schools, especially where there are significant numbers of pupils with special educational needs. Many schools are finding the recommended termly review of IEPs with parents and external agencies very difficult to carry out.

A small minority of schools do not complete the annual reviews for pupils on a statement of special educational needs on time. Transition reviews, which are the responsibility of the LEA, are frequently not completed. The bulk of this work has fallen on SENCOs and has proved very onerous and time-consuming. Even so, in the great majority of schools SENCOs have succeeded in applying the Code, often at the expense of many hours of their own time. In most schools senior managers undervalue the significance of providing clerical support to help SENCOs with administrative tasks. The effect of this, at the worst, is that the work of the SENCO in compiling large quantities of documentation is wasted because, for lack of the necessary time, they have not been able to carry it forward through contact with other teachers or with pupils.

Good progress on the part of pupils with learning difficulties is promoted by effective teaching by special needs support teachers. Support teaching is most effective where the teacher has a good specialist knowledge of the subject and has been able to plan work jointly with the class teacher. The work of support teachers often tends to be more beneficial than that of special support assistants, who are not usually trained teachers. The effectiveness of either depends on their ability to help pupils who are having difficulties in tackling the concepts, knowledge and skills of the subject at levels appropriate for them, rather than merely providing encouragement or occupying them with tasks which, although subject-related, are not very worthwhile. Good support work can help low attaining pupils to make genuine progress in the subject, but its efficacy usually depends also on the quality of class management exercised by the class teacher. These features are present at

Mulberry School for Girls, Tower Hamlets.

The learning needs of a large number of pupils with special needs are met and there is full compliance with the Code of Practice. All staff are aware of the individual education plans (IEPs) and they are used to matching learning to the ability level of pupils. The many pupils who need support in learning English are well catered for in lessons and by provision of good teaching material which is matched to their levels of English language proficiency. The quality and range of material, which matches levels of teaching and learning to the specific needs of pupils, is a strength of the school.

OFSTED INSPECTION REPORT, 1997

Over the four years of the cycle, there has been a steady improvement in the quality of support offered by subject teachers and learning support assistants, partly as a result of additional training that some have received. Where learning support is weak, the main features are poor planning and low expectations, and pupils with special educational needs consequently make only very limited progress.

5.5 Teaching pupils with English as an additional language

The teaching of pupils with English as an additional language (EAL) requires particular skills, not least because at one extreme such pupils may also have special educational needs, while at the other, they may be capable of very rapid progress as they acquire fluency in English. Pupils with EAL tend to make the most progress when the class teacher has both a good grasp of their abilities and attainment in the subject and a clear idea of their language development needs.

Class teachers are, however, often insufficiently aware of these needs and are dependent on the help of Section 11 funded staff. Effective Section 11 teachers operate in partnership with mainstream teachers, working with pupils in order to develop their understanding of new concepts in the specialist subject, or modifying the resources they use to ensure that inexperience in their English skills does not unduly inhibit their progress in the subject. Essentially, they maintain a dialogue with

EAL learners which underpins the work of the class, providing access to the subject matter of the lesson and developing pupils' skills in listening, responding and writing in English.

A Section 11 teacher and a geography teacher had planned together, as part of a broader scheme of work, a Year 7 lesson on patterns of settlement. The planning gave due attention to oral components of the work. The lesson began with a clear review, focusing on specialist vocabulary such as settlement, activity, and function. Pupils were given sets of cards with words and phrases illustrative of each of these, referenced to different places. In pairs, they discussed the cards and placed them on a matrix. Each of the teachers worked with pairs of pupils to support language and conceptual development. Incorrect placement of a card on the matrix showed teachers where misunderstandings had occurred, and teachers focused their support accordingly. Pupils collaborated well, and overall the lesson supported language development and progress in geography.

HMI INSPECTION, 1997

When mainstream teachers lack the benefit of support or advice from Section 11 staff, the materials they use are often inappropriate for EAL pupils, as sometimes are the strategies they employ.

5.6 Teacher assessment

Assessment remains the weakest aspect of teaching in most subjects. Despite improvement, it remains poor overall in almost one school in eight in Key Stage 3 (Chart 60). The assessment of pupils' progress in a subject is fundamental to effective teaching. Good practice requires an understanding of the reasons for assessment and the systems and structures adopted in the school. It entails regular and purposeful marking of pupils' work; consistent and accurate judgements of pupils' attainment; effective use of day-to-day assessment to provide pupils with feedback and to inform the setting of targets; and manageable systems for recording pupils' progress.

Whole school approaches to teacher assessment

High-quality assessment of specific subjects

requires specialist knowledge and expertise and perhaps for this reason senior managers generally leave it to subject departments to determine their own procedures. However, there are certain common elements which can be addressed at whole school level in order to promote consistently good practice. Where assessment is good, schools have a comprehensive and realistic whole school policy providing a clear rationale for assessment which is accepted and implemented by all staff; this can be tracked into departmental schemes of work which incorporate assessment objectives; there is also a marking policy which sets out an expectation of the role of marking in directly raising standards. Despite much energy expended on assessment, nearly all whole school assessment policies have weaknesses or gaps which are reflected in corresponding weaknesses in the assessment practice of teachers.

In almost all schools an assessment co-ordinator has an overseeing role of development and implementation of the policy on assessment, recording and reporting. This role is usually held by a member of the senior management team.

*At **Lady Lumley's School, North Yorkshire,** assessment is well managed. A document sets out what is required of heads of department and heads of year. For example, heads of department are expected to translate the school policy into effective department policy and practice, ensure that reviews take place as new schemes of work are developed, monitor the effectiveness of the policy and contribute to revisions of the whole school policy, design appropriate formative and summative records, and ensure - if relevant - the completion of a portfolio of exemplar work. Each of these aspects is fully amplified. There is an assessment calendar for each year-group, providing a checklist for staff and information for pupils and parents. This quite imposing system works because the assessment co-ordinator has a realistic and sensitive vision of what is required and how to achieve it. There has not been a headlong rush to implement change, but the emphasis is on thinking, discussion and developing practice in the light of emerging and proven experience.*

HMI INSPECTION, 1996

Often, however, there is not enough designated time for this purpose, and as a consequence the co-ordinator is ineffective in ensuring consistency of approaches. Overall, schools need to give more consideration to the implementation and monitoring of policies to improve day-to-day assessment and marking, statutory teacher assessment, testing and examinations, and for recording and reporting.

The National Curriculum review of 1993 resulted in significant changes to assessment procedures. In the early stages of implementation of the National Curriculum the focus in many schools was on recording strategies rather than more fundamental consideration of the use of day-to-day assessment for improving standards. This burden of assessment and recording practice was a major issue addressed in the review.

The review replaced the structure provided by Statements of Attainment with Level Descriptions, against which to make "best fit" end-of-key stage judgements; emphasised the minimal nature of the statutory requirements for assessment, recording and reporting; underlined the importance of teachers having the freedom to exercise professional judgement in making teacher assessments and devising manageable day-to-day assessment and recording strategies; and, for the core subjects, affirmed that the two statutory elements, teachers' assessment and the tests, have equal status.

In general, schools have been slower to respond to the revised assessment arrangements of the National Curriculum than to changes in structure and in the programmes of study. In many schools statutory end-of-Key Stage 3 teacher assessment still carries relatively low status, the main focus being on the GCSE examination: as a consequence overall assessment practice in Key Stage 3 is less good than in Key Stage 4.

The range and quality of assessment in the core subjects in Key Stage 3 is improving, but considerable weaknesses remain. There is a greater variety of assessment approaches in English than in other core subjects. These provide opportunities for pupils' skills at a range of levels to be recognised, and help pupils to be aware of the assessment criteria used by their teachers so that they are clear about what they need to do to improve their standards. Teachers are increasingly addressing the assessment of speaking and listening skills. For example, teachers have become more adept at using the opportunities arising from presentations and subsequent question and answer sessions to keep informal records of pupils' speaking and listening skills. Nevertheless, formal assessment of these skills is still the weakest aspect of assessment in English.

In mathematics and science, the quality of formal tests, which are the mainstay of assessment in these subjects, is improving, and increasingly reflects the quality and style of the Key Stage 3 national tests. Effective assessment of the process attainment targets, Using and Applying Mathematics and Experimental and Investigative Science, is becoming more common but frequently remains the weakest aspect of assessment in these

subjects. In mathematics good practice involves the use of regular major and minor investigative tasks which are assessed using specific mark schemes derived from Level Descriptions. Similarly, in science good assessment practice includes a range of practical investigations throughout Key Stage 3, assessed to provide evidence of progress and attainment; at first the emphasis is often on assessing the development of practical skills in the context of the ongoing teaching of topics, with more formal practical investigations becoming progressively more important. By Year 9 this evidence provides a sound basis for end-of-key stage assessment.

Overall, however, many schools and subject departments have been slow to realise the implications of the changes in National Curriculum

Chart 60 Assessment of pupils' performance

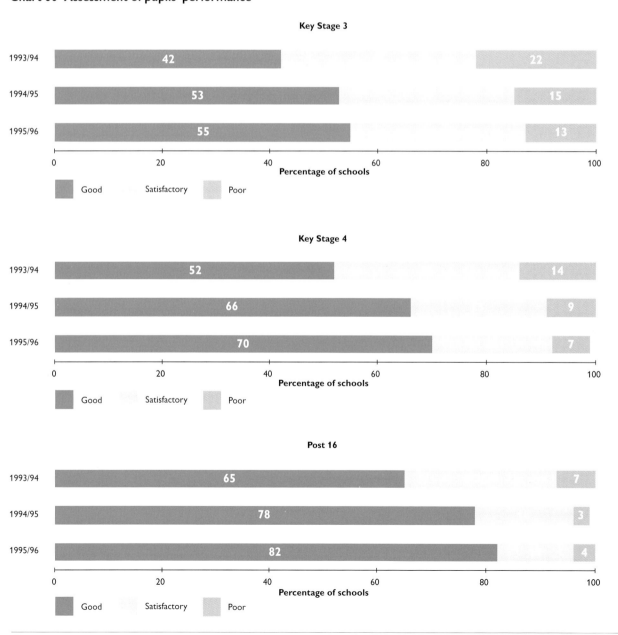

assessment arrangements for policy and practice. For example, in some schools departments have undertaken end-of-Key Stage 3 assessment without making use of national benchmark materials or agreement trialling to ensure the consistency and accuracy of the assessments.

Assessment approaches in Key Stage 4 are strongly influenced by the requirements of the GCSE. These have increasingly provided a basis for good practice in assessment: by ensuring attention to all aspects of the syllabuses, providing explicit assessment objectives, and drawing on a range of evidence throughout the course. The GCSE also ensures that consistency of assessment is enhanced through moderation procedures. Since the introduction of the GCSE, teachers have generally gained a sound understanding of grade standards in relation to both coursework assessment and to the estimation of pupils' likely GCSE grades. It is, however, unfortunate that few schools use the sound assessment practice established in Key Stage 4 to inform their assessment in Key Stage 3.

In sixth forms, assessment is similarly generally well geared to the requirements of examination courses. Clear and specific guidance by examination boards on the marking of GCE AS and A-level coursework ensures that it is assessed thoroughly and accurately. Internal examinations continue to be an important feature of many courses, in preparing students for their final external examinations, although the advent of modular examinations has removed the need for them in an increasing number of departments.

The complexity and overall burden of assessment and recording requirements for GNVQs have proved a major problem in the introduction of these new qualifications. In the early stages of operation of these courses, teachers found it difficult to interpret the specifications in relation to just what a student had to produce to achieve a full GNVQ, and, in more than a third of schools visited, staff did not clearly understand the grading system. Highly bureaucratic recording systems were introduced involving staff and students in an excessive amount of paperwork. The grading criteria for award of merit and distinction were initially flawed since they did not include the standards achieved in the vocational work itself, being concerned only with generic process skills. Modifications to the GNVQ framework have made

some improvements to the system, and a revised framework, being piloted from 1997, is intended to simplify assessment requirements and put much greater emphasis on the quality of students' work.

With increased experience of GNVQ, most teachers have refined their assessment and recording procedures, and their assessment has become better focused and more effective. Formative assessment has been a particular strength of GNVQ courses, with teachers generally marking work thoroughly, and providing very detailed and specific feedback to the student on precisely what more needs to be done to ensure that an assignment fully meets the specified requirements. Regular tutorial discussion between teacher and students has been an important feature, helpfully supplementing the teacher's written assessment. What teachers have needed, but have lacked so far, have been exemplification and clear guidance on the standards of work required to fulfil the requirements for pass, merit and distinction. In their absence, many have sensibly made judgements about standards in GNVQ based on their experience of teaching GCE A-level and GCSE courses in associated subjects.

A system of internal and external verification has been in place to ensure consistency of assessment and grading in GNVQ, within and between different schools and colleges. However, until very recently, the emphasis within the verification procedures has been on coverage and process skills, rather than on the standards of students' work. It is still the case that a significant number of internal verifiers, and some external verifiers in one of the vocational awarding bodies, are not specialists in the areas for which they have responsibility, and therefore cannot be realistically expected to make judgements about vocational standards. The verification of key skills is even less satisfactory. In a few schools, specialist English, mathematics and IT staff have recently taken responsibility for internal verification of key skills, and they generally do this in a rigorous way. However, much more commonly there is just checking of whether recorded material is present in portfolios, without regard to its quality, and external verification is even more cursory, especially where the external verifier is not a specialist in the relevant key skill area.

Overall, the purpose of assessment is to improve standards, not merely to measure them. Although the quality of formative assessment has improved perceptibly, it continues to be a weakness in many schools. For example, in sixth-form English and mathematics, where candidates in some syllabuses produce a number of separate pieces of coursework at different times, the potential to provide feedback which helps students to understand their strengths and weaknesses and learn from them in subsequent work is often missed.

Marking and responding to pupils' work

Regular marking should inform the teacher of pupils' progress, stimulate dialogue about the work and encourage pupils to improve. However, these powerful potential benefits of marking are only sometimes realised. The frequency and quality of marking vary unacceptably, within and across departments and between schools. Even at A level, where work is almost always marked regularly and conscientiously, the quality and quantity of teacher feedback vary considerably.

Almost all schools, and most subject departments, have marking policies which aim to secure consistent practice between different teachers. Such policies are often well established and include guidance on such things as the frequency of marking and the use of marks or grades. At **Cranbourne School, Basingstoke,** the marking policy begins with a statement of purpose:

Marking is necessary:

For the pupil, as it

a) gives feedback on work

b) gives praise for work correctly completed

c) shows errors

d) shows how work could be improved

e) establishes good working habits

f) shows that work is valued.

For the teacher, as it

a) diagnoses individual pupils' needs

b) helps in planning work for the future

c) sets targets

d) ensures that work has been completed

e) provides evidence for moderation purposes

f) checks on presentation.

Additionally, the benefits of marking for parents and the school are listed. There follows guidance on the nature of marking, including rules for target setting, correction of errors, and the use of marks and grades, 'only to be used if they relate to criteria that pupils and parents understand'.

HMI INSPECTION, 1995

Marking policies in a significant minority of schools have important weaknesses. For example, some overemphasise the need for a positive response to pupils' work. As a result teachers are sometimes over-generous in their appraisal of the work in a misplaced attempt to motivate the pupils. This can encourage complacency and militate against increasing the sharpness of the pupils' self-evaluation. A further common weakness is that the criteria for the award of grades or marks are often unclear, and pupils become confused between grades for effort and grades for attainment. There is sometimes also a lack of clarity between grades used to indicate absolute attainment and attainment in relation to the capabilities of the pupils; for example in ill-defined distinctions between good attainment for a high achiever and for a lower attainer.

Whatever the quality and detail of marking policies, there are few schools in which marking practice is consistent, even within departments. In the best departments assessment is built into lesson plans in the form of targets for pupils to meet. Marking is then based on these specified targets and on the extent to which pupils have met them. The quality of such marking is generally high, involving a written comment and a mark, and providing additional targets for the next piece of work.

In addition to formal assessment all teachers engage in more informal assessment, through observation, listening to pupils, discussing work with individuals or small groups, and questioning pupils about their developing knowledge and understanding. The quality of teachers' questioning is very variable in the degree to which it extends pupils' thinking, draws out their ideas, and encourages them to volunteer points and explore further, thus providing evidence of achievement. Too often, teachers engage in closed questioning, limiting pupils' responses or even neglecting to take up issues pupils raise, and ultimately failing to register how far they have understood the objectives of the work.

At best, pupils are aware of the assessment objectives and understand how far they have been successful in achieving them. A common misconception among teachers is that pupils marking their own work amounts to self-assessment. In fact, this is often no more than an administrative device to save the teacher's time, and there is frequently little real engagement by the pupils in the process. Occasionally pupils abuse the teachers' trust by cheating.

Among the core subjects, English is the subject in which pupils are most often given good feedback. This is most evident in pupils' writing, where teachers' written and oral comments encourage them to draft and redraft work against clear criteria. English departments often involve pupils in the assessment process. For example, in drafting pieces of writing pupils are provided with assessment criteria against which they can review their own work before and after it is marked. This leads to a self-awareness that greatly assists in setting targets for improvement in future pieces of work.

In mathematics and science it is less common for schools to share with the pupils the assessment criteria. Where it does happen it is most commonly for work in the process attainment targets, Using and Applying Mathematics and Experimental and Investigative Science, though this is not often done before Year 9. In the few schools which collect and retain individual pupils' portfolios of work as an evidence base for end-of-key stage assessment, pupils are helped to understand the assessment criteria applied. Pupils are occasionally involved in the selection of work for this purpose.

More commonly, however, pupils see assessment and marking as a process which is done for them, and to them, and they are not greatly aware of, or involved in, that process. The most common and sometimes quite effective approach to feedback from assessment, particularly in subjects where assessment is mainly through regular tests, is by a post mortem on the pupils' test responses. This is usually conducted with the whole class. Where the pupils' difficulties have been carefully analysed, and the subsequent attention to them is well-focused, this can be a successful approach. Too often, however, pupils are not asked to analyse their own responses to tests in order to identify their strengths and weaknesses. Furthermore, such a post mortem may fail to engage the whole class in discussion and some pupils who might benefit most pay little attention.

Even where teachers' comments on work are thorough and point the way to improvement, pupils often do not engage with or respond to them. Corrections are frequently not made. Inadequate work is seldom improved. Even when pupils attempt to respond to comments, teachers do not sufficiently acknowledge this when next marking their books. The full potential of marking to support progress is rarely capitalised upon.

Records of pupils' progress

Recording of pupils' progress has improved but the results are generally under-used. Although some misunderstandings about the purposes of pupil records and of the statutory requirements have been dispelled by the National Curriculum review, much remains to be done to devise practicable and useful records. Prior to the review, there was a common misconception that attainment needed to be recorded against each Statement of Attainment in each Attainment Target for each subject. This led to much ticking of boxes and an unmanageable administrative burden with little educational

Chart 61 Records of pupils' achievements and progress, Key Stages 3 and 4 and Post-16, 1993-96

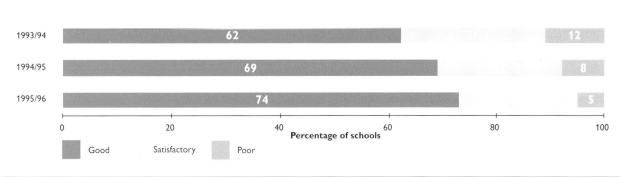

benefit. Also, many teachers recorded pupils' coverage of the National Curriculum rather than their attainment within it. The National Curriculum review made clear that teachers should use their professional judgement in making rounded end-of-key stage teacher assessments; as a consequence the "tick-box" approaches in most schools have fallen into disuse. However, they have only rarely been replaced by alternative strategies which provide records from which secure judgements can be formed. In many schools these issues have still not been sufficiently addressed across subjects, and in general assessment policies and procedures have not been amended to recognise the new statutory assessment requirements.

5.7 The availability and use of learning resources

There are significant variations between schools in the quantity and quality of resources available to support teaching and learning. At one extreme there are schools where pupils have a wide choice of reference material, easy access to information technology, the use of a range of modern equipment and materials, and books which they can use at home. In contrast, in other schools pupils have to share textbooks, rely on poor-quality photocopied material, have access to a very limited range of sources of reference, have to make do with out-of-date and inadequate technology and do not have books to support homework. Most schools fall somewhere between these two positions but the proportion which have unsatisfactory learning resources is a cause for concern.

Poor levels of resources limit the range and effectiveness of teaching, and in some subjects a lack of books may even prevent the full implementation of the National Curriculum. There

are deficiencies of books in almost all subjects. Sometimes books have to be shared in lessons. The lack of resources, particularly in practical subjects, results in a limited range of teaching approaches and a narrow development of pupils' skills. In other subjects pupils sometimes fail to develop satisfactory research skills. Learning resources are frequently not appropriately matched to the age or ability of the pupils, leading to pupils becoming demotivated and producing poorer quality work. A further critical aspect of poor book provision in many schools is that there are insufficient texts to provide pupils with an individual copy which can be used for homework: the lack of adequate resources for homework constrains both the type of homework task that teachers set and the quality of the work that pupils produce.

While inadequate learning resources partly contribute to the observed weaknesses in teaching, learning and standards, it would be wrong to assume that they are the only or necessarily the major cause. It is also the case that poor teaching and poor planning often lead to the poor use of resources. It is therefore simplistic to assume that increasing expenditure on learning resources would by itself ensure improved teaching and standards of work in schools. Low expenditure per pupil on resources is not in itself sufficient to warrant a judgement that learning resources in a school are unsatisfactory. However, schools judged to have unsatisfactory levels of resources more often have standards of attainment and quality of teaching which are below average.

Resources, like teaching, need to be well matched to the ability and skills of pupils. As Chart 64 shows, subject teachers vary enormously in how well they use resources, but a common weakness across subjects is that resources are inaccessible to lower-ability pupils in terms of level of difficulty. In particular the reading demands of many texts used in lessons are beyond the capabilities of at least some of the group. Some departments, in

Chart 62 Use of resources

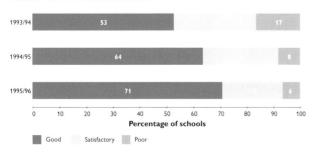

Chart 63 Quantity of resources

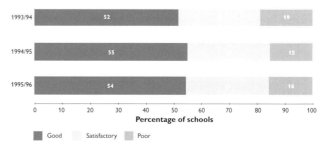

conjunction with special educational needs staff, routinely review the readability of textbooks and worksheets; a few also consider the extent to which pupils with reading difficulties can make use of 'raw' resources, such as the Internet, whose material makes no concessions. Similar consultations sometimes occur about the numeracy and graphicacy demands and general conceptual complexity of learning resources. Less commonly, there is a lack of suitable resources to provide sufficient challenge to support the progress of the more able.

Across a wide range of subjects there is significant overuse of under-challenging, ill-conceived or poorly-presented worksheets. Such a surfeit of worksheets can limit the attainment and progress of pupils of all abilities. On the other hand, good teachers produce worksheets, sometimes of very high quality, to provide their pupils with resources matched as closely as possible to their needs and interests.

In a Year 10 chemistry lesson particularly good use was made of a range of differentiated resources. The teacher first reminded pupils of the particle model of matter and then demonstrated a reaction between gases as they diffused along a tube. This part of the lesson was whole class with pupils responding to directed questions, asking their own questions

and being encouraged to explain what was happening in the demonstration. All pupils responded in some way and the teacher adjusted the demand of questions to match pupils' differing levels of understanding, always pressing them to develop their ideas. After an introduction by the teacher, pupils then carried out their own practical work in pairs. Although all pupils attempted very similar experiments the supporting materials were written at three levels with the detail of instruction and depth of questions varying to match pupils capabilities. Homework sheets were similarly differentiated. Pupils were encouraged to use those materials which would enable them to substantially succeed yet be challenged. Excellent negotiation took place during practical work and at the end of the lesson as the teacher decided with pupils which resources they should use. All pupils made good progress.

HMI INSPECTION, 1996

In some schools, teachers are provided with guidance on how to prepare and present worksheets. For example, a geography department carefully considered the characteristics of good worksheets, producing exemplars annotated to bring out detailed features of content, presentation and language level, as well as the extent to which

Chart 64 Teachers' use of resources by subject

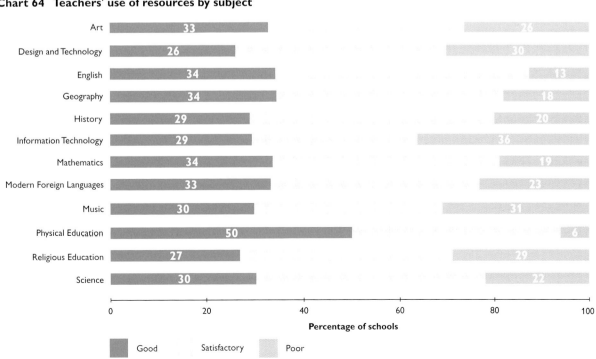

Subject	Good	Poor
Art	33	26
Design and Technology	26	30
English	34	13
Geography	34	18
History	29	20
Information Technology	29	36
Mathematics	34	19
Modern Foreign Languages	33	23
Music	30	31
Physical Education	50	6
Religious Education	27	29
Science	30	22

Percentage of schools

Good   Satisfactory   Poor

the material would support independent work. The worksheets were intended to supplement, not replace, the main textbook used. SENCOs can play a useful part in monitoring the quality of worksheets used across departments. In one school, for example, checks on readability led to the discovery that text was more accessible when presented in columns rather than across a full page, and this influenced future practice.

Where pupils make use of the new technology, such as information technology, there are many examples of how this can enrich their learning and produce work of a high standard. Equally, new technology is often used for trivial purposes or in ways which offer no extra benefits. This includes extraction of text from electronic sources in a way which is essentially no more than copying; indeed, it is even less worthwhile if the sophisticated tools at their disposal allow pupils to copy text without even reading it and to reassemble it into so-called 'essays' or 'projects' without the need to critically refashion the material to present a personal account or argument. Similarly, while genuine redrafting to improve quality is a valuable activity to which word-processing is ideally suited, copy-typing from a handwritten draft is poor use of time, especially if the pupils lack, as many do, the ability to type at anything approaching a sensible speed.

Productive uses of the new technologies demand essentially the same 'access' skills as other resources: many pupils are adept at the technical manipulation of electronic resources but where their reading is weak, if they are untrained in interpreting graphical messages, or if they do not know how to define clearly the object of their search, then the vastly increased range and immediacy of information available via the Internet or, for example, from an encyclopedia on CD-ROM can use a significant amount of time unproductively. Even so, as shown in 2.5 and 7.8, the new technology has vast potential which a growing minority of teachers are beginning to investigate and exploit.

There is frequent criticism in inspection reports of the limited use made of the resources available to support the teaching. This underuse of available resources may be a result of ineffective planning or the poor management of a central resource, such as the library or information technology

equipment. It can also be for logistical reasons, in particular lack of physical accessibility. Most subject lessons are taught in specialist accommodation and, particularly where a department's rooms are suited, access to the appropriate resources is generally unproblematic. However, where a department's rooms are scattered around a large site or on split-site accommodation, problems arise in the sharing of resources and the use of bulkier items. Where non-specialist rooms are used, the range of resources routinely used is generally more restricted. For example, modern foreign languages teachers do not make regular use of the overhead projector, a very important aid in this subject, if they have to transport it from another part of the school. Similarly, it may simply not be possible to take a television/video unit to an outlying room. Too often the teachers most affected by these problems are the least experienced members of the department or non-specialist teachers.

Centrally held resources are used with different degrees of effectiveness by schools. For example, many schools possess IT hardware and software in sufficient quantities for the number of their pupils, but nevertheless, this equipment is frequently underused. If the school library or central IT rooms are to be more efficiently and effectively used, opening hours and booking systems have to be clear, fair and reliable. The school must also recognise and address the implications of pupils' freer movement to and from 'their' classroom and sometimes the need to supervise and support pupils working away from the rest of the class. Teachers are sometimes deterred from using such resources by a general school ethos which inhibits movement during lesson time. Equally, however, teachers need to realise the potential of central resources. Although it can be argued that many libraries have inadequate book stocks, it is also the case that libraries are too often insufficiently used by subject departments to strengthen their curriculum provision or to provide pupils with challenging work calling for information search, retrieval and handling skills. So although there are resourcing problems, the failure to make good use of reading for subject learning stems in the main from inadequate policy and practice.

5.7 Homework

The use of homework is generally one of the weaker aspects of teaching in Key Stages 3 and 4. Although it is well used in over one-third of schools in Key Stage 3, it is poor in one-sixth. There is a little improvement in Key Stage 4, where just over two-fifths of schools use homework well, but use remains poor in nearly one-eighth.

Most schools affirm the importance of homework and many have a clear statement of policy which indicates its use to parents as well as to pupils and teaching staff. Homework generally has the wide support of parents. In those schools where homework is effectively planned to extend learning, it also serves as a significant tool in raising levels of pupils' attainment. However, although there are many examples of schools which strive to make homework an integral part of pupils' learning experience across the whole curriculum, in a large number practice is unacceptably variable among subjects and even within subjects.

The school homework policy typically sets out the aims of homework, indicates the range of appropriate tasks, and sets out responsibilities for monitoring that homework is set, completed and marked. Most subject departments also make similar statements in their departmental handbooks or schemes of work, although these policy statements vary widely in how well conceived and comprehensive they are. Many schools give clear information to teachers, pupils and parents about the approximate time, per subject or per evening, that homework should occupy in successive years. In general, the quantity of homework increases as pupils progress through their secondary education.

In many schools there is great variation, even within departments, in the extent to which the overall school policy on homework genuinely informs practice. A frequent complaint of pupils and parents is that agreed timetables for setting homework are not adhered to. This makes it difficult for pupils to establish regular homework routines and to manage their homework effectively.

Where work in a lesson is closely matched to pupils' ability, the homework which follows tends

Chart 65 Use of homework 1996/97

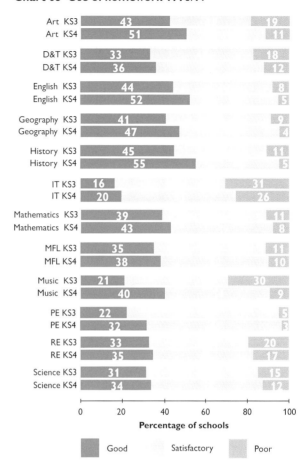

also to be better matched. Where homework is well used, teachers ensure that it is integrated with, reinforces and capitalises on classwork.

Homework can be a powerful tool in developing independent study habits by promoting research and initiative. It can also help to develop pupils' self-organisation, perseverance and self-discipline. Very practically, homework allows more ground to be covered and enables classwork to concentrate on activities that require the presence of the teacher. Often, however, homework involves simply 'finishing off' work begun in class and frequently fails to stimulate, challenge or extend.

The quality of homework is often limited by the poor resources available. In modern foreign languages, for example, when pupils can not take home a copy of the textbook, worksheet-based written tasks are seldom sufficiently stimulating and, more importantly, pupils lack essential reference sources to elaborate their response or check its accuracy. Vocabulary learning homework is often less challenging when restricted to only those items which pupils have copied out themselves. More broadly, if pupils' reading is to improve more should be done at home, and this requires the availability of attractive and relevant books across the curriculum to support and extend the homework that teachers have set.

When homework is consistently checked by the teacher it tends to have high status with the pupils. Where teachers set good-quality homework and mark it promptly and thoroughly it contributes significantly to pupils' learning. On the other hand, where pupils spend time on homework and it is ignored, or where the teacher's response is inconsistent, motivation and attainment suffer as a consequence.

Homework is significantly better used post-16: use is good in almost two-thirds of schools and poor in very few. For sixth-form students, homework blends with private study within the school day. Arrangements and expectations for private study vary considerably. A minority of schools provide structured programmes and supervision; others only require students to be in school when they are being taught. The effective use of private study depends more on students' attitudes and their ability to work independently of the teacher than on specific arrangements. Sixth-form students are normally set an appropriate amount of work to carry out in their own time. The content is usually suitable, though sometimes the style of working required of students does not directly contribute to the development of their independent study skills. On occasions, activities which require the students to work by themselves in lessons could be more efficiently set for homework.

Many schools check that departments have homework policies, but it is much rarer to find senior managers or heads of department monitoring whether the policies are consistently and adequately implemented. This is done in some schools on a relatively informal basis, for example as part of a periodic review by senior managers of pupils' homework diaries. Ensuring that homework is not only consistently planned, set and followed up, but that its nature and quality are appropriate, requires monitoring by the head of department. Such monitoring is rare. In practice, the monitoring of homework by middle and senior managers is often limited to dealing with pupils referred to them for not completing tasks.

Parents generally express strong support for the principle of homework and great concern when they see it neglected. Schools can, therefore, benefit greatly from parents encouraging and assisting pupils with their homework. Many schools provide homework diaries which parents are asked to sign, usually weekly. This is only effective where it is supported by clear information from the school as to what is expected of the pupil, the time to be spent on the homework and the objectives of the task set. Few schools, however, take full advantage of homework diaries to engage parents in a real dialogue about the work their children are doing. When this happens, well-informed comment by parents provides a valuable form of evidence for schools' monitoring of homework.

In recognition that some pupils have less than ideal conditions in which to work at home and less support and encouragement than they need, an increasing number of schools have set up 'homework clubs'. These provide some or all pupils with the opportunity to do homework on school premises, after the end of normal lessons and/or during the lunch break. The amount of adult support provided during these sessions varies, but overall they have resulted in many teachers giving considerable amounts of their time. Significant numbers of pupils take advantage of these opportunities and there is every indication that they can enable pupils to make more rapid progress with their work.

Pupils with English as an additional language find such sessions particularly beneficial in enabling them to keep up with their peers, to gain access to help in English which may not be available at home, and to reinforce language development in the context of new classwork and homework.

Looking to the future, developments in information and communication technology have the potential to change, substantially and positively, the educational relationship between home and school. Schools and pupils' homes can be linked by Internet or Intranet. Some pupils already have access, outside school hours, to particular interest groups or experts. The exploitation of these new resources is just beginning but individual pupils already demonstrate their potential value in extending the range of their learning and fostering their ability to work independently.

6
THE CURRICULUM

A secondary school's curriculum is a compromise between a number of competing pressures which include statutory requirements, school aims, the nature and circumstances of the particular school and logistical factors including staffing, accommodation and resources. Balancing these pressures is not easy for any school. During 1996/7, **Dartford Girls' Grammar School** was the only secondary school inspected where the overall curriculum provision was judged to be excellent. The only identified weakness was in curriculum continuity between Key Stages 2 and 3, a very common problem, examined in detail on pages 103-5.

Chart 66 The curriculum reflects the aims of the school

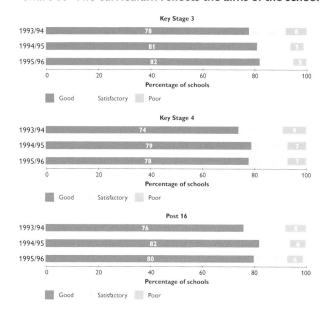

The school's curriculum aims are very clear and focused on achieving academic excellence whilst at the same time fostering a caring and hardworking community in which pupils can recognise their worth and that of others. The day-to-day curriculum fully supports these aims and effectively promotes pupils' intellectual, physical and personal development.

The curriculum in this school is unique, offering as it does not only the full National Curriculum and religious education, but also an extremely wide range of other subjects and opportunities. There is a good emphasis upon science and technology. At present the curriculum in Key Stage 3 is not building directly upon that covered in the primary school. The school provides comprehensive written information on the curriculum for parents and pupils. The deputy headteacher, who is responsible for the curriculum, ensures management and monitoring are very good.

The school timetable includes a very valuable optional 'enrichment programme' at the end of the school day. This time is used to enable pupils to study other subjects or to take part in extra activities. At lunchtime there is a well attended and impressive range of extra-curricular activities including clubs, music

and sports. The provision for teaching all aspects of health, drug and sex education is good and meets the appropriate statutory requirements.

The well-balanced curriculum at Key Stage 3 is further enriched by the addition of personal and social education (PSE), dance, drama and a classical language in Year 7. This is supplemented by a second language in Year 8 and from Year 9 classics can be studied through the enrichment programme. All pupils are offered a residential experience.

The curriculum at Key Stage 4 fully meets the statutory requirements of the National Curriculum and for religious education. All pupils are interviewed prior to their Key Stage 4 option choices and given good advice which is valued by pupils. Currently all girls study courses in at least nine GCSE subjects. The curriculum is broad and well balanced and ensures that the pupils' further choices beyond Year 11 are not restricted. With the addition of the extra opportunities offered by the 'enrichment programme' the breadth of the curriculum is exceptional.

The breadth and quality of the curriculum in the sixth form are very good... Pupils have a choice from 33 A-level and a number of A/S level subjects. The complementary programme for all students is very good with extremely valuable courses in physical education, information technology, religious studies, careers and health education and a foreign language.

The well-planned programme of extra-curricular activities enhances and extends pupils' experiences and personal development across all year groups. This is further supplemented by residential visits, fieldwork and work experience.

OFSTED INSPECTION REPORT 1997

6.1 School aims and curriculum planning

A school's curriculum satisfies the 1988 Education Act if it is balanced and broadly based, promotes pupils' spiritual, moral, cultural, mental and physical development and prepares them for the opportunities, responsibilities and experiences of adult life. The basic curriculum, as provided for by the Act, consists of RE and the National Curriculum. **Holbrook School, Suffolk**, has embodied all of these requirements within its own curricular aims.

These aims are designed to provide an enjoyable framework of teaching and learning which will help all pupils to become confident, competent individuals by the time they leave school. They will be kept under review.

1   To ensure that pupils experience a wide range of knowledge, skills and values.

This requires a broad and balanced curriculum reflecting all the areas of experience (language, mathematics, science, technology, physical education, the arts, the humanities and the moral, spiritual and social dimensions) and includes the requirements of the National Curriculum. It also requires that all pupils have a good preparation not only for further education and employment, but also for leisure.

2   To emphasise the particular importance of the basic skills of literacy, numeracy, communication and study.

3   To enable individual talents and interests to flourish.

4   To help pupils respond to experience with sensitivity, creativity and imagination.

5   To help pupils acquire the confidence to ask questions, tackle problems and make choices/decisions in a rational way.

6   To help pupils acquire social and inter-personal skills which enable them to listen to and accommodate the views of others and to work co-operatively and constructively with them.

HOLBROOK SCHOOL STATEMENT OF AIMS

These are ambitious aims which go well beyond the subject curriculum to permeate the work of the school. The inspection report demonstrates that they are largely fulfilled: 'Holbrook High is a very successful school where pupils achieve high academic standards and also develop well as individuals.' Most schools, like Holbrook, have statements of curricular aims, although some are rather too intangible to serve as a basis either for developing the curriculum or for self-review.

Only a minority of schools with sixth forms have distinct curricular aims and written policies for their post-16 provision. Without the specific context that such aims and policies provide for establishing priorities or making decisions, in many schools new courses and practices have been introduced incrementally without any overall rationale. Curricular decisions are often left to subject departments or faculties and are not seen as part of a distinct sixth-form policy. Where there are distinct aims and policies, however, they provide a framework and focus for the sixth-form

curriculum and a useful yardstick against which its effectiveness can be measured.

The great majority of secondary schools are successful in providing a broad and balanced curriculum for their pupils in Key Stage 3. Nine out of ten also do so in Key Stage 4 although, with the introduction of more vocational courses including Part One GNVQ, schools are increasingly finding a tension between their commonly stated aims of breadth and balance and providing choice for all pupils as a route to higher motivation.

Schools are also generally successful in providing equality of access and opportunity within their curriculum provision. There is little evidence of limited access or opportunity for either boys or

Chart 67 Content, breadth and balance of the curriculum for all pupils

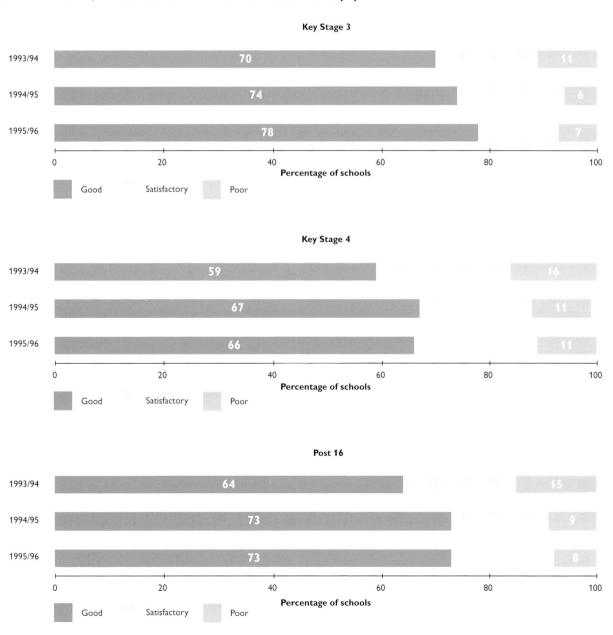

girls. However, although most schools are aware through their monitoring and GCSE results that boys' attainment is generally lower than that of girls, few have established curriculum strategies to address the issue. Specialist provision for pupils with SEN is generally good and these pupils have reasonable access to the curriculum. Indeed, some of the best curriculum planning is for pupils with SEN, where teachers take into consideration the individual education plans (IEPs) and targets for pupils with learning difficulties. However, where IEPs are too vague, individual subject teachers have difficulty in using them as a basis for planning and, as a consequence, the curriculum can become restricted.

Whole school and departmental planning for curriculum progression and continuity is at least satisfactory in the majority of schools in both Key Stage 3 and Key Stage 4. However, it is unsatisfactory overall in nearly one in five schools in Key Stage 3 and nearly one in eight in Key Stage 4. Moreover, in one in three schools there is clear evidence of variation in the quality of planning between departments and poor and ineffective curriculum monitoring by the senior management to address this shortcoming. Characteristics of the one in three schools where planning is good include clear objective setting and due consideration to the ability range of pupils in classes. Where planning for progression is weak the curriculum fails to take into account the needs of the whole ability range; assessment is not used to inform curriculum planning; there is a lack of consistency in approaches to the sharing of learning objectives with the pupils; a lack of setting by ability where it would be appropriate; and insufficient attention is given to individual education plans of pupils with special educational needs.

Departmental schemes of work help to underpin progression and continuity in pupils' curricula. Effective schemes of work are central to good teaching and a key factor contributing to high standards in all subjects. Although schemes of work are commonplace in schools their impact upon the quality of teaching and standards attained is more variable. Not all schools provide guidance to heads of departments as to what a scheme of work should contain and as a consequence their quality is variable even within the same school. In general, planning for coverage

is given higher priority than planning for continuity and progression. This weakness is particularly apparent at the points of transfer between Key Stage 2 and Key Stage 3 and often between Key Stage 3 and Key Stage 4. Some schemes of work, too, merely restate the programmes of study or examination syllabus, or cross-refer to a published scheme upon which the teaching programme is based, rather than providing detailed guidance on how they should be taught.

In schools which have provided effective guidance on schemes of work, there is generally much greater cross-subject consistency in departmental documentation, which facilitates liaison between departments about the content and timing of common topics. Schools with good schemes frequently place a strong emphasis on developing teachers' understanding of teaching and learning strategies. They also ensure that schemes specify assessment objectives and give clear guidance on the departmental approach to statutory assessment.

In planning their curriculum, schools are urged by the DfEE to provide a minimum of 25 hours of teaching per week in Key Stage 4 and 24 hours for Key Stage 3. In practice, the vast majority of schools have the same length of teaching week for all pupils. One in five secondary schools has a teaching week of less than 25 hours. Available teaching time for the curriculum at both Key Stages 3 and 4 varies widely, for example in schools inspected in the 1996-7 school year from 22.5 to 27 hours, and higher in some City Technology Colleges. This difference in taught time equates to nearly 100 hours per year, or the equivalent time allocation expected for a National Curriculum subject. In about 80 per cent of schools neither governors nor parents have been effectively involved in decisions about the length of the taught week.

There is a relationship between the length of time devoted to a subject and how well the course succeeds in covering the requirements of the National Curriculum Order. In practice, however, there is little evidence of timetabling reviews, undertaken as part of an effort to improve standards, being underpinned by any systematic auditing of the work in subjects or the time needed to deliver an aspect of the curriculum. Allocations of time for a subject are usually a compromise between past practice, timetabling convenience and availability of staffing. The senior management of schools often concede to requests for changes in subject time without evidence of how efficiently the time available is currently used in lessons or of the impact of allegedly inadequate time on the standards achieved in the subject. An intention of the National Curriculum review was that some additional time should become available to meet the needs of particular groups of pupils, such as the more able. There is little evidence that schools have identified any additional non-National Curriculum time in Key Stage 3, let alone used it to provide curriculum enrichment. Where there is additional provision for able pupils, for example, it generally continues to take place at lunch-times or after school.

6.2 Continuity from Key Stage 2 to Key Stage 3

Ensuring effective curriculum continuity from primary to secondary schools remains a major issue to be addressed by senior and middle managers in many schools. Most schools invest a great deal of time in ensuring that incoming pupils settle quickly and feel confident and secure in their new secondary school environment. To this end much liaison activity concentrates on pastoral rather than curriculum issues. The information sought on pupils is often fairly general in nature, for example the general ability of pupils, the nature of special needs, and pastoral issues. Far less time is expended in promoting continuity and progression in learning, and although for many pupils new demands from specialist subject teachers bring rapid acceleration, for too many the experience is one of marking time or even regression. The practical difficulties facing schools in ensuring progression are, admittedly, complex. As a consequence of more open enrolment many secondary schools receive pupils from an increasing number of primary schools. Some schools and departments, particularly those in an urban setting, are overwhelmed by the logistical difficulties of liaising with large numbers of primary schools and assimilating the large quantities of transfer documentation that this requires. Primary school staff are often uncertain as to what information will prove useful to their

secondary colleagues and sometimes receive different requests from each of the schools to which they send pupils.

A number of useful local initiatives have promoted curriculum continuity across Years 6 and 7 in particular clusters of schools, or between middle and upper schools. For example, in some cases primary school co-ordinators and secondary staff have met to exchange their teaching programmes in order to improve co-ordination.

Mathematics is a subject where close liaison is particularly important. However, in large clusters where schools use different commercially produced mathematics schemes, planning a common teaching programme across the two years presents significant problems which relatively few schools have addressed.

The Castle School, South Gloucestershire, takes pupils from six main feeder schools and some 24 other schools. The school's policy on liaison derives from productive cluster meetings and is supported by a detailed statement of liaison procedures for the academic year, which involves staff from the mathematics department. Mathematics teachers also meet the curriculum co-ordinators from feeder schools and occasionally provide some specialist teaching in Year 6. Cross-phase agreement trials have promoted shared insights about standards. The secondary mathematics representative interviews groups of pupils who are to transfer. The useful and informative record they complete is passed to the Year 7 mathematics teachers. These records, together with notes from the Head of Year 7 liaison co-ordinator, enhance the agreed transfer document used well by all feeder schools. The document has helpful notes on its completion. It includes teachers' assessment against each Attainment Target with a useful section for comment. The information gathered informs Year 7 mathematics provision and pupils embark on work that builds on their previous knowledge and experience. Pupils too recognise the clear continuity in their mathematics learning across Year 6 and Year 7.

HMI INSPECTION, 1997

The recently introduced National Numeracy Project is developing a year-by-year planning framework in mathematics for use by primary schools. Secondary schools receiving pupils from primary schools involved in the project will find the framework helpful in identifying the mathematics that has been taught and in planning their Key Stage 3 teaching programmes to ensure more effective progression.

It remains the case, however, that links between the subject specialists of the National Curriculum core are rare. It is still uncommon, for example, for all relevant information on the curriculum covered or on attainment to be made available to departments, or for subject staff to be involved in liaison arrangements. Transfer data is consequently not used systematically within subject departments to organise pupils, to plan work, to track pupils' progress or to make judgements about the department's added value. For example, inadequate attention is given to pupils' attainments on entry to secondary schools in about half of mathematics departments, and this frequently hinders pupils' progress. Many mathematics departments claim to give pupils a 'fresh start', which often results in pupils being given work which is too easy. Such pupils fail to make appropriate progress and some become bored or lose interest in the subject.

Frequently departments disregard Key Stage 2 test data, preferring to administer a common test to the new intake from which setting is derived. For example, very few science departments make systematic use of primary transfer documentation when planning their Key Stage 3 programme and some still plan their introductory topics without regard for the Key Stage 2 Programme of Study. This results in the repetition of work already encountered. In Year 7, for example, work on the conditions for plant growth (Life Processes and Living Things), the properties and uses of materials (Materials and their Properties) and the construction of electric circuits (Physical Processes) often fails to build on pupils' learning in Key Stage 2. Similarly, teaching in Year 7 often does not capitalise on pupils' well-developed investigational skills. The use of Key Stage 2 statutory assessment data for science is poor in about half of schools.

Even where good account is taken of primary school work in science difficulties arise because of differences in the context or language used. Where schools are part of a local cluster, continuity is often stronger as teachers are able to meet to

discuss cross-phase curriculum and assessment issues, so developing mutual understanding and confidence.

*The science department at **Tabor High School, Essex,** has worked hard to develop links with partner primary schools over a period of five years. They now meet regularly to share ideas, agree contexts for teaching, and to standardise assessments. A list of activities has been drawn up linked to each topic area so that the secondary school science teachers know the context in which their primary colleagues have introduced scientific ideas, and primary school teachers know which contexts to avoid. Samples of work from both phases have been assessed and moderated with a view to reaching a common interpretation of end-of-key stage Level Descriptions. The primary schools are adopting a common approach to the transfer of information on pupils' achievement in science. This work has led to an improvement in mutual confidence, a clearer view of the common elements in pupils' science experience in Key Stage 2, a shared understanding of standards, and the underpinning of a progressive curriculum across the break of key stage. Secondary teachers have found that starting points can be adjusted and more rapid progress made in Key Stage 3 as a result.*

HMI INSPECTION, 1997

Some LEAs have played a valuable part in improving co-operation between subject teachers in primary and secondary schools, for example in music. In general, liaison in music is weak. Many secondary music teachers know very little about the music curriculum in their partner primary schools, or pupils' prior attainment in music. The transfer records that they receive from primary schools often contain little other than lists of pupils who are taking lessons from peripatetic instrumental teachers. Secondary teachers do not know whether their new Year 7 pupils have any repertoire, for example songs, in common. Some of them are not familiar with the programmes of study for Key Stage 2, and pitch their Year 7 curriculum at a level that is more appropriate to Key Stage 2, or in some extreme cases, Key Stage 1.

*Advisers and teachers in **Dudley LEA** have developed a package of curriculum materials* *for music that primary and secondary schools can use to promote progression from Key Stage 2 to Key Stage 3. During the last half term of Year 6, pupils learn four contrasting songs about transport that were composed for them by secondary teachers. In addition, there are some optional related composing activities and appraising activities based on music composed by pupils in Key Stage 4. The songs are taught by primary teachers, with the support of backing tracks on cassette if they wish, but may also be rehearsed during pupils' induction visits to secondary schools.*

As a result, when secondary teachers meet a Year 7 class for the first time, they know that everyone has four songs in common. In practice, almost all pupils know the songs by heart. In their first lesson at secondary school pupils sing the songs with their teacher, and are taught to improve the quality with which they sing. They perform aural exercises based on the melodies of the songs. They learn to play parts of the melodies of the songs on tuned percussion instruments or keyboards. By half term each class has turned the songs into a medley with links between songs that they have composed.

HMI INSPECTION, 1997

Occasionally, liaison is boosted where primary and secondary teachers have jointly planned work which bridges the transition from Year 6 to Year 7, for example in design and technology. When most pupils transfer from primary school, there are significant discontinuities in their experience of design and technology. Few departments make effective use of records and most do not build sufficiently on pupils' previous experience in the subject.

*Attempting to improve pupils' continuity of design and technology learning from Key Stage 2 to Key Stage 3, teachers in **Fowey, Cornwall**, developed a range of activities involving the local Education Business Partnership. Pupils in several primary schools visited a local factory as part of an agreed design task. Some design work with precise learning objectives was started in the primary schools with associated practical work being completed in the secondary schools during their introductory visit to the secondary school in the summer*

term. The teachers worked in each other's schools during the project to improve their understanding of the activities and pupils' capabilities. A display of their work greeted the Year 7 pupils when they started at the school in September and early design and technology work built on this experience.

HMI INSPECTION, 1997

Secondary schools are increasingly using baseline assessment, including non-verbal reasoning tests, to identify the potential of pupils on entry in an attempt to promote individual pupil progression. Although such testing has benefits, there is a danger that this further underplays the previous curriculum experience or attainment of pupils. Secondary teachers often voice doubts as to the depth of previous coverage and the variability of subject specialist provision in primary schools: rarely is this substantiated with rigorous assessment. If there is not to continue to be considerable waste of pupils' time, secondary schools need to work more closely with the primary feeder schools to ensure better continuity and progression when pupils transfer to the next school and stage of their education.

6.3 The basic curriculum in Key Stages 3 and 4

Most schools broadly meet National Curriculum requirements in Key Stage 3, and most provide religious education which conforms to a locally agreed syllabus. Additionally, as required, most provide sex education. In a minority of schools, provision of RE and IT falls well short of the statutory requirements. Most schools also provide some form of personal and social education. Many schools devote more than the recommended 80 per cent of the curricular time available to meet these statutory requirements, and thus have difficulty in finding sufficient time for other courses. The pressure points in Key Stage 3 are the additional curriculum subjects which some schools wish to offer, particularly dance, drama, classics and a second modern foreign language. Many schools have debated whether there should be a second foreign language for all, or just for some pupils. Some schools effectively maintain a second modern foreign language for more able linguists by giving them rather less time in other subjects, notably

English and mathematics. Some schools provide for 'extra' subjects, for example classics, outside normal curriculum time.

Since 1993 the secondary curriculum has undergone significant changes. Principally, these were revisions to the National Curriculum programmes of study, the relaxation of the National Curriculum requirements at Key Stage 4, the introduction of new GCSE criteria and subject syllabuses, and, in pilot schools, the introduction of the Part One GNVQ. On the whole, schools have managed the changes well in both Key Stages 3 and 4, with nine out of ten schools providing at least a satisfactory curriculum and around two-thirds judged good or very good.

The original National Curriculum Orders were introduced in schools in 1989 on a rolling programme which would have seen all subjects in place up to Year 11 by 1996. It soon became clear that early revision of the National Curriculum would be required. In particular, as acknowledged by the National Curriculum review of 1993, 'Urgent action is needed to reduce the statutorily required content of its programmes of study and to make it less prescriptive and less complex'. The first cycle of inspection therefore coincided with a period of considerable curricular change. Early inspections found in some schools and some subject departments considerable frustration at the pace and scale of central intervention in the curriculum; a scepticism in those subjects which

had already experienced revision; and some dismay at the perceived inadequacies of the statutory assessment arrangements. The National Curriculum review was widely welcomed not only because it sought to slim down the statutory requirements, but also because it sought to give back some of the initiative to schools and teachers, and, not least, because it promised a five-year moratorium on further change. Inspection has shown that the revised curriculum has had a beneficial effect across a range of subjects.

In most subjects the review brought a welcome rationalisation. In design and technology in particular it clarified what was expected and helped teachers to organise a sensible programme with a more appropriate balance between designing and making work. In both history and geography the reduction in content, and in geography the simplification of the requirements, enabled teachers to respond more flexibly and in greater depth to the requirements of the Order.

In several subjects the review brought a useful broadening of the range of work. While in English the greater range required has been a cause of difficulty in some schools, overall the requirements for pre-twentieth century literature, drama, media education and IT have proved beneficial. Revisions to the process attainment target in science were welcomed as they broadened the types of investigative work and the range of contexts through which the skills could be developed. In

Chart 68 Median length of taught time in Year 9 by subjects 1995/96

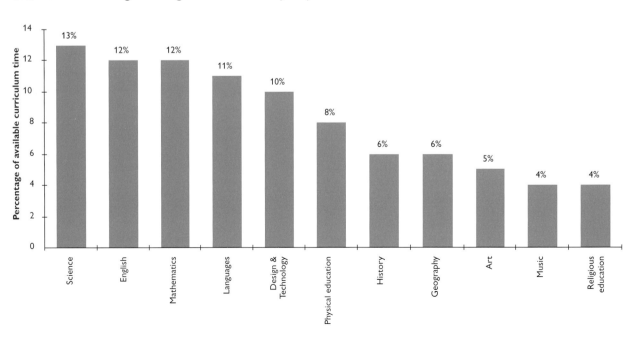

music, listening and appraising are now being taught more effectively through performing and composing, where this is appropriate.

In contrast to this broadly positive picture, the revision was problematic in some respects in mathematics, IT and PE. In mathematics the simplification of the assessment system, which was intended to improve manageability, caused difficulty because Statements of Attainment had worked effectively as learning objectives under the old model, but did not transfer easily to the new. In IT the language used in the new Order was very useful in ensuring that the text stayed relevant and up to date even as technology advanced. Such generic language meant, however, that extra guidance was needed for the Order to be effectively used. Moreover, because IT requirements were not spelled out in all subjects, many schools tended to concentrate on teaching only the low-level skills formally required, without affording all pupils opportunities for applying these IT skills in other subjects. This resulted in some low expectations and lack of independent use of IT by pupils. In PE the emphasis on traditional games in schools has created substantial imbalance in the present curriculum and an over-narrow curricular experience, especially for boys.

In Key Stage 4 the majority of schools have responded successfully to the new mandatory core curriculum in most respects. However, at the time when they were inspected nearly one in ten schools failed to comply with the requirement to teach all pupils design and technology, and one in ten failed to do so in modern foreign languages, usually for lower-ability pupils. Non-compliance in IT in Key Stage 4 is common. This is often linked to weaknesses in curriculum monitoring by senior management and thus a failure to ensure that the intended cross-curricular delivery of IT actually takes place. Compliance in RE in Key Stage 4 often relies upon time being made available within a personal and social education programme, an arrangement which is often unsatisfactory and fails to meet with statutory requirements.

The National Curriculum review was intended to allow schools greater freedom in planning their own Key Stage 4 curriculum than they had experienced under the previous arrangements. In particular, reducing the required core was intended to leave schools with time to be used at

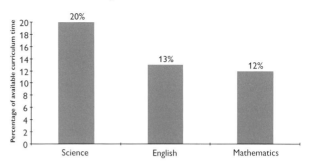

Chart 69 Median length of taught time in Year 11 by core subjects 1995/96

their discretion, with the possibility of offering 'vocational pathways' including GNVQs. In practice, for those schools which did not already have a compulsory modern foreign language and design & technology, the effect of the review has been to extend their "core" curriculum, which now occupies between 70 per cent and 90 per cent of the time available in the great majority of schools: many schools which are unhappy at the loss of mandatory history or geography from the curriculum have extended the core with constrained options so that, for example, all pupils take either history or geography, or a course from a broader pool which might also include humanities, sociology, business studies or RE; a relatively small number of schools have a further constrained option in the creative arts. Roman Catholic and other denominational schools make a full GCSE course in RE compulsory for all pupils. Even so, an inevitable effect of this curriculum pressure in Key Stage 4 has been a squeeze on those subjects including history, geography, music and a second modern foreign language which are not part of the core.

While the majority of schools offer pupils in Key Stage 4 two free option choices, about one in eight schools offers only one. Schools with a larger core tend to be most successful in fulfilling the aims of breadth and balance, but it often becomes difficult for pupils to pursue a particular programme or develop individual strengths, for example studying two modern foreign languages and two humanities courses. Creative subjects are often clustered together in the same option group and the requirement to select only a single subject can constrain pupils' choice. The most able pupils occasionally have to choose between a second modern foreign language and art, or between a language and humanities subject. The range of subjects in the free option pool or pools varies considerably. Most schools offer the non-mandatory National Curriculum subjects and a range of other courses, including, in over half of schools, at least one vocational GCSE course such as business studies. Some schools also offer community languages, some of which, including Urdu, are increasingly popular and have high success rates.

The National Curriculum review explicitly urged schools to create the possibility of a vocational pathway in Key Stage 4. Around three hundred schools participated in the first two years of the Part One GNVQ pilot, and some other schools have introduced GNVQ units. These new courses, along with a range of well established GCSEs which have a vocational element to them, provide an extension to the conventional Key Stage 4 subject diet which many pupils find motivating and which provide valuable insights into the world of business and industry.

In general, schools with below 800 pupils find it difficult to introduce new curriculum options. This is particularly so for Part One GNVQ, because of the demands made on staff expertise, and the overall impact on the existing option structure of a course that requires the curriculum time of two GCSE subjects. Smaller schools, too, have difficulty in providing a wide menu of options in Key Stage 4, and some of them are unable to offer courses such as music, drama, or classics because of the uneconomic size of the option groups.

It was with this curriculum pressure in mind that short course GCSEs were introduced in 1996. These are intended to help create space for vocational options in Key Stage 4 and to help schools to combine depth with breadth and balance in pupils' curricula. A significant number of schools have adopted at least one short course, with IT, RE and PE being particularly popular. Some schools which were reluctant to comply with the requirement for all pupils to study particular subjects, especially RE and design and technology, offer them as short courses, thereby ensuring least impact on a well established curriculum model. A few schools, however, have introduced a full menu of short courses from which all pupils are required to select as a means of broadening their curriculum. Combined courses such as Business Studies with Design and Technology which were first offered at an earlier stage of National

Curriculum development have not been introduced in many schools.

A further pressure on the Key Stage 4 curriculum was the introduction of new GCSE courses written on the basis of the revised GCSE criteria. Subject departments received a range of new syllabuses from which they selected the courses they would offer for first examination in 1998. Many departments understandably chose courses which offered the greatest continuity with those previously studied, but some took the opportunity to innovate. In either case, the changes required the writing of new schemes of work and a review of assessment strategies. Early indications are that departments have managed these changes successfully.

6.4 The sixth-form curriculum

Most schools have recently reviewed, and are continuing to review their sixth-form curriculum, and are conscious of the need to extend their provision to cater for the larger numbers and differing abilities of the students who are staying on. The subjects and courses offered in sixth forms are determined by several factors - continuity of teaching, the availability of staff, students' choice and the need to offer an appropriate range of subjects to meet their requirements. Most schools go to considerable trouble to accommodate students' requests.

Most sixth forms now provide GNVQ courses in addition to a range of GCE A levels, and usually a much smaller number of AS courses. Intermediate level GNVQ is offered most commonly for one-year students, with a somewhat smaller, but growing proportion of schools offering Advanced GNVQ. A few sixth forms, often in grammar schools, continue to concentrate just on GCE A levels, and a smaller number of schools, usually former secondary moderns, have set up new sixth forms providing only GNVQ courses.

The large majority of students in school sixth forms follow GCE A-level programmes of study. With the introduction of GNVQ courses, the proportion of students studying GCE A levels fell slightly from 91 per cent in 1993 to 86 per cent in 1996, but A levels form the basis of the post-16 curriculum in all but a few sixth forms. About 60 per cent offer some AS courses alongside A levels, but take-up has remained very modest, and few students take more than one AS course.

Entry numbers for most GCE A-level subjects remained fairly stable over the period 1993-97. Numbers for physics declined up to 1996, and then steadied in 1997, whilst those for biology increased, particularly in 1997. Numbers in English, the most popular A-level subject, also increased markedly in 1997. A substantial drop in entries for economics was largely offset by increases in business studies. Numbers in mathematics showed encouraging increases in 1996 and 1997 after falling throughout the early nineties. AS entries in total amounted to only 8 per cent of those for A level. Long-established gender patterns in choice of A-level subjects have persisted, with mathematics, physical sciences and economics predominantly studied by boys, and English and modern foreign languages by girls.

The quantity of work undertaken by A-level students can vary quite considerably. Although three A-level subjects is the norm, a small number of students successfully complete four; most commonly these are science students, often taking further mathematics as a fourth A level. Some students also combine an AS course with three A levels, and this often serves to broaden the range of their studies. In contrast, in most sixth forms there are some students who find three A levels too demanding, and drop down to two subjects by the second year of their course; the additional non-taught time thus created is often not used in as effective a way as it could be. The potential for extending the amount and variety of advanced level work undertaken by A-level students is illustrated by the small group of schools offering the International Baccalaureate in place of, or in addition to, GCE courses. Here, students successfully study what is broadly the equivalent of three A levels and three AS courses, in addition to other requirements for the International Baccalaureate Diploma.

The period 1993-97 has seen the progressive introduction of GNVQ courses into many schools, providing for the first time a realistic alternative, at Advanced level, to GCE A levels. Take-up of Advanced GNVQ has not been as great in school sixth forms as in FE colleges, but the proportion of sixth-form students taking these courses increased

from 0.4 per cent in 1993 to 9 per cent in 1997. Business has been by far the most popular GNVQ vocational area, followed by Health and Social Care, Leisure and Tourism and Art and Design; very few schools offer GNVQ Engineering or Manufacturing, partly because of their resourcing demands.

The introduction of GNVQ has transformed the provision for those students who choose to stay on in the sixth form for one year to improve on their GCSE performance. Most schools have now dropped their one-year GCSE resit courses, where students just repeated previously unsuccessful work, and which were largely ineffective in significantly raising attainment; it is usual now to provide resit facilities only in the core subjects of English and mathematics. The GCSE resit programmes have been largely replaced by GNVQ Intermediate courses which generally motivate students, enable them to be successful, and provide a more worthwhile educational experience than was previously available.

Most schools accept the importance for effective sixth-form education of providing a broad programme of "enrichment" studies, in addition to students' main A-level or GNVQ courses. Though very well intentioned, the range of this additional provision, and the time allocated for it, vary widely, and few schools have a clear rationale for defining the content provided. Programmes often include general studies, sports studies, courses on IT, personal and social education, modern foreign languages and drama, as well as activities suggested by the students themselves.

Many girls achieve very high standards in mathematics and science at GCSE but are still seriously under-represented in the sixth form in subjects which lead to careers in mathematics, science, engineering and technology. This has two effects: it narrows their opportunities for personal development, and it limits national resources in a crucial area for economic development. This is all the more disturbing given that girls achieve at least as well as boys in mathematics and the sciences at GCSE and that the minority of girls who study these subjects at A level perform well.

Strategies likely to promote greater take-up by girls of mathematics and science at A level include a review of the courses provided at Key Stage 4, the use of outside agencies to demonstrate the career opportunities and the applicability of these subjects, and the further development of relevant extra-curricular opportunities. Individual mentoring of pupils has also been found to be successful in similar fields in boosting girls' confidence about entering male dominated careers. Schools need to continue to improve careers-related initiatives to broaden pupils' thinking about subject options post-16, especially with regard to boosting the confidence of girls who have the potential to do well in science and technology.

There is an increased interest nationally in key skills being incorporated into the programmes of study of all students following post-16 courses. However, the wide agreement about their importance is not matched by a common view of precisely what is meant by key skills, what purpose they serve, and how they are to be taught, learned and assessed. This uncertainty, combined with what has been until very recently their relatively low status in schools, has resulted in their forming the least satisfactory part of the GNVQ programmes; in many cases they have been regarded as a somewhat irritating add-on extra to the main vocational work.

The number of GCE A-level subjects taught tends to depend on the size of sixth form, but can vary from as low as 5 up to more than 30. A minimum of 12 A-level subjects is needed if students are to be offered a reasonable choice, and most schools are able to provide this. Since GNVQ is a self-contained course, schools do not need to provide a large number of vocational areas, but more options do provide greater choice for students.

For a school deploying current levels of resourcing equitably between the sixth form and main school, a minimum of 80 students is needed to provide economically a basic curriculum of 12 A-level subjects. To provide, for example, 16 A levels, two Advanced and three Intermediate level GNVQ courses a school needs to recruit a total of 200 students. Where numbers in AS and A-level classes are small, schools are frequently able to operate more efficiently by combining Year 12 and Year 13 groups, for at least some of their lessons; there is no evidence that these arrangements have an adverse impact on examination results.

Some schools enhance their sixth-form curriculum provision through links with other institutions. The extent of such co-operative arrangements varies considerably. There are some integrated sixth-form consortia with joint planning and publicity, shared resources and timetables and jointly delivered programmes. An example is in Lowestoft, Suffolk, where three upper schools, in a compact geographical location, have co-ordinated timetables and students travel by consortium-operated buses to whichever school provides the subject they are taking. There are clear advantages to the schools, both in terms of breadth of curriculum and economies of scale. When the smallest of the three schools was visited in 1995, it would have required an extra six staff to have been allocated to the sixth form to provide the curriculum available to its students at that time, if the consortium had not been operating; for a school with a total staff of 42, this would have been quite impractical.

In other areas, co-operative arrangements are frequently on more of an ad-hoc basis, with another institution providing the teaching of a particular course for a small number of students in a school where teacher expertise is lacking or whose numbers do not merit timetabling the course in the school.

Although these link arrangements are not without their difficulties, when they work well students benefit considerably from the greater choice of courses and diverse experience which institutions working together can offer. Such arrangements have recently become more problematic, and in some cases have ceased because of the increased competition between schools themselves and between schools and colleges.

6.5 The whole curriculum: spiritual, moral, social and cultural development

The contribution of National Curriculum subjects to pupils' spiritual, moral, social and cultural development in schools is usually ad hoc. However, in some schools attempts have been made to draw out the threads in order to evaluate the strength of provision and make it more explicit.

*The senior management team at **Heathland School, Hounslow**, identified SMSC as an area for development in advance of their OFSTED inspection. To this end, they agreed that a post of responsibility would be given to a member of staff to investigate and develop this area. There followed a comprehensive curriculum mapping exercise, accompanied by a survey of all staff from the perspectives of teacher and tutor. Additionally a questionnaire was sent to parents, and other members of the local community were interviewed to gain perceptions of the school's ethos. The mapping exercise revealed that a great deal was already being done, both explicitly and implicitly. In Year 8 drama, for example, pupils' moral development is promoted by consideration of moral dilemmas, examining the rights of the individual versus those of the community, considering the concepts of good and evil, power and revenge. As a result of the mapping exercise a number of recommendations were made, including that each department should have a statement on SMSC and that the subject contribution should be explicit in the schemes of work. Since then there have been several important departmental initiatives. For example, the mathematics department has begun to use approaches and tasks from a commercially produced Key Stage 4 scheme; during the course, explicit links were made between tessellations and Islamic art and design work and data were used which drew upon topics from areas with social and cultural links. The department is now designing its own materials for Key Stage 3 based on these principles. In English, Year 9 pupils studying "The Merchant of Venice" deepened their understanding of prejudice through an analysis of Shakespeare's portrayal of Shylock and his relationships with his Christian neighbours, understanding the need to look carefully at the positive and negative aspects of a person's character rather than make a judgement on the basis of superficial knowledge. The scheme of work for geography incorporates explicit reference to moral issues. For example, when studying flooding in Bangladesh, pupils consider moral issues related to deforestation, international aid and corruption. Particularly significant is the fact that subjects' contribution to SMSC is continually monitored by the*
member of staff responsible. Interviews with heads of department identify progress made and look at plans for making SMSC more explicit. The explicit nature of SMSC elements is seen as particularly important: implicit messages may be obvious to teachers, they are not necessarily so to pupils.

HMI INSPECTION, 1997

Where subject departments give due thought to their contribution to SMSC, and emphasise it in schemes of work and in planning, this supports pupils' development and enriches the subject. Rarely, however, is this a consistent position across a school.

Effective schools provide their pupils with knowledge and insight into values and religious beliefs and enable them to reflect on experiences in a way which develops their self-knowledge and spiritual awareness. The main responsibility for spiritual development in the curriculum naturally rests with the teaching of RE, but other subjects can also promote spiritual development. In art, for example, where teachers are able to set tasks which call on pupils to express emotion and reflect on abstract concepts, the results can say much about the unspoken spiritual nature of art. In one school, a sixth-form student had made abstract paintings about his family's experience of the Holocaust in an unmistakeable demonstration of the capacity of painting to show feelings. English teaching can also make a significant contribution to spiritual development.

*At **Broughton High School, Liverpool**, the English department regularly uses opportunities to explore the nature of spirituality through language and imagery. For example, in a Year 10 class studying "Twelfth Night", pupils explored the notion that the Duke was in love with Cesario's 'spirit'. The concept of 'spirit' and the range of meanings of 'love' were discussed by the class. Pupils concluded that qualities such as loyalty and love describe our spiritual nature and give individuals their unique character.*

HMI INSPECTION, 1997

Although most schools have difficulty with the idea of spiritual development that is not directly associated with religion, the effect of good practice of the kind described above can be seen at

St Michael's School, Southwark.

Pupils' spiritual development is excellent. Religious education, inspected separately under Section 23, is planned to enable pupils to examine the Roman Catholic faith, the progress of Christianity and note the variety of faiths which help people develop a reasoned set of values, attitudes and beliefs. Other subjects make suitable reference to and contribute to pupils' spiritual growth. For instance, in history, pupils discover the significance of persecution in reinforcing people's faith. In English, poetry provides an opportunity for spiritual reflection. Spiritual awareness is reinforced during listening to music and from time to time in the performance and composition of pupils' own pieces.

OFSTED INSPECTION REPORT, 1997

In sixth forms, with the exception of denominational schools, there is generally little formal provision for spiritual development. Some general studies courses include modules on religious issues, but otherwise, unless they are in church schools, the large majority of sixth-form students have no religious education within their programmes. Many students have strong beliefs or views about religion, but these are largely sustained by their experience out of school.

Where schools are making good provision for pupils' moral development across the curriculum, teaching strategies successfully emphasise school values. Perhaps most important of all, teachers and other adults effectively promote moral principles through their interaction with pupils and each other. For example, in PE and games, teachers provide good role models and successfully encourage a sense of fair play. RE makes an important contribution to pupils' moral development by teaching principles which distinguish right from wrong, and developing rational thinking. For example, in examination classes, in particular, a wide range of personal, social and ethical concepts are explored in depth and pupils are challenged to reflect on their own values and principles. In other subjects, too, moral development is supported where pupils are

encouraged to think for themselves and to discuss a range of moral issues.

Geography lessons in many schools involve pupils in discussing population, settlement and environmental issues relating to equity, compromise, fairness and tolerance. Some science lessons include planned opportunities to discuss moral issues arising from their work, such as genetic engineering, nuclear power, AIDS and drug abuse. In history lessons pupils are encouraged to discuss issues such as war and conflict, prejudice, and rich and poor. In sixth forms, moral issues are often addressed through general studies and other enrichment activities, as well as sometimes within students' main studies. In art, for example, a GNVQ graphic design brief required a powerful symbol for a victim support agency; students had discussed and researched at length the feelings and attitudes of victims of crime as part of their preparation for this task.

The extent to which pupils and students are encouraged to think about moral issues varies considerably between, and sometimes within, schools. A dilemma for schools and individual teachers is the degree to which moral issues should be dealt with in a 'value free' way, in particular in order to avoid any danger of indoctrination. The danger of this is that opportunities for exploring moral issues are sometimes lost. As noted in HMCI's Annual Report for 1993/4, even in schools which have strong policy documents and high levels of awareness, 'more often than not moral issues appear to be ignored, ducked or else explored in a "value neutral" manner. It is clear that for many pupils, the one opportunity to hear the views of a significant adult on an important issue of the day - not least those pressing on their lives - is often missed'.

Where the provision of opportunities for social development is good, schools provide many opportunities for pupils to develop their inter-personal skills across subjects. These include, for example, paired and group work used to develop collaborative skills, sharing ideas and equipment and participation in team games. Explicit attention to pupils' personal development is usually found in Personal and Social Education lessons or tutorials (see below, section 7.15)

In most schools, however, more thought could be

given to strategies for the development of pupils' social awareness through the subjects of the curriculum. For example, it is assumed that pupils know how to work co-operatively in pairs and small groups; often this is not the case, and mixed groups quickly resort to gender stereotypes, particularly where computers are involved. Insufficient attention has generally been paid by schools to analysis of pupils' behaviour to identify successful and unsuccessful forms of grouping, organisation and activity. In a significant number of lessons pupils are allowed to sit where they choose, and as a result behaviour patterns are based around the friendship groups of the pupils; sometimes this can conflict with the purpose of the lesson.

Around a half of secondary schools make good provision for pupils' cultural development, as at **Helston School, Cornwall.**

Cultural development is a major strength of the school. Pupils are provided with very good opportunities to follow an area of personal interest in a range of music, sporting and other clubs and societies. Awareness of local traditions is high. Personal writing in English researches family background and shows respect for local life and tradition and the Celtic dimension is celebrated in some religious education work and in music, where Cornish Christmas carols are sung. Pupils are made aware that they are part of a much wider community through some multicultural work and through the culturally diverse novels and poetry which form the GCSE English syllabus. There are trips and visits to further pupils' cultural awareness, and their involvement with the local community through art and musical performances is very strong.

OFSTED INSPECTION REPORT, 1997

RE generally makes an important contribution to pupils' cultural development by teaching about Christianity and its influence on British culture and about the world's major faiths, so giving pupils some insight into a range of cultures. Well chosen syllabuses take into account the range of cultural diversity in the school and the scheme of work includes units which make pupils aware of the richness of cultural diversity in Britain. Where schools take cultural development seriously, a range of lessons include the use of paintings, pottery, music, literature, poetry, architecture and costume to develop pupils' cultural awareness and appreciation. Often RE rooms also contain artefacts which provide pupils with tangible contact with a range of religions.

Art provides many opportunities for cultural development through contact with the work of artists in the form of reproductions, books and videos. Displays of "live" art are important, as when one school set out some superb ceramic pieces and allowed pupils to touch and explore the work. Art plays an ever-increasing role in developing awareness of cultural diversity through, for instance, the use of Asian styles of stitchery, learned by pupils at home from their mothers and grandmothers and used in a GCSE textiles project. Where schools employ artists-in-residence, a clear agenda set out at the start of the placement is invaluable in making the best use of this potentially powerful resource for cultural development. This has become a regular and important feature of art in secondary schools. Other subjects can also make valuable contributions to pupils' cultural education, although often this dimension of the work is insufficiently explicit.

Some schools offer opportunities for cultural development to some pupils but not to all. In sixth forms, for example, the level of involvement and range of experience of cultural activity is highly dependent on the particular A-level or GNVQ courses chosen. Increasing opportunities for sixth-form students to travel abroad as part of their studies, including for example, GNVQ units in business or leisure and tourism in Europe, allow them to experience cultures other than their own.

Some schools fail to reach a sensible balance in the development of pupils' understanding of the cultural traditions of the United Kingdom, of modern multicultural Britain, and of other European and world cultures (see also pages 60-61). At **Shelley High School, Huddersfield**, a school with predominantly white pupils in an area with significant ethnic minority communities, provision for cultural development is well balanced and specific opportunities are exploited to the benefit of all pupils.

The school gives some consideration to an appreciation of the pupils' own cultural traditions through, for example, the study of history and geography and the choice of fiction in English. Their own musical and dramatic culture is celebrated and is recognised by the school community in the extended annual school assembly. They also pay frequent visits to galleries, concerts and theatres and the school environment itself is rich in display. There is a programme of exchange visits and educational field study activities in mainland Europe as well as a variety of work placements in the community and further afield. The link with Tanzania is a unique feature of the school and one that is valued by those pupils who are able to participate. At any one time a number of ex-students are spending time on voluntary service in Tanzania. This link, especially at times when Tanzanians visit the school, permeates the life of the school and successfully raises the multi-cultural awareness of pupils. This is consolidated by the subject material often chosen for devised drama productions, which have also been toured to other communities, including the Royal National Theatre. Similarly, in English effective use is made of literature from black and non-European writers.

OFSTED INSPECTION REPORT, 1997

6.6 The whole curriculum: cross-curricular themes

The subjects of the National Curriculum do not in themselves wholly fulfil the general requirements of the 1988 Education Act, particularly in respect to preparing pupils for the opportunities, responsibilities and experiences of adult life. In order to promote a broader view of the curriculum, in 1990 the National Curriculum Council issued guidance to schools on the planning, co-ordination and management of five cross-curricular themes: careers education and guidance, health education, education for citizenship, environmental education and economic and industrial understanding (EIU).

Schools vary widely in the degree to which they have taken these cross-curricular themes seriously. The great majority plan adequately for careers education and guidance, health and sex education, but only a minority have a planned approach to environmental education, citizenship and economic and industrial understanding.

Personal and social education (PSE) programmes are often seen as a 'catch all' for areas of the curriculum which cannot be subsumed into the content of the National Curriculum subjects, including the cross-curricular themes (see section 7.15). Sometimes PSE courses are effective in tackling particular issues, but often units of work are isolated and fail to guarantee progression as pupils mature. There are also some difficulties where PSE is taught by tutors or generalists who are ill-equipped to deal with the specific or sensitive issues which parts of the course involve. Additionally, PSE courses become increasingly crowded. There are, therefore, good reasons for National Curriculum subjects to play a more explicit part in providing elements of the cross-curricular themes.

However, where schools have implemented cross-curricular themes by permeating them through other subjects they have not always been successful. In the majority of schools the cross-curricular themes lack status and resources. Few schools have systematically reviewed the effectiveness of their planning. In general, there is a need for schools to raise the profile of these themes if they are fully to meet the curricular aims of 'breadth and balance' and 'preparation for adult life'.

Careers education

Careers education and guidance is good in one-third of schools and satisfactory in a further one-third. In the remaining schools it is poor and provides limited benefit to students. Careers education typically starts in Year 9. The best programmes offer systematic information about careers, access to individual guidance, direct experience of the world of work, access to up-to-date information about education, training and careers opportunities, and the opportunity to compile and review a personal Record of Achievement. In the majority of schools careers guidance provides opportunities for students to develop self-awareness and so to recognise their talents, strengths and weaknesses and explore future options. Such programmes are normally provided at the end of Key Stage 3 and through to school leaving. They are generally sound and links between schools and local careers services are generally good. An example of a very successful careers programme was seen at **Mill Hill School, Derbyshire.**

Provision for careers education and guidance is very good. Well-organised modules within the PSE programme at Key Stages 3 and 4 and through the students' tutorial system at post-16 help students to make informed choices and develop a good understanding of their future needs and an appreciation of the world of work. The good standard of work in this area is attributable to students' ability to recognise and reflect upon their own strengths and weaknesses, and upon their personal aspirations for the future. They are developing the ability to access information about careers and related personal and academic requirements and to analyse such information in a critical fashion. Students value their careers guidance, want to do well and are encouraged by the support and guidance provided by staff. They are frequently presented with activities which help them to develop effective skills in research and decision-making. Students with particular learning needs are well supported in their careers guidance and examples of good liaison with the special educational needs department and Careers Service are evident. Well-planned inputs delivered at crucial stages mean that appropriate attention is paid to students' progressing needs and external requirements of them. Careers education and guidance is well co-ordinated within the wider PSE and pastoral programmes of the school and links are made with subject departments, through study skills inputs and support for the work experience programme. Where possible, form tutors are also involved with the students' work experience and further opportunities to extend this should be encouraged. The school has established very good relationships with both the local Careers Service and employers.

Good use is made of the local business community through a wealth of opportunities including work experience and specific input into careers programmes. An effective service-level agreement has been negotiated with the Careers Service and regular termly review of this responds to programme needs and specific student requirements. The Careers Service is extensively involved in student interviews and assists the school in ensuring that impartial advice is available both from them and from staff within the school.

OFSTED INSPECTION REPORT, 1997

A key element of the careers education and guidance programme in schools is the opportunity to undertake work experience. There is a strong commitment to work experience from schools, parents and employers, and the large majority of placements have the potential to provide worthwhile learning opportunities for pupils. Organisation of work experience is usually effective. It is generally co-ordinated by careers teachers and most placements are based on pupils' career interests, but are also influenced by their general attainment, and to a lesser extent by the courses they are studying. Preparation for work experience usually occurs in tutorial periods or PSE lessons. It often includes preparation of a curriculum vitae, consideration of health and safety issues, and more broadly, the practice of skills associated with the workplace including communication, taking responsibility, resolving problems and working in groups and with adults.

Overall about three-quarters of placements are well matched to the interests and capabilities of pupils, and two-thirds provide an appropriate level of challenge. In general, there is a high degree of satisfaction from the successful completion of a placement, and pupils value the opportunity to demonstrate qualities which are not given the same emphasis in their day-to-day work in school.

However, around one in five pupils find their work experience unsatisfactory, usually because tasks are undemanding, limited in range, and allow them no scope for taking responsibility. Some pupils are frustrated by the limited contribution made by their work experience to school work, for example to support coursework on a vocational GCSE course. Only a half of schools have written policies for work experience. At best, such policies provide a rationale for work experience, guidance for consultation with parents and employers, rules for supervision and arrangements for review. In many schools, however, policies are absent or only implicit, and this is often matched in practice by the lack of a suitable structure to support work experience and poor communications between the parties involved. Overall, and with the exception of its use as a stimulus for English coursework, work experience is not well used to support other courses in schools, or built upon in subsequent classwork. Preparation of evidence for the National Record of Achievement is uneven.

In the majority of schools careers education and guidance is provided through the tutorial system and the programme of PSE. Weaknesses are often found where there is no policy on guidance, and the role of tutors has been insufficiently defined. Tutors are frequently expected to undertake guidance without sufficient training. Further, the tutor periods in which guidance has to take place are often too short for effective procedures to be introduced. While most staff provide sound advice to students on Key Stage 4 option choices, this is not always the case. Better understanding by the students themselves of their strengths and weaknesses would enable them to take greater responsibility for their choice of options at this time. In general, sixth-form students are well informed about higher education courses, reflecting the attention given to this by schools. They mostly make realistic decisions and are clear about entrance requirements. However, they are generally less well informed about the world of work.

Health education

Schools generally seek to promote the health and well-being of their pupils by providing a safe, secure and stimulating school environment which encourages them to be conscious of health and safety issues, and which seeks to develop their self-esteem and self-confidence, so enabling them to take the initiative, make choices and exercise responsibility for their own and others' health. Within this context many schools provide for health education as part of their PSE programme,

often supported where appropriate by the subjects of the National Curriculum and Religious Education.

The best provision is in schools which have a co-ordinator responsible for planning and implementing a coherent health education curriculum which complies with statutory requirements and is accessible to all students. They ensure that the agreed curriculum and related policies are implemented effectively and monitor the outcomes in terms of knowledge, skills, attitudes and behaviour. At best, the co-ordinator ensures that teaching is informed, is of a consistently high quality and is based on an approach which recognises the importance of starting with students' existing levels of understanding of and attitudes towards health issues. Additionally, effective co-ordinators , with the support of senior managers, develop liaison with other schools, with parents and guardians, with the community, and with outside agencies and specialist services on a range of health-promoting initiatives.

*At **Bordesley Green Girls' School, Birmingham**, the planning of health education across the curriculum is good. It sets out a clear rationale for teaching the subject. Its aims and objectives are detailed and wholly appropriate. The Health Education Co-ordinator has defined the areas of experience for the girls. For each of these areas the scheme of work indicates when aspects will be taught and within which subjects. Major contributions to health education are from PSE, RE and science with further inputs from technology, PE, geography and English. The scheme of work is then supported by a good range of resources that relate to each year of the programme with helpful advice on how they could be used.*

HMI INSPECTION, 1996

Sex education is a required element of the curriculum of all secondary schools. Nine out of ten secondary schools have recently revised their sex education policies: the majority now meet statutory requirements. Where there are problems these usually relate to the accuracy of advice given to parents concerning their right of withdrawal. Levels of withdrawal from sex education lessons are very low at less than one per cent of pupils.

*Heathfield Community School, near Taunton,
developed its sex education programme after
extensive consultation with teachers, governors,
pupils, parents and the wider community, and
in association with the Exeter University
Schools Health Research Unit. Parents have
been informed of their right to withdraw their
child from sex education where it does not
feature as part of the National Curriculum.
Parents are also informed when sex education
is to take place: as sex education is provided
across the curriculum, sensibly the school has
indicated to staff that they do not have to
inform parents every time issues relating to sex
education might occur when it is not the main
focus for the lesson. In this and previous
academic years no parent has exercised their
right to withdraw their child from the taught
programme. There were three enquiries last
year concerning the sex education programme:
in each case the parent was satisfied that the
contents of the lessons were commensurate
with the values taught at home. There has been
a focus on sex education in line with the Health
of the Nation objectives.*

HMI INSPECTION, 1996

Overall, the quality of the sex education
programme is good in over half of secondary
schools and adequate in a further third. Teaching
the facts about sexual reproduction is often done
very well.

*In a Year 11 science lesson the pupils were
revising human reproduction and, in particular,
the role of hormones. The excellent subject
knowledge of the teacher was demonstrated*

*through the clear and well delivered exposition.
The pupils were enjoying the work, and showed
good recall. The majority were able to explain
the stages of human development.*

HMI INSPECTION, 1996

Education about relationships is always more
difficult and requires skill and sensitivity from the
teacher. An experienced and well trained teacher
can, however, explore relationships and personal
issues to very good effect.

*A class discussion of sexuality and the age of
consent was part of the Year 10 social and
religious studies programme. The pupils were
arranged in two groups. In their groups they
were asked to discuss various scenarios set by
the teacher: these focused on the development
of resistance skills, coping strategies and
negotiating skills. The lesson was well planned.
The content was reassuring to pupils as the
scenarios were close to the pupils' experiences.
The teacher established a secure and
encouraging learning environment in which the
pupils could work. The pupils were willing to
share their opinions, and were involved and
challenged throughout the lesson. Some good
ideas developed particularly when the pupils
applied the situations to their own lives. The
excellent rapport within the class and with the
teacher was a major factor in the success of the
lesson. No one ridiculed others' ideas;
discussions were very good-natured and often
humorous. All pupils were very open and
honest when discussing their personal
experiences.*

HMI INSPECTION, 1996

Chart 70 Policy for sex education

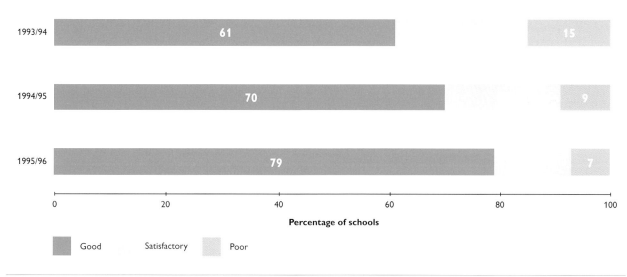

Percentage of schools

Good   Satisfactory   Poor

Such lessons are unfortunately rare. The quality of teaching about sexuality is generally not good and this has potentially damaging consequences. The UK has the highest teenage pregnancy rate among 15-19 year olds in the whole of Western Europe. While the rate of conceptions in the 16-19 year-old age group has been decreasing since 1990, in the under-16 year-olds the rate has been steady over the last 20 years.

The great majority of schools are aware of the key role that they must play if drug misuse is to be reduced, and this is reflected in their policies and their teaching. In both Key Stage 3 and Key Stage 4, school drug education programmes assist in broadening and deepening students' knowledge of drugs (including tobacco and alcohol) and their effects. This includes not only the immediate effects, such as the link between intoxication and accidents, but also long-term effects such as increased risk of cancers, HIV and cardio-vascular disease, and the effects on family, friends and communities. As a consequence pupils' and students' knowledge about drugs and their effects is at least satisfactory and often good. The majority of students are also taught the skills believed to assist them in resisting drugs when they are offered to them. In some schools, however, provision is inadequate or patchy, and overall too many pupils remain vulnerable to pressures inducing them to smoke or experiment with banned substances. The high incidence of young smokers, especially girls, suggests that the best efforts of schools on their own are often not enough.

The quality of teaching about drugs is often good. Poor teaching is frequently linked to lessons taught by tutors who lack the necessary knowledge and skills. Even where the teaching is good, however, it is sometimes insufficiently co-ordinated, failing to take account of prior learning and so reducing the overall coherence and impact on pupils. Better monitoring would enable schools to improve co-ordination, assess the effectiveness of their teaching and remedy perceived deficiencies.

Where drug education is taught as part of National Curriculum science there is often an assessment of the extent to which students' knowledge and understanding of drugs has improved. Discussions with the students and follow-up questionnaires are sometimes used to determine the extent to which

their attitudes towards drug use have also been affected by the drug education programme. What is more difficult to determine is the effect on their behaviour, particularly in the longer term.

Citizenship, environmental education, and economic and industrial understanding

Citizenship, Environmental Education, and Economic and Industrial Understanding (EIU) are the poor relations of the curriculum in many schools; such schools need to consider whether, in the light of this neglect, they are fulfilling their curricular aims.

The aims of citizenship education are to establish the importance of positive citizenship and provide the motivation for pupils to participate as citizens at school, community, national and international level. Citizenship education also involves the acquisition and understanding of essential information on which to base the development of pupils' skills, values and attitudes towards citizenship. This includes knowledge of how a community works, of democracy, and of the law.

Education about the environment is a requirement within the Orders of a number of National Curriculum subjects, particularly geography and science, and there are opportunities to teach about the environment in all subjects where teachers have a choice of contexts for that which they are teaching. At the heart of environmental education is the development of world citizenship and care for the planet. The period since 1988 has been a very active one for discussions about and the promotion of environmental education. These initiatives can be seen within the framework of the British Government's acceptance of the proposals of the Rio Earth Summit in 1992 about sustainability and biodiversity and the need to promote understanding and action by citizens. Where environmental education is good it provides all pupils with opportunities to acquire the knowledge, understanding and skills required to engage actively with environmental issues including those of sustainable development; it encourages pupils to appreciate the environment from a variety of perspectives; and it arouses their awareness and curiosity about the environment and encourages active participation in resolving environmental problems.

The aims of teaching EIU are to help pupils to

acquire a range of knowledge, understanding and skills sufficient to enable them to analyse and understand current economic issues. All good teaching in this area seeks to develop a proper respect for evidence and the ability to separate facts from opinion. It also helps pupils to recognise different value positions and how those different values reflect on the judgement of past events or the formulation of future policies. Inter-dependence is a key factor in economic problems and it is important for pupils to see that the best outcome involves trade-offs and is determined ultimately by a series of value judgements. This comprehensive and coherent view is only acquired through a planned programme of study. In Key Stage 3 pupils are often introduced to industry and commerce through industry days or presentations by speakers from local businesses. For many pupils, the development of EIU is supported by well planned work experience and other links with industry, including special events such as industry days.

The majority of schools have formulated a policy for at least some of these cross-curricular themes. However, the quality of the policies varies considerably: some are very basic with mere lists of headings while a very few others draw a clear distinction between content and process as well as detailing planned outcomes in terms of skills and attitudes with suggestions as to how these might be evaluated. The curricular statements which support the best practice show a clear link between the themes and the National Curriculum subjects.

These themes are sometimes successfully promoted in the school at large, in its ethos and assemblies. For example, at school level citizenship education is implicit in the daily life of the school and is manifested in the attitudes, values and behaviour of pupils. Broadly, secondary schools produce good citizens at this level.

In more concrete terms, these themes are often part of a personal and social education programme. Units on citizenship dealing with issues such as elections can be very successful, but often work is decontextualised and fails to address key concepts and what they mean in real life; such work can be dull and often carries low status with pupils. Environmental education is frequently one of the more successful features of PSE provision,

with units of work on aspects such as vandalism, litter, rainforests and pollution. A few schools have chosen to locate their EIU programme wholly within a PSE, tutorial or careers education programme, so giving it definition in terms of content and curricular placement. At best, the resulting schemes of work include important concepts such as supply and demand, scarcity of resources, and opportunity costs. More frequently, however, such key concepts are absent, and there is a narrower focus on practicalities such as job applications and bank accounts. What is almost always missing within these schemes of work are links with the work in other subjects across the school and, invariably, an indication of how any EIU learning might be evaluated. Work of high quality does occur but it rarely leads to the systematic acquisition of knowledge and understanding, and equally rarely are pupils given opportunities to apply that knowledge to an array of everyday situations as part of a planned teaching programme. In most schools, more thought needs to be given to strategies for the development of pupils' social awareness through the subjects of the curriculum.

Few schools fulfil the original intention of weaving these themes into the subjects of the National Curriculum, although opportunities for doing this can be found in plenty. In history, for example, the Key Element 'Organisation and Communication' in Key Stage 3 requires that pupils know, understand and can use terms such as government, parliament, monarchy, republic, communism, fascism, dictatorship and democracy. Some history departments have given due thought to ways in which these concepts can be explicitly linked to citizenship education; often, however, explicit links are not made to pupils' other knowledge and their own experience in order make the lessons of history transferable. Similarly, bits of seemingly relevant Economic and Industrial Understanding acquired in separate subjects do not add up to an intelligible whole for most pupils. Overall, therefore, this is an area where much remains to be done.

6.7 Extra-curricular activities

The extra-curricular provision in secondary schools has maintained its strength throughout this first four-year period of OFSTED inspections and is good or better in four out of five schools. In a small number of schools the provision of extra-curricular activities is restricted by logistical factors or a lack of enthusiasm on the part of staff and pupils and the overall benefits to pupils are reduced accordingly. Most schools, however, through the goodwill of teachers, provide an extra-curricular extension to their curriculum which includes some team sports, both within the school and in the broader community, and opportunities for the pursuit of particular interests such as art and travel. Extra-curricular activities are often supported by parents who contribute to activities such as theatre visits and field trips. A growing area of development in a number of schools is the use of extra-curricular time to provide an extension of the curriculum. For example, an increasing number of schools provide homework clubs, some both early morning and after school. In some schools pupils are able to study for an extra GCSE subject. For example, in one school where art could not be taken by pupils who opted for double science or a second modern foreign language, thirty students studied for art GCSE by attending a weekly after-school session. Also, community languages are offered as an extra-curricular option in some schools.

Many schools use extra-curricular activities to foster pupils' social development. Such activities include the school orchestra and sports which promote teamworking. More broadly some schools use residential visits and summer camps, sometimes for a whole year group, to foster a sense of community. Community links are well established in many schools. In some small towns and villages the school has become the cornerstone of the community. In sixth forms an increasing number of students are undertaking some form of community service, as a formal part of their sixth-form programme. This can provide valuable opportunities for involvement in old peoples' homes, local hospitals, and working with community groups including disabled or disadvantaged people.

Where extra-curricular provision for cultural education is strong, opportunities are provided for pupils to make studies of the local community, its history and architecture, to compare local culture in the past with the present and to work with local artists, musicians and dancers. More broadly, many schools are able to offer visits to museums including trips to London. This provides pupils with opportunities not only to see the works of western artists, for example, but also to recognise the diversity of expression within a cultural tradition.

Some schools have recognised that extra-curricular activities are a good opportunity for providing more effectively for able pupils. An enriched curriculum and good teaching will encourage these pupils to take advantage of extra-curricular activities or local events, sometimes involving higher education institutions, which can increase their engagement with the subject, broaden their experience of it and offer additional challenges. They can give pupils a chance to extend their normal classroom work into new activities, such as debating, philosophical discussion, mathematical competition or large-scale technological projects. This can help them to gain a broader view of the subject and of its value within the adult world.

Chart 71 Extra-curricular provision in Key Stages 3 & 4

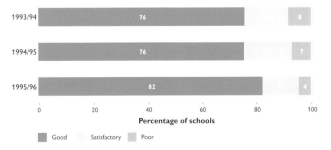

1993/94	76	8
1994/95	76	7
1995/96	82	4

Percentage of schools

■ Good   Satisfactory   ■ Poor

7 STANDARDS IN SUBJECTS

Standards, as indicated by the examination results at GCSE and A level (shown in charts 72 and 73), vary among subjects, between boys and girls and in the extent of improvement since 1994. Charts 15 and 51 showed similar variations in inspectors' judgements of standards of achievement in relation to pupils' progress and the quality of teaching. Some of reasons for this are discussed in the separate subject sections below, as are the key issues to be faced in improving standards in these subjects.

Chart 72 GCSE results 1994 and 1997

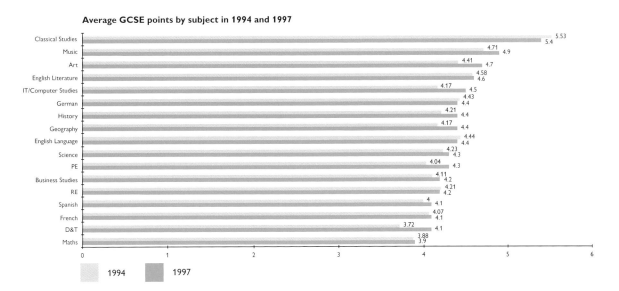

Average GCSE points by subject in 1994 and 1997

☐ 1994   ■ 1997

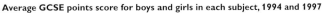

Average GCSE points score for boys and girls in each subject, 1994 and 1997

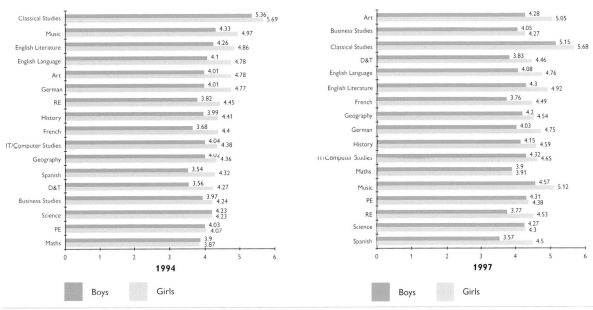

1994

■ Boys   ☐ Girls

1997

■ Boys   ☐ Girls

Chart 73 GCE A-level results 1994 and 1997

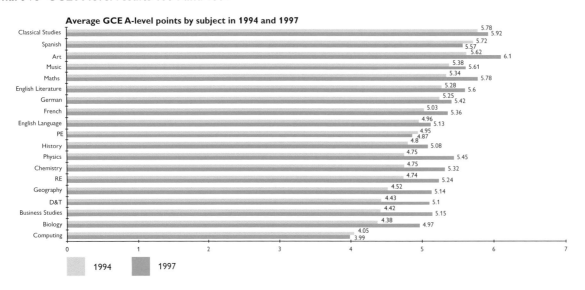

Average GCE A-level points by subject in 1994 and 1997

Subject	1994	1997
Classical Studies	5.78	5.92
Spanish	5.57	5.72
Art	5.62	6.1
Music	5.38	5.61
Maths	5.34	5.78
English Literature	5.28	5.6
German	5.25	5.42
French	5.03	5.36
English Language	4.96	5.13
PE	4.95	4.87
History	4.8	5.08
Physics	4.75	5.45
Chemistry	4.75	5.32
RE	4.74	5.24
Geography	4.52	5.14
D&T	4.43	5.1
Business Studies	4.42	5.15
Biology	4.38	4.97
Computing	4.05	3.99

1994 1997

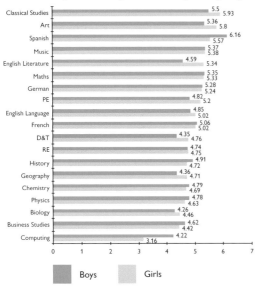

Boys/Girls average GCE A-level points by subject 1994

Subject	Boys	Girls
Classical Studies	5.5	5.93
Art	5.36	5.8
Spanish	6.16	5.57
Music	5.37	5.38
English Literature	4.59	5.34
Maths	5.35	5.33
German	5.28	5.24
PE	4.82	5.2
English Language	4.85	5.02
French	5.06	5.02
D&T	4.35	4.76
RE	4.74	4.75
History	4.91	4.72
Geography	4.36	4.71
Chemistry	4.79	4.69
Physics	4.78	4.63
Biology	4.26	4.46
Business Studies	4.62	4.42
Computing	4.22	3.16

Boys Girls

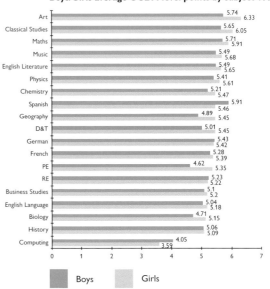

Boys/Girls average GCE A-level points by subject 1997

Subject	Boys	Girls
Art	5.74	6.33
Classical Studies	5.65	6.05
Maths	5.71	5.91
Music	5.49	5.68
English Literature	5.49	5.65
Physics	5.41	5.61
Chemistry	5.21	5.47
Spanish	5.91	5.46
Geography	4.89	5.45
D&T	5.01	5.45
German	5.43	5.42
French	5.28	5.39
PE	4.62	5.35
RE	5.23	5.22
Business Studies	5.1	5.2
English Language	5.04	5.18
Biology	4.71	5.15
History	5.06	5.09
Computing	4.05	3.59

Boys Girls

7.1 ENGLISH

Trends in English, 1993-7

Standards in English have shown steady improvement, especially in Key Stage 4. English is now usually a well-managed subject with good development planning, strong departmental teamwork and good teaching. Schemes of work often have clear objectives, and provide improved coverage of the revised National Curriculum Programmes of Study. All of this has had a positive impact on pupils' learning. Most pupils enjoy the subject and respond well to it.

The revisions to the National Curriculum have led to significant gains in terms of both coverage and standards: there has been increased focus on technical accuracy; due attention has been paid to speaking and listening during a period when debates about literacy have dominated educational headlines; the specified range of reading and writing, including Shakespeare and other pre-twentieth century texts in Key Stage 3, has broadened the diet of most pupils, as has the inclusion of drama, media education and IT. However, there have been some difficulties in implementing the new Order. In particular, some schools have not yet established a clear rationale; the focus of the national tests has tended to distort some programmes; some teachers find it difficult to include in their planning and practice the full range of reading and writing specified; "standard English and language study" are not handled well in many cases; and drama, media and IT coverage is uneven. In Key Stage 4 the requirements for more extensive reading, while generally beneficial, have put further pressure on resources and time, and make particularly heavy demands on lower-attaining pupils.

Overall, despite an improving picture, there remain national concerns about standards of literacy (see 2.5 where these are considered from a whole-school point of view), about boys' performance in English and about the failure of too many pupils to build on their early skills in each of the English attainment targets. For a sizeable proportion of pupils there is a need to improve their reading, writing and speaking and listening capabilities. National Curriculum tests continue to show that about 40 per cent of fourteen-year-olds fail to reach expected levels of performance. The proportion of candidates gaining grades A*-C in English GCSE has levelled off at about 56 per cent. Inspection evidence suggests that many pupils reach a plateau in their reading and writing skills as they enter Key Stage 3 and face the demands of the full secondary curriculum. The challenge for schools in the immediate future is to be clear about the things which most pupils do well and to identify those aspects of English which need further attention.

Although the provision of drama varies considerably from school to school, its place in the curriculum was strengthened by the revision of the English Order. Standards have steadily improved, especially in Key Stage 4, where it is a rapidly expanding option at GCSE. Drama provides good opportunities for sustained talk, often missing in other subjects. Pupils learn to adjust their language to the needs of different audiences and situations. There is good training and practice in dramatic conventions, techniques and skills. Pupils explore complex themes, emotions and both familiar and new situations: they learn to empathise; and they learn about the characteristics of a good performance. Some weaknesses remain: teachers lacking the skills and/or confidence to teach drama effectively or

Chart 74 English

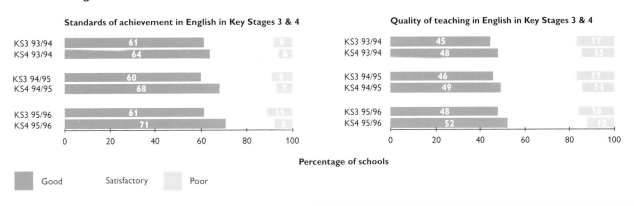

Standards of achievement in English in Key Stages 3 & 4

KS3 93/94	61
KS4 93/94	64
KS3 94/95	60
KS4 94/95	68
KS3 95/96	61
KS4 95/96	71

Quality of teaching in English in Key Stages 3 & 4

KS3 93/94	45
KS4 93/94	48
KS3 94/95	46
KS4 94/95	49
KS3 95/96	48
KS4 95/96	52

Percentage of schools

Good Satisfactory Poor

include it in their lessons; pupils not being fully engaged in an activity; good ideas remaining undeveloped; and insufficient progression.

English continues to be a popular A-level subject. Alongside English literature, English language entries continue to grow and it is now common for schools to offer a number of courses: communications, theatre studies, film studies, English language and literature. Examination results have improved from year to year and the best work at this level is characterised by students sustaining a detailed critical discussion of a set text or issue and using specialist terminology confidently and accurately. Through their reading they develop a good personal response based on firm understanding, and their critical abilities are well developed. Students whose writing is good produce excellent critical essays, marshalling opinions, examples and quotations well; and their writing is technically accurate.

English at A level attracts a number of weaker candidates. Such students fail to make the progress needed to do well and teachers need to identify approaches which will help those students who lack the critical vocabulary to talk or write about subject matter and who find it difficult to back up opinions with pertinent examples. In literature courses, too many students find it difficult to move beyond surface meanings of a text and language students find it difficult to cope with the concepts and models of language being presented. The writing of the weaker candidates is often immature; spelling, punctuation and grammar are insecure; and they are unable to rise to the demands of formal essay writing.

As in many other subjects, modular A-level courses have been introduced in recent years. Some students have done less well than expected in early modules, indicating that staff and students are taking some time to adapt to this new form of assessment and structuring of courses. Early results, combined with the fact that a high proportion of candidates for modular syllabuses in 1996 took all their module assessments at the end of the course, suggest that many teachers need to consider carefully the suitability of the modular style of assessment for English.

Issues in English

Reading skills in Key Stage 3

Most pupils enter secondary schools with sound basic reading skills. They can identify, select and use information from library books and they have good comprehension skills. The revised Order for English has helped to ensure that pupils become familiar with a wide range of literature. Despite the early concerns of many English departments, the teaching of Shakespeare and other pre-twentieth century literature in Key Stage 3 has improved.

A low attaining group in Year 11 were introduced to "Romeo and Juliet" through video extracts, a simplified text role play and a cloze exercise to consolidate pupils' grasp of the plot. The teacher then worked on extracts from the original text and pupils showed a good understanding of Shakespeare's language and concepts in the play.

HMI INSPECTION 1997

Pupils often approach new reading with skill, confidence and discrimination and as they complete GCSE courses, many can offer confidently their own interpretations and views on the texts they have studied. Teachers have improved their handling of class readers and are more likely to include poetry in their lessons. This includes poems of high quality, written before 1900.

In an ambitious lesson with a Year 8 class on "The Lady of Shalott", the teacher set differentiated tasks and had high expectations. Pupils sought prosodic patterns, investigated the case of telling rhymes and discussed the poet's intentions.

HMI INSPECTION 1997

Some of the best lessons which encourage an interest in reading are those when a gifted English teacher shares with a class his or her own enthusiasm for literature. Successful departments ensure that pupils receive guidance on their private reading and that non-fiction and media texts are included alongside the 'canon' and the best contemporary teenage literature.

A small number of secondary schools receive intakes where the majority of pupils have reading ages of two years or more below their chronological age, and consequently they are ill-equipped for the demands of the secondary curriculum. Targeting these schools for specific support with reading is a responsibility of LEAs. In schools, the gap between good and poor provision for such pupils has widened over the last four years. While some schools have well-developed strategies, including classroom support, withdrawal, paired reading and home-reading projects, others offer little. A larger number of pupils, while possessing adequate skills, make little further progress. They are capable of using only basic reference material and their comprehension skills remain at a literal level: they find it difficult to grasp alternative meanings, make inferences or see different points of view. All this limits their appreciation of literature and their understanding of non-fiction texts in other subjects. Secondary pupils still need to be taught to read different types of text and directed towards sustained reading if they are to make progress and, for increasing numbers of pupils, if the reading demands of many post-16 courses are not to come as a surprise.

A significant number of schools have an insufficient range of books to support the reading requirements of the National Curriculum in English. Some schools lack pre-twentieth century fiction while others lack modern works. Relatively high expenditure on set texts leaves insufficient funds for a range of other textbooks, novels, plays, poetry and writing from different cultures. There are sometimes not enough books for less able pupils, who consequently lack motivation to improve their reading skills.

Raising standards in writing

Standards in writing generally lag behind those for speaking and listening and reading and there is evidence of poor standards in just over one in five schools in Key Stage 3 and one in ten in Key Stage 4 in this attainment target.

As with reading, the main problem to have emerged over the four years has been the failure of too many pupils to go on developing and improving their basic skills. For example, even able youngsters continue to make elementary technical errors; redrafting is little more than making a neat copy; formal essays contain many colloquial usages and moving beyond narrative and description to discursive writing presents pupils with insurmountable difficulties with regard

to structure, vocabulary and style. The current concern for standards of literacy has rightly focused attention on the significant minority of pupils who have real difficulties with their writing. Again, as with reading, there is now a wide gap between schools making good and poor provision for these pupils. Too much work by low-attaining pupils remains unfinished. They need considerable help in gathering and ordering their ideas and developing them in writing: they need to be taught the essential rules of spelling, grammar and punctuation; and they need to acquire a more varied vocabulary.

Good attainment in writing is characterised by accurate, confident work in a steadily increasing range of genres. Pupils are taught specific forms of writing by teachers' effective use of models and they begin to acquire a distinctive style of their own. One vital skill listed in the National Curriculum Order for English is that of distinguishing varying degrees of formality, selecting appropriately for a task.

A Year 9 class worked on the notion of "register", altering a piece of writing about a television programme which they had watched from informal to formal style: pupils understood the need to change grammar and vocabulary depending on the purpose and intended readership of the piece.

HMI INSPECTION 1997

Pupils benefit from well-targeted work on spelling, punctuation and grammar and from regular practice in drafting and editing their writing. In GCSE and more particularly at A level, many produce creditable critical essays and use specialist terminology effectively. Coursework is often of a very high standard and based on a carefully planned sequence of work. Often it involves a firsthand experience of a real problem.

Year 10 pupils wrote letters to the local council about road traffic problems in the area. This involved the class collecting and selecting information from newspapers and reference books and then drafting and revising their letters, which were accurate, carefully structured and in an appropriate style.

HMI INSPECTION 1996

The teaching and learning of speaking and listening

Teachers are used to assessing pupils' oral skills in GCSE but the substantial demands of the other attainment targets and some uncertainty about what constitutes progress in speaking and listening have meant that many pupils fail to do themselves justice. For example, too much discussion, whether in a whole class or in groups, is unfocused. Pupils are not encouraged to use sustained talk to argue, explain, plan, evaluate, respond to questions or develop an idea. Often, they fail to distinguish between formal and informal speech and do not listen carefully. A significant minority of students enter A-level courses with weaknesses in these areas. As schools have been encouraged to concentrate on improving pupils' standards of literacy, a real danger has emerged of teachers failing to intervene sufficiently to improve pupils' oral skills. There is an urgent need to plan more opportunities for speaking and listening in long units of work; to challenge pupils more to justify their opinions; to ask demanding questions and encourage considered responses; to train pupils to listen carefully; and, perhaps above all, to show them the different needs of formal and informal situations.

The many pupils who make good progress can read aloud with accuracy and expression and are able to work well in groups and in role play, where they build on the contributions of others. They adjust their speech according to the context, and by the end of Key Stage 4 and in the sixth form they make confident presentations to the rest of the class, holding the interest of others and answering questions well.

A Year 11 class played a definitions game in which pupils had to explain to a group of Martians some difficult concepts, such as religion, emotions, relationships and the family. Pupils learned to express themselves clearly and concisely and to explore language which had numerous connotations. Many pupils were operating at the highest levels, structuring their explanations carefully, using standard English effectively, and being encouraged to reflect on the purpose and nature of their talk.

HMI INSPECTION 1997

Increasingly, pupils are able to conduct a simple interview to gather information or seek the views of others.

In a Year 10 communications lesson pupils improved their oral skills by telephoning a number of local firms to arrange a series of visits in connection with their GNVQ work. They had to explain their needs clearly, negotiate a programme and agree dates. This showed pupils using language for a real purpose, listening carefully and bringing the conversation to a successful conclusion.

HMI INSPECTION 1997

The poor performance of boys in English

Boys' performance in English has increasingly lagged behind that of girls. In Key Stage 3 tests, boys are now 20 per cent adrift and in GCSE the difference is 16 per cent at A*-C grades. Too many of the lowest sets in secondary schools contain many disaffected boys. Departments need to look at the implications of grouping patterns and to identify strategies which will improve boys' attitudes and attainment. The lessons of the National Literacy Project in primary schools need to be applied to literacy work in secondary schools. For example, many pupils need more direct teaching of essential skills in all three attainment targets. More pupils - girls as well as boys - need to see reading as a pleasurable and useful activity and this involves teachers providing effective guidance and models. Some gains can be made by helping pupils to distinguish carefully between formal and informal language usage, by providing more opportunities for careful listening and sustained writing in a variety of forms and by using drama and role play more, as ways of strengthening oral skills.

7.2 MATHEMATICS

Trends in mathematics, 1993-7

Standards in mathematics did not improve significantly in Key Stage 3 over the period of this review, although steady improvements were made in Key Stage 4 and post-16.

In Key Stage 3 the proportion of pupils reaching national expectations in mathematics fell slightly after 1994, when some 60 per cent of pupils achieved level 5 or better in the national tests, to 57 per cent in 1995 and 1996. In 1997 the proportion returned to 60 per cent. The results of the Third International Mathematics and Science Study (TIMSS)[6] presented a gloomy picture of the performance of Year 8 and 9 English pupils in mathematics tests when compared to those in many other European and Pacific Rim countries. More encouraging was the performance of English 13-year-old pupils in practical, problem-solving tasks which relate more closely to Attainment Target 1, Using and Applying Mathematics. Here, they did as well as, or better than pupils in most of the other European countries involved.

GCSE results in mathematics have improved after a dip in 1995. At GCE A level, results have steadily improved. At GCSE and post-16 examinations, girls are now achieving higher scores than boys in mathematics. Over the four years, the proportion of girls attaining GCSE grade C or better has caught up that of boys. At A level, results achieved by girls have improved faster than those of boys, and girls now account for about a third of the entries.

[6] *The Third International Mathematics and Science Study (TIMSS),* National Foundation for Educational Research, 1996.

There have been significant increases in take-up of A-level mathematics in a number of schools following the introduction of modular courses. The impact of these courses is also reflected in national trends. A-level entries rose significantly for the first time in 1996, after years of serious decline, to be followed by a further, smaller increase in 1997. A-level results have improved considerably in some of the schools which have introduced modular A-level mathematics syllabuses. Improvements have been most marked at the lower end of the ability range, but in some highly selective schools the most able are also being stretched by being able to complete basic modules at an early stage and progress quickly to more demanding work.

While there has been some improvement in standards in mathematics, the overall picture is of patchy progress. Over the four years, there have been quite fundamental changes to the National Curriculum Order, to GCSE syllabuses and structures, to post-16 courses and to related assessment procedures. In some schools, mathematics departments have been slow to react to these changes, sometimes suspecting that other changes will supersede them. Clearly the improvement at GCSE and post-16 is positive and deserves credit. However, there remain key areas which require attention if all pupils are to leave our schools equipped to deal with the mathematical demands and challenges of the next millennium.

Issues in mathematics

Pupils' progress in Key Stage 3

Inspection evidence indicates consistently that pupils make quicker progress and reach higher standards, relative to their age, in mathematics in

Chart 75 Mathematics

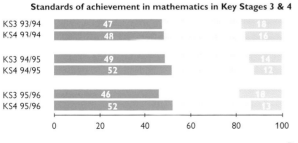

Standards of achievement in mathematics in Key Stages 3 & 4

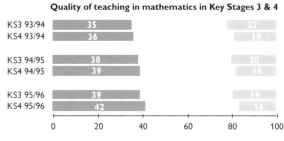

Quality of teaching in mathematics in Key Stages 3 & 4

Percentage of schools

Good   Satisfactory   Poor

Key Stage 4 than in Key Stage 3. The quality of mathematics teaching has also been marginally better in Key Stage 4. One reason for this is that the GCSE examination has provided schools with a clear goal, the detailed syllabuses and past examination papers helping to identify teaching and learning expectations. This is generally not the case in Key Stage 3 where the changes made to the National Curriculum Order in 1995 caused problems for some departments. The loss of statements of attainment, intended to reduce the assessment load, also removed much of the detail used previously by schools to identify learning objectives. Some departments continue to refer to the statements of attainment in the earlier Order, but they do not transfer well. However, where departments have entirely abandoned objectives at this level of detail, the quality of lesson planning often varies unacceptably among teachers.

In some departments, the scheme of work is little more than a list of chapter headings from the textbooks in general use. Most commonly, learning objectives are not stated, are unclear or, where an individualised learning approach is in use, are often understood to be determined by the pupil's route through the scheme. Planning to ensure clear progression within the subject across the whole of Key Stage 3 remains a weakness in many schools. In some schools good use has been made of the national tests, which have provided schools with helpful guidance on standards. This has resulted in some improvements in curriculum planning for progression and the quality of teaching in Key Stage 3, and teachers have become better at assessing pupils at the end of the key stage.

Theale Green Community School, Berkshire, makes good use of primary school records to group pupils and to diagnose their strengths and weaknesses. Pupils' progress in Year 7 is enhanced by this analysis which informs planning and teaching. Planning for the short and long term is good. The scheme of work is developed from the revised Order and provides pupils with a broad and balanced mathematics curriculum. Teachers' planning is frequently adapted in response to pupils' assessed needs and attainment and to take account of intended learning objectives and the length of the lesson. Teachers deliberately vary their teaching approaches which include exposition and discussion, with opportunity for pupils to practise and consolidate their knowledge and skills. Pupils are encouraged to determine and use the most appropriate method to use when calculating, including mental methods and estimation. Homework is regularly set and discussed in lessons. Standards attained in the Key Stage 3 national tests are well above the national figures. The results are carefully monitored by the Head of Department, who attributes the improvements in pupils' performance to the successful implementation of the agreed planning and teaching approaches.

HMI INSPECTION, 1996

More commonly, poor lesson planning often results in ineffective teaching with uncertain and slow starts to lessons, inconclusive endings with no summary or consolidation, and pupils spending too much time left to themselves even when they are experiencing difficulties with the work. In such lessons pupils make little or no progress. Younger pupils in Key Stage 3 can regularly spend time in mathematics lessons working at texts, queuing for help, and collecting and exchanging materials, but rarely engaging in the interactive whole class learning which helps to elucidate key concepts.

A key weakness of much mathematics teaching in Key Stage 3 is that is fails to take into account prior attainment and to build on it at good pace (see pp 103-4). Setting is used in the majority of mathematics departments, and increasingly so during Key Stage 3 so that by Year 9 nine out of ten classes are set. Although the match of work to pupils' prior attainment is generally helped by setting, this does not guarantee that the match of work is good. The demands of the work given to different sets are often determined by the series of textbooks used. Teachers' lesson planning may simply indicate the textbook exercise pupils are to complete after the teacher's introduction. Such lessons often have an unsatisfactorily slow pace and pupils make poor progress. The work is routine and undemanding. Homework is commonly to complete the exercise or, when teachers are caught out by the amount of work pupils have completed, to start the next one. Slower pupils resent the quantity of homework they have to complete. Over time, exposure to this one style of teaching can lead to pupils becoming disaffected with mathematics; some pupils become deliberately obstructive and antagonistic.

The recall and transfer of mathematical knowledge to new situations

Many mathematics lessons have a common pattern: some introductory whole-class teaching, followed by pupils working from a textbook or worksheets, when they generally work on their own and receive support from the teacher who circulates around the class, checking and marking work. The introductory teaching is usually a sound and straightforward explanation of the technique needed to complete the exercise and to practise the method. Other techniques are then introduced and practised. Over time this should build up pupils' mathematical knowledge and skills. In practice, however, it often provides an atomised curriculum consisting of a set of unrelated items and techniques. Pupils are not taught how to identify and make connections between the underlying structures and concepts which aid understanding and assist with memory and recall of information. Higher-attaining pupils can make the links for themselves, but lower-attaining pupils cannot, and are confused by an excessive range of seemingly discrete techniques which they cannot remember. Neither is sufficient attention given to identifying and correcting pupils' errors and misunderstandings.

Inspection evidence has shown how important discussion and mental work are in mathematics teaching, together with appropriately monitored practice and consolidation, to promote good understanding. Where this is done well, the teacher integrates a question and answer technique into explanations to stimulate discussion. Pupils' responses to challenging questions provide insights into their understanding which are used by the teacher to direct teaching during the whole class introduction, and later to groups or individuals. Mental mathematics provides further opportunity for consolidation and assessment. It strengthens pupils' recall of facts and relationships, establishes and reinforces mental strategies for calculation and simplification, and stimulates the skill of visualising numbers, objects and patterns. If pupils are to succeed they must remember many different bits of mathematics and be able to transfer their knowledge, understanding and skills. Unfortunately, they frequently do not. Consequently, many pupils confuse ideas and methods they can only loosely recall. Evidence from international and national tests highlights this problem.

The teaching of algebra

Standards of attainment in algebra have continued to vary widely both across and within schools. The algebraic knowledge, skills and understanding that pupils bring to A-level and higher education courses have come under a barrage of criticism from some quarters. Issues include approaches to the teaching of algebra and the impact of new technologies on standards.

Most secondary schools assume that pupils have not previously been introduced to algebra and start from scratch. However, this teaching rarely starts with generalising arithmetic ideas, drawing upon equivalent forms to establish algebraic statements such as $4+4+4= 3 \times 4$ to establish $x+x+x= 3x$. Although many pupils explore and describe pattern in number or geometric sequences, relatively few use algebra to make generalisations. The use of symbols to formulate a problem which can be solved by equations is given insufficient attention. Pupils lack confidence in using and applying what skills they have to solve problems and to simplify and manipulate algebraic expressions, to explain and justify choices, and to prove results.

Increasingly pupils are taught how to employ trial and improvement methods using calculators. When this is successful the work draws together different approaches and pupils can confidently choose which approach to use for which purpose. Increasing access to and use of graphics calculators enables pupils to solve equations using tables, iteration and graphics in addition to finding exact solutions using manipulation skills. Good teaching draws in the number, the geometric and the algebraic features of this work. However, excessive reliance on trial and improvement leads to a superficial grasp of the algebraic concepts involved and pupils are not able to grasp the mathematical structures that support other approaches. Trial and improvement is an effective strategy which pupils are confident in using. However, it does not provide them with the skills needed to manipulate algebraic symbolism in order to find exact and general solutions rather than approximate solutions.

The regularity of mathematics lessons

In primary schools the National Numeracy Project has focused attention on the importance of providing pupils with daily mathematics lessons. Regular oral and mental work sharpen and extend pupils' mental mathematics. The impact in raising standards of the National Numeracy Project and the forthcoming National Strategy for Numeracy will need to be sustained in secondary schools. Frequent regular teaching must be maintained to ensure that pupils retain and build on their computational skills. Schools should therefore guard against further erosion of mathematics time and evaluate the effectiveness of the pattern of lessons over the teaching week. There is a clear need to improve secondary pupils' mental mathematics and a danger that the primary impetus might be lost because of limited and dissipated teaching.

The use of graphics calculators

The potential to improve standards in mathematics through the appropriate use of graphics calculators and other technologies is considerable. Their role in teaching and equally importantly in public examinations has, however, yet to be agreed. Such an agreement is necessary to rationalise the currently undirected and inequitable system. Graphics calculators are increasingly being used by students on Advanced-level courses and by pupils preparing for the GCSE. They provide pupils with the opportunity to observe, interpret, test and explain behaviour, which teachers can then capitalise upon, for example, to show the effects of different values for a, b and c on the graph of $y=a(x-b)^2+c$ to establish turning points and establish curve sketching techniques. Even the display of the full expression to be calculated can help pupils to recognise errors and to identify the precedence given to operations. They are not, however, a substitute for using methods that give exact solutions.

7.3 SCIENCE

Trends in science, 1993-7

From 1993 there has been a steady improvement of standards in science. In particular, a sharper focus for lessons, clearer objectives identified by teachers, and better use of class time have contributed to an improvement in pupils' knowledge base. The proportion of pupils in Key Stage 3 reaching the expected level in science national tests has risen slowly to six out of ten, a similar proportion to other core subjects. International comparisons confirm this broadly positive and improving picture, with standards comparing favourably with those in other Western European countries. Results in the double award science GCSE have shown steady improvement, while at A level, although overall numbers of entries for science subjects have declined, students taking science subjects achieve well and obtain good grades in relation to their previous GCSE performance. A-level results in modular science courses have also been good, despite the fact that lack of success in early modules has raised questions about the preparedness and maturity of some students for these elements of the syllabus.

This is a particularly encouraging picture, given that the science National Curriculum Order has been subject to a number of changes. The most significant change has been the revision of Attainment Target 1 (Experimental & Investigative Science): schools have welcomed the reduced requirements which allow them to broaden the types of investigative work undertaken by pupils. In Key Stage 3 there are signs that investigatory skills are being developed in a wider range of contexts and with less emphasis on whole investigations. The impact of the new requirements has, however, been relatively small so far in Key Stage 4.

A major challenge for teachers of science in Key Stage 3 is to take account of the science learned in primary schools (see also page 104). The picture has changed rapidly; pupils now arrive at secondary school with a good grounding in scientific knowledge, practical skills and terminology. Many encounter an abrupt change in teaching style and a very different context for the teaching of science when they transfer to secondary school. In many schools the science curriculum at the start of Key Stage 3 has not been modified to allow for pupils' achievements in primary school so their progress is slow. Much can be gained by improving the interchange of ideas and information across the primary - secondary boundary and by teachers improving the questioning used to find out what pupils have already learned. For example, the teacher of a Year 7 class investigating the cooling of a beaker of water was told by pupils that they had not done anything similar before. Later it was discovered that some pupils had investigated 'what material would be best to keep the baby Jesus warm', at Christmas in Year 5. Knowledge of this would have enabled the teacher to approach the activity rather differently so as to build on pupils' previous experience and existing understanding.

Science teaching is almost invariably well organised and purposeful; during the last four years lessons have become even more sharply focused on scientific content, particularly in Key Stage 4. Almost all teachers have good subject knowledge and science is confidently and accurately presented. Practical work is given high priority and laboratory work features in a high proportion of lessons. The variety of activities and experiences used to teach science decreased in

Chart 76 Science

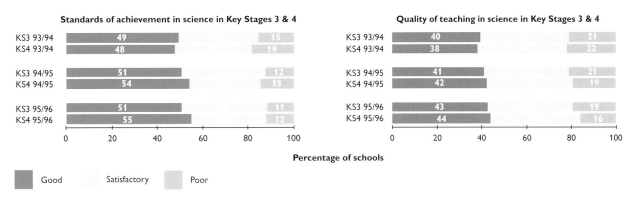

Standards of achievement in science in Key Stages 3 & 4

	Good	Poor
KS3 93/94	49	15
KS4 93/94	48	19
KS3 94/95	51	12
KS4 94/95	54	15
KS3 95/96	51	11
KS4 95/96	55	12

Quality of teaching in science in Key Stages 3 & 4

	Good	Poor
KS3 93/94	40	21
KS4 93/94	38	22
KS3 94/95	41	21
KS4 94/95	42	19
KS3 95/96	43	17
KS4 95/96	44	16

Percentage of schools

Good   Satisfactory   Poor

many schools as planning was revised to cover National Curriculum content and GCSE syllabuses. Now that there is greater curriculum stability teachers are beginning to employ a greater range of techniques and activities with positive effects on pupils' response and standards achieved.

Issues in science

Pupils' understanding of underlying scientific concepts

Inspection evidence across the four years of the cycle has shown that, whereas their knowledge of the material in the Programmes of Study has improved, pupils' understanding of underlying scientific concepts frequently remains insecure, and they are insufficiently able to apply their knowledge in new contexts. For example, pupils may know about energy transfer in physical systems but not be able to apply these ideas to plant nutrition or chemical reactions. Where pupils' conceptual understanding is well developed, they are able to apply knowledge in different situations, make inferences, offer hypotheses and make generalisations. In the schools where pupils show greater facility in transfer of ideas, understanding is well founded and teachers have given systematic attention to the development of ideas across the science curriculum.

Part of the problem of pupils' inability to apply their knowledge in new contexts arises from the way in which many departments have approached the changes demanded by revisions to the National Curriculum. Often topics or modules have been prepared by individuals or small groups of teachers with insufficient time or opportunity to co-ordinate approaches to key scientific concepts across different topics. For example, chemists and physicists may have planned and taught energy transfer in chemical and mechanical systems without using the same vocabulary or drawing parallels. For pupils, what is received is therefore fragmented, and an intellectual leap is required to make important connections.

Many teachers fail to capitalise on opportunities to develop conceptual understanding. Where this is done well, a starting point is the teacher's ability to relate new work to pupils' existing experience and to challenge any misconceptions, for example through questioning which reconstructs the foundations upon which new material can be built.

More rarely do teachers ask the questions necessary to bridge gaps with related topics and engage in extended discussion to make pupils aware of the wider significance of the work in hand.

In a Year 10 lesson preparing for experiments on the rate at which marble chips react with acid, excellent questioning techniques were used to make sure that all pupils understood what factors could be changed, and could predict how these might affect results. Examples from everyday life and other chemical topics were discussed which showed that some pupils thought that dissolving sugar in water was a chemical reaction. After the experiment sufficient time was given to reviewing outcomes in order to generalise about the effect of the exposed surface area on the rate at which a reaction proceeds.

HMI INSPECTION 1996

Standards in experimental and investigatory science

Whereas pupils have consistently demonstrated the ability to carry out routine practical tasks, the ability to plan, execute and evaluate their own investigations has only slowly improved despite the revision of Attainment Target 1 (Experimental & Investigative Science) made in the National Curriculum review. Problems with the original attainment target included difficulties in interpreting the statements of attainment, access to higher levels, especially in biology, and the perceived time demand of investigatory work. The review has eased these difficulties, and in particular reduced the requirement for all assessment to be in the context of whole investigations. Many schools have been slow to take advantage of the greater flexibility which this offers to integrate investigatory work with work in other areas of the Programme of Study. Additionally, many schools continue to pursue a relatively narrow range of set-piece investigations without preparing pupils effectively through the practice of skills in other contexts. For example, very many schools use the same established investigations for GCSE assessment at Key Stage 4: photosynthesis in pondweed or an enzyme experiment (Life and Living Processes); rates of reaction using marble chips and acid (Materials and Their Properties); and the resistance of a wire (Physical Processes).

Departments which are more successful in developing experimental skills have reflected on the purposes of the full range of practical activities which they undertake in order to make sure that scarce time and resources are most efficiently used. They include planned opportunities for the development of the constituent elements of Experimental and Investigative Science. For example, good teaching encourages pupils to draw scientific conclusions from practical work rather than just describing outcomes. It also makes overt links between the evaluation of a routine whole-class practical activity and the requirements for evaluation of individual investigations. Good planning defines the range of objectives which practical activities can most effectively fulfil, while avoiding the danger of doing practical work only for its own sake.

In spite of the generally rather slow progress in relation to National Curriculum expectations, evidence from an international study shows that, at age 13, English pupils perform relatively well in a range of practical tasks. The Third International Mathematics and Science Study (TIMSS) report on Performance Assessment ranked English pupils as second only to those from Singapore in their mean score for the six practical tasks used in the survey. English pupils were better at using scientific procedures such as recording, measuring and conducting experiments than at applying their scientific knowledge to explain practical outcomes or solve problems. This is consistent with inspection findings and suggests that the priority for schools should be to ensure that pupils are challenged to use their knowledge and understanding of science in a range of practical contexts.

The status and popularity of science

Since 1989 all pupils have been required to study science to the age of 16. Those pupils who have experienced the full National Curriculum from age five are now reaching the end of Key Stage 3, bringing with them a broader and deeper experience of science than their predecessors. It remains to be seen whether the benefits of this expansion will feed through to an increased take-up of science subjects post-16. However, there is evidence that more needs to be done to raise the status and popularity of science with pupils at all levels in secondary schools to sustain the good start made in Key Stages 1 and 2. In particular,

research suggests that while pupils' views of science are not strongly negative, they are less positive than for most other subjects, and increasingly so as pupils move through secondary school. There are some immediate ways in which schools can address this issue.

Key Stage 3 is a crucial time. In schools where science is thriving, pupils of all abilities are provided with a varied and stimulating programme supplemented by extra-curricular activities such as 'Science Challenge' or the CREST award scheme. In lessons teachers use textbooks selectively, avoiding the danger of over-dependence on schemes or worksheets which tend to promote a uniformity of approach and which set a ceiling on achievement. Here, and more so in Key Stage 4, these schools have given careful thought to the deployment of staff in order to make optimum use of their specialist subject expertise.

St Aidan's School in Harrogate has experienced steady growth in the numbers studying science subjects post-16, far outstripping the national trend. This is attributed to good-quality specialist teaching across Key Stages 3 and 4, with teachers readily available to provide support outside lessons. Whilst planning is good, teachers are flexible and willing to change track in a lesson in response to pupils' questions or interests. Pupils are given 'the confidence to succeed' by this regime which is reinforced by examination success at GCSE. Teachers are enthusiasts for their subjects and constantly seek ways of conveying this to pupils. Extra-curricular activities thrive; pupils are, for example, involved in producing two science magazines ("Young Einstein" and "The Mad Scientist") which are sold to pupils and staff.

HMI INSPECTION 1996

Post-16, the teaching of science subjects compares unfavourably with that of most other subjects. In the 1993-4 OFSTED Review of Science inspection findings it was reported that 'there is a tendency in too many classes to "spoon feed" rather than to encourage students to think ideas through for themselves. In some cases there is an over-reliance on dictated notes and duplicated hand-outs'. This is still too often the case. However, in the best A-level lessons students are excited by the realisation of how their learning can be applied in an increasingly wide range of fundamental, modern and relevant contexts.

7.4 ART

Trends in art, 1993-7

Standards of achievement in art have improved steadily, with an increase in the proportion of good work in lessons seen, as well as improvement in grades at GCSE and at A level. In 1996 just over 35 per cent of the Year 11 cohort of pupils from maintained secondary schools in England took Art and Design GCSE, and 55 per cent gained A*-C grades. It is difficult to make direct comparisons of standards achieved in art in schools in England with those achieved in other countries, but art in English schools is generally held in very high regard internationally.

Over the four-year period, the Key Stage 4 curriculum has been driven by the GCSE syllabuses and has remained essentially unchanged. However, the effect of more systematic teaching in Key Stage 3 has begun to filter through to Key Stage 4, with pupils tending to be more conversant with the work of artists and more able to discuss work using technical language. The best Key Stage 4 work involves the refinement of skills and the development of depth and breadth of knowledge. Pupils are capable of planning their own work, investigating, researching, experimenting with materials and creating imaginative and innovative responses to a set brief. They can show their individuality through the accomplished handling of imagery, which often shows original ideas and reflects the influence of other artistic works. Indeed, many teachers are now looking beyond the basic requirements of the GCSE syllabus to explore 'issues-based' approaches which involve more moral and ethical questions, and touch more on the issues which are of concern to the pupils themselves.

Post-16 work is very highly rated in inspection in terms of attainment, progress and teaching. Inspectors judged progress post-16 to be better in art than in any other subject in 1996-97. Sixth-form students can make very rapid progress in art as they come to realise the creative possibilities of a project. Good teaching is well supported by the examination framework of A level, and teachers often share their own extensive knowledge of art, craft and design with students. Some Advanced GNVQ Art and Design work goes beyond the scope of GCE A level in terms of breadth and relevance to design practice.

Issues in art

The impact of the National Curriculum

In spite of the reservations of some teachers, the National Curriculum Order in Art has had a positive impact on the overall national provision in Key Stage 3. The concept of a curriculum entitlement has benefited those pupils in schools where Years 7 to 9 were seen as little more than preparation for Key Stage 4, or were thought of as a period when pupils were marking time until the subject could be dropped. It has forced a re-think in those schools where Key Stage 3 lessons were restricted to less expensive activities, usually in two dimensions, so that more valuable resources could be saved for those taking public examinations.

In better departments the National Curriculum has often reinforced existing good practice, and has helped to give the curriculum continuity and progression. Before the introduction of the National Curriculum the majority of Key Stage 3 lessons concentrated on a practical approach to investigating and making. Although many teachers were already teaching lessons involving the study

Chart 77 Art

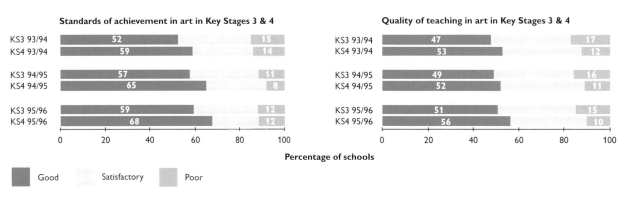

Standards of achievement in art in Key Stages 3 & 4

	Good	Poor
KS3 93/94	52	15
KS4 93/94	59	14
KS3 94/95	57	11
KS4 94/95	65	8
KS3 95/96	59	12
KS4 95/96	68	12

Quality of teaching in art in Key Stages 3 & 4

	Good	Poor
KS3 93/94	47	17
KS4 93/94	53	12
KS3 94/95	49	16
KS4 94/95	52	11
KS3 95/96	51	15
KS4 95/96	56	10

Percentage of schools

■ Good   Satisfactory   Poor

of the work of other artists in response to a growing professional awareness of the importance of critical studies in art, it was not until the introduction of the National Curriculum that such study became a requirement. Although many art teachers with graduate qualifications in the subject had the historical and critical knowledge required, it was only with the introduction of the National Curriculum that they were required to use that knowledge systematically in planning schemes of work in Key Stage 3.

Teachers have gained confidence in using the study of the work of artists to develop pupils' own practical skills. As yet the emphasis is on fine art. Although design has always been a required component of the National Curriculum Programmes of Study, the fraught developments surrounding design and technology in the early nineties discouraged art teachers from seeing design as part of their legitimate domain, with the consequence that the study of design and designers has been neglected in Key Stage 3. It is only now, with the development of GNVQ courses, that design activities are returning in strength to art departments. More recently, there has been more widespread use in Key Stage 3 of art and craft from other cultures.

In a Year 9 project based on Australian native art pupils began by making line drawings of the original motifs, adapting them for use in printing and collage, then developing them further as containers constructed in the shape of Aborigine images of animals, using card and adhesive tape. These were exquisitely decorated with paints and collage materials to produce skilfully made craft objects.

HMI INSPECTION 1996

Although initial suspicion of National Curriculum art has been replaced in most cases by an awareness that more systematic teaching in Key Stage 3 can have benefits at Key Stage 4 and beyond in terms of improving attainment and progress, there are still undercurrents of dissatisfaction, based on the view that an "imposed" curriculum framework stifles creativity. There is the view that if only art teachers were able to have freedom to plan their own work then standards would rise, and that the National Curriculum has led to a uniformity of practice, with little scope for pupils to express their individuality. There are in fact many examples of schemes of work, entirely consistent with the National Curriculum, which result in highly creative work in Key Stage 3. In practice, therefore, a National Curriculum provides valuable planning support, and over the past four years has given a better deal to pupils.

Assessment in art

Assessment has been a difficult area for art teachers in Key Stage 3 throughout the four-year period. In the absence of early guidance teachers successfully drew on GSCE experience and their own past practice. Some teachers mistakenly assumed that the emphasis should be on complex records rather than the communication of their judgements about pupils' work. The end-of-key stage statements introduced following the review of the National Curriculum have given teachers a clearer set of national expectations, but there are, and will continue to be, problems in describing the quality of visual work in words. The recently published document from QCA on expectations in Key Stage 3 has been unjustly criticised by teachers for showing too much of the middle range of work rather than a full range, including the very best work. This document is thought by them to have contributed to the feeling that the National Curriculum has encouraged mediocrity in Key Stage 3. The end-of-key stage optional tests were, however, seen by those who used them as well thought-out, and giving a clearer picture of how end-of-key stage assessment should be conducted.

Resources and the use of IT in art

In the best cases, schools have invested in resources to provide a comprehensive range of materials and equipment. This helps to provide sound coverage of the National Curriculum programmes of study and forms a good base for Key Stage 4 and post-16 work, including GNVQ, especially where the investment has included IT.

The broadening of the range of work to include three-dimensional activities has, however, caused resourcing problems for many departments, and forced them to reconsider the allocation of resources amongst their Key Stage 3, Key Stage 4 and post-16 groups. Even so, deficiencies are evident. In some schools the emphasis in Key Stage 3 remains on two-dimensional work. The National Curriculum requirement for the use of sketchbooks to record ideas and visual notes has helped to introduce much good practice into Key Stage 3 which had previously only been seen in Key Stage 4. Nevertheless, in many schools the expense of providing suitably robust sketchbooks has limited their availability.

There are examples of art departments being put under considerable pressure by lack of funds. Some schools have only just enough resources to sustain the range, type and scale of work that National Curriculum and examination courses demand. Where expenditure is low, three-dimensional work, and ceramics in particular, is most affected. In too many schools facilities such as those for ceramics or photography are lying idle for want of teacher expertise or funds.

Visual source material plays a vital part in expanding pupils' repertoire of knowledge in art. In some schools, for example, pupils have access to a catalogued collection of reproductions, postcards, visual ephemera, videos and slides. Although schools have acquired more art books in recent years, there is still a shortage of materials to cover the full range of art, craft and design. For example, few schools have books about the many British designers and craftspeople with international reputations.

There is evidence of an increase in the creative use of IT in art in Key Stage 3, but this is still not widespread. Where Key Stage 4 and post-16 work in IT have developed successfully, this often feeds down into Key Stage 3. In too many schools teachers are simply not aware of the potential of IT within art, and fail even to provide the statutory IT entitlement in the subject. In some cases this is due to inadequate IT resources in the department, or lack of access to centrally held computers. In too many schools teachers simply do not exploit the huge potential of IT, and the power of the computer to change pupils' ways of thinking in art is left untapped.

In many schools, good and flexible teaching overcomes some deficiencies in resourcing, and pupils continue to make good or at least adequate progress, but where resources are predominantly poor, progress is affected in spite of teachers' best efforts. In other schools, pupils are seriously disadvantaged by a combination of poor resourcing and poor teaching.

7.5 DESIGN AND TECHNOLOGY

Trends in design and technology, 1993-7

Standards in design and technology (D&T) have improved markedly. This is mainly due to the introduction in 1995 of the revised National Curriculum Order for D&T where a clearer Programme of Study helped teachers plan more effectively. There has been a return to a higher proportion of practical work with pupils developing better general D&T capability.

Many teachers found the original Order for D&T problematic: not only was it difficult to understand and open to wide differences in interpretation, but also there was insufficient time for teachers to plan the required new approaches. It was subject to early revision, but it was not until 1995/6 that teachers were able to work with an Order with which they felt comfortable. During the years 1993-7, therefore, three versions of D&T could be found in schools: the largely discredited original Order; the new Order in Key Stage 3 from 1995 and Key Stage 4 from 1996; and some schools used the suspension of the mandatory status of D&T in Key Stage 4 to continue with GCSE syllabuses for craft, design and technology (CDT) and home economics.

Despite these difficulties, D&T education has attracted considerable interest from around the world. Pupils' ability to demonstrate true technological competence, by combining their skills with knowledge and understanding in order to both design and make products, is highly regarded by educationalists overseas. The popularity and vocational potential of the subject may have contributed to the ten per cent rise in numbers of students taking A level in the last four years. Post-16, standards of attainment have risen too and work is often of outstanding quality, especially where students' designing and making projects are linked to industry. Some of these students have had ideas patented or designs registered, for which they receive royalties and experience the excitement of seeing their designs being manufactured or influencing production. Many students show sound understanding of important environmental and other social and cultural issues.

The majority of D&T teachers provide workshops at lunchtime and after school, enabling pupils, particularly in Key Stage 4, to use the specialist facilities and guidance available; and post-16, because of small group sizes, many lessons are co-taught with other classes. Over the last four years there has been a steady rise in the number of schools involved in Young Engineers Clubs and schemes aimed at strengthening links with industry, such as Neighbourhood Engineers or the Engineering Education Scheme. All this strengthens pupils' education in D&T.

Issues in design and technology

Pupils' attainment in design

At best, pupils rigorously apply their knowledge of the working properties and performance characteristics of materials and of tools, equipment and processes in developing design specifications. They also use their experience of hand-tools, larger pieces of equipment and machinery to specify, at the design stage, how the materials will be prepared, cut, shaped, formed, joined and finished. Their sketching and drawing skills, together with the use of appropriate modelling techniques, are used effectively to illustrate their

Chart 78 Design & Technology

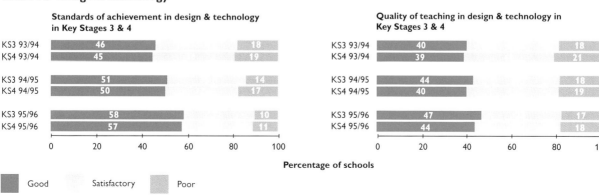

Standards of achievement in design & technology in Key Stages 3 & 4

	Good	Poor
KS3 93/94	46	18
KS4 93/94	45	19
KS3 94/95	51	14
KS4 94/95	50	17
KS3 95/96	58	10
KS4 95/96	57	11

Quality of teaching in design & technology in Key Stages 3 & 4

	Good	Poor
KS3 93/94	40	18
KS4 93/94	39	21
KS3 94/95	44	18
KS4 94/95	40	19
KS3 95/96	47	17
KS4 95/96	44	18

Percentage of schools

Good   Satisfactory   Poor

design ideas. Their thinking is made explicit: their resulting designs are used as valuable working documents to guide the manufacture of the product and to help the pupils work autonomously.

However, although an increasing proportion of pupils work at this level, they remain a minority, and in general pupils' attainment in designing lags behind that in making. This is because pupils are either not introduced to a sufficiently wide range of designing strategies in Key Stage 3 or are not taught to use them effectively. Pupils are generally confident where work is closely directed by the teacher, but less so when working independently to their own plans, with little awareness of how their work will develop in the later stages of their projects. This inhibits attainment and progress in Key Stage 4 when the work becomes less directed by the teacher: pupils are not sure how to define the design task and develop a specification, or how to generate possible solutions and optimise their choices. Thus, for example, pupils working on major coursework projects in Key Stage 4 tend to lack a sufficient overview of the designing, planning and making tasks. Therefore they have no sense of urgency, manage their time poorly and are able to make only limited progress without the direct support of the teacher.

Similarly, when teaching designing, teachers frequently make insufficient use of product analysis where pupils 'investigate, disassemble and evaluate familiar products and applications' as required in the National Curriculum; they rely instead on designing only with paper and pencil, sometimes retrospectively so that design-sheets become an end in themselves rather than a means to an end.

Progress in design is often hindered by lack of co-ordination of the different elements of D&T. In Key Stage 3 most schools operate a rotational modular system to enable pupils to work with the variety of materials and activities specified in the National Curriculum Order. Departments need to give more attention to providing continuity of experiences and progression in building pupils' knowledge, skill and understanding as they move from one project and material area to the next. Where these modular courses work well, teachers are careful to build on pupils' earlier experience, and increase the level of challenge in a module when they teach it later in the year. This develops rather than just repeats the generic designing and making skills.

Planning to meet the identified needs of particular groups of pupils

Most teachers set the same work for all their pupils and expect them to work to the best of their ability, often without making their expectations clear. Relatively few teachers differentiate effectively, for example, by setting different tasks, or by specifying required outcomes from pupils of different abilities working on the same task. In particular, the most able pupils are frequently under-challenged; many activities fail to develop pupils' research skills sufficiently and offer little opportunity for initiative or creativity.

Girls have increasingly made better progress and achieved higher levels of attainment than boys in all areas of D&T except systems and control. In general, girls manage their work more effectively, meet deadlines and take greater care over the quality of presentation. They frequently write at greater length, but not necessarily more analytically or creatively than boys. Few D&T departments analyse the reasons for such differences in performance, and so they have no strategies for raising standards overall.

*When national and local inspection showed evidence of underachievement by boys in D&T to be a significant issue, **Cornwall LEA** D&T advisers analysed data from examination results and other research evidence. At a county-wide meeting of D&T Heads of Department they discussed monitoring strategies and remedial action that might be taken. As a consequence, teachers at **Cape Cornwall School** identified the need to help boys improve their time-management and presentation skills; schemes of work have now been modified to set shorter project deadlines and provide more feedback on pupils' progress.*

HMI INSPECTION 1997

Equipment and resources

Although there have been improvements in the teaching materials, equipment and other resources on the market, the funding to acquire them is rarely available except in Technology Schools or Colleges. The gap between provision and need as well as in the range between schools is widening. Overall capitation levels for the subject have declined in real terms over the four years - as a consequence, in some schools expensive equipment lies idle for lack of the necessary consumable materials.

Some schools have difficulty in providing resources for systems and control work, computer aided drawing and computer aided manufacturing (CADCAM) - all required by the National Curriculum. The curriculum in some schools is limited by dependence on donated scrap materials from industry. Despite the appearance of a new generation of up-to-date book and non-book resources, provision of books is poor in more than a third of schools. Where teachers compensate for lack of books with worksheets, they are often insufficiently matched to the ability of the pupils using them and frequently restrict the development of pupils' research skills. Additional funding has, however, allowed many Technology Colleges to provide better access to a good range of CADCAM equipment. This is promoting the development of pupils' capability in computer control, designing and manufacturing.

In D&T pupils should use IT to control mechanical, electrical and pneumatic systems either in their own right or as part of CADCAM systems. They should also be able to learn the importance of microprocessor control systems in domestic and industrial products. Increasingly, systems are being developed for computer control and CADCAM that are within the financial reach of schools. In both key stages, however, the majority of teachers lack sufficient knowledge of the systems and control aspects of D&T. In Key Stage 3, for example, this means that many pupils do not develop electronic systems and most do not develop a sufficient understanding of the concepts of feedback and how they can be used to ensure the correct functioning of systems. Where teachers have had appropriate in-service training, including distance learning materials for on-site training and the sharing of expertise between local groups of schools, there are direct benefits.

*In **Churchill Community School, Avon**, through great staff commitment to learning about control, sharing experience and building equipment, all pupils are able to devise control sequences to operate large school-made models such as washing machines and car-parking systems prior to developing their own computer-controlled projects.*

HMI INSPECTION 1996

Too often, however, opportunities for training are unavailable or inaccessible, usually for financial reasons. Senior management teams need to ensure that their expenditure on new resources is not wasted because they have given insufficient priority to professional development. This is particularly true for the use of information technology in D&T.

Design and technology accommodation

The pressure on accommodation for design and technology has grown steadily as the numbers of pupils taking the subject overall, and especially the size of class and the range of activities, have increased. D&T rooms were almost always designed for a maximum of twenty pupils but one-half of Year 7 classes and one-quarter of classes in Key Stage 4 are above this number. This has implications for health and safety as well as for teaching, learning and standards. In some schools where specialist accommodation is under pressure, classes have been split between practical and theory work, limiting time for practical activities and leading to incomplete or rushed work, and ignoring the greater weighting in the National Curriculum Order on developing capability in making products. Additionally, in one-quarter of schools accommodation is unsatisfactory, with poor decoration, limited space for designing, inadequate access to IT facilities, and unhygienic or dusty and unsafe furniture and fittings. There are health and safety issues, for example, where inadequate dust extraction in workshops or chipped work surfaces in food technology compromise safe working. These problems will require significant financial outlay if they are to be remedied.

7.6 GEOGRAPHY

Trends in geography, 1993-7

Standards in geography at GCSE and A level have improved steadily since the beginning of the inspection cycle and could go higher still, given more substantial foundations in Key Stage 3. Some 50 per cent of geography candidates in maintained schools now achieve a higher grade (A*-C) at GCSE, and 80 per cent a pass at Advanced level, 50 per cent in the high grades A-C. Good standards in geography continue to be closely associated with a regular programme of practical work and field study in Key Stage 3 and in examination courses. In many schools much care is put into organising this work, where pupils learn the essential skills of observation, recording, analysis, explanation and presentation. The work engenders enthusiasm and motivates most pupils of all abilities to higher standards. The quality of some individual studies at GCSE and A level is especially high, often based on detailed study of local geographical matters. Post-16 residential courses provide particularly good training for the individual studies in human and physical aspects of geography.

More generally, the study of geography appeals to pupils, particularly when the teaching has encouraged a questioning approach to the study of places and issues in human and physical geography and can be seen to be relevant to topical geographical matters. When the time comes to choose options in Key Stage 4, geography is the most popular non-statutory GCSE subject, taken by almost half of pupils. Progress improves in Key Stage 4 and post-16, reflecting more good teaching and the greater use of specialist geographers.

Although this picture of geography is one of a flourishing subject towards the end of the secondary curriculum, the past four years have seen significant changes to the curriculum in Key Stage 3, GCSE and at GCE A level. By the time of the National Curriculum review, most geography departments had devised a satisfactory scheme of work for Key Stage 3, although the content required by the original Order was clearly too much for the teaching time available. The review involved substantial changes, shortening and simplifying a complex programme of study with five attainment targets. As with the original, however, the flexibility of the new Order allowed places, themes and skills to be mixed in many different ways over the three years of Key Stage 3. This required a significant revision of schemes of work and lesson planning which geography departments have undertaken in greater or lesser degrees of detail. Some departments chose at this time to give a lower priority to revisions in Key Stage 3 because of the need to develop a scheme of work to match the new examination syllabuses chosen for Key Stage 4 and A level.

Just as pupils' progress has consistent features over the inspection cycle, so has the quality of teaching. The majority of teachers have secure subject knowledge, though in Key Stage 3 some are not specialists and are not up to date with recent geographical thinking. In some schools this is compensated for by detailed schemes of work which identify clearly the specific teaching objectives, learning outcomes and assessment opportunities. Most lessons are well planned and include a variety of teaching methods, though these continue to be narrowed or limited at times by the availability of resources, an issue which persists in one-fifth of schools. There are inadequate numbers of atlases and textbooks, as well as a limited range of other visual resources, and this affects classroom practices and also the nature and style of homework.

Chart 79 Geography

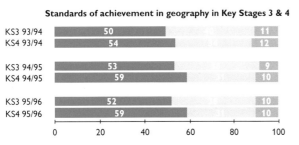

Standards of achievement in geography in Key Stages 3 & 4

	Good	Poor
KS3 93/94	50	11
KS4 93/94	54	12
KS3 94/95	53	9
KS4 94/95	59	10
KS3 95/96	52	10
KS4 95/96	59	10

Quality of teaching in geography in Key Stages 3 & 4

	Good	Poor
KS3 93/94	41	17
KS4 93/94	45	14
KS3 94/95	43	17
KS4 94/95	48	14
KS3 95/96	44	16
KS4 95/96	49	12

Percentage of schools

Good   Satisfactory   Poor

Issues in geography

Raising standards in Key Stage 3

Key Stage 3 is the weakest area of secondary geography teaching. It often begins from a low base in Year 7. Liaison between schools on the geography curriculum is poor: the diversity of organisation of the geography curriculum in Key Stage 2, and its weaknesses in many schools, ensure a slow start in Year 7 for many pupils. This is not unique to geography, but the flexibility and structure of the geography Order, and the substantial revisions in 1995 have made planning for continuity particularly difficult. The lower years of Key Stage 3 in many schools are often taught geography by non-specialists, sometimes as part of combined humanities courses, and this is reflected in the slow progress made by pupils and the weaker quality of teaching. Some teachers find it difficult to plan the intellectual progression of some themes and concepts, and to specify clear learning objectives to share with pupils. Some teachers, too, are uncertain about how to develop some concepts within a theme; for example, pupils in Year 9 being taught about population migration processes in the same manner they were taught in Year 7, without consideration of more complex variables such as age and sex structures or the changing economic circumstances which promote urbanisation. The new Order is a significant improvement for Key Stage 3 in general structure, but teachers need to go further in identifying and clarifying detailed teaching objectives in order to overcome these problems.

Where teaching is well planned and places high demands on pupils, the quality of the experiences and of the tasks set results in good standards.

In a Year 9 class the pupils were studying their nearby coastal area, looking at the impact of a new sewage outfall. They had visited the site, met an engineer and constructed and administered a questionnaire to local people, including residents, hoteliers, fishermen and tourists. They used IT to present results and in a classroom presentation pupils spoke on behalf of an interest group about the new development. The teacher ensured that questions were asked and answered about coastal processes, economic activities in the area and how environments could be managed. The tasks set required the pupils to use the evidence of observation and questioning, the making and presentation of maps and the use of a specialist vocabulary. The debate in class was lively, with pupils very animated. By skilful and sensitive questioning the teacher encouraged pupils to reflect on the effects of the sewerage work on different groups in the community, whilst consolidating their knowledge of coastal processes and environmental change.

HMI INSPECTION 1996

In a few schools limitations in the amount of teaching time available for geography affects the quality and depth of work. In Key Stage 3 this may vary from one to two hours per week and in Key Stage 4 from two to three. Guidance documents for geography from the School Curriculum and Assessment Authority (now QCA), have helped some teachers by exemplifying standards which can be achieved in Year 9 and by interpreting level descriptions. The processes of statutory teacher assessment at the end of Key Stage 3, first undertaken in 1997, have provided a timely opportunity for schools to reflect on the Key Stage 3 geography curriculum and the match between opportunities offered and levels which pupils can attain as a result. In some schools, the range and depth of work have been limited by teachers' over-dependence on textbooks which were based on the original geography Order and which suggest exercises which are insufficiently challenging; for example with insufficient requirement for pupils to use extended writing to explain or justify.

Knowledge, explanation and analysis

There are some consistent strengths and weaknesses in pupils' progress in geography. At levels appropriate to their development, pupils have sound knowledge and understanding of the places and geographical themes they have studied, with an ability to offer some explanations for changes taking place and to apply these to new contexts; for example how processes of population migration apply regionally and internationally. Many pupils have satisfactory recall of locational knowledge and are able to use appropriate geographical terms and vocabulary, increasingly so in Key Stage 4 and post-16. Investigative skills are well developed through the study of places, through themes such as geomorphological processes and settlement, and in topical issues and problems locally and worldwide. Teachers ensure pupils can sequence their enquiries logically, resulting in some excellent individual studies, particularly in public examinations. Increasingly pupils understand the connections between physical and human themes and apply them to their studies of places and environments. Field-based studies, local and further afield, are well organised, generate enthusiasm and consolidate conceptual thinking through practical involvement. Although there is scope for more explicit approaches, there is sound support of pupils' social, moral and cultural development through the study of geographical topics such as development, settlement and environmental issues which address major concerns of society such as equity, compromise, fairness and tolerance.

Weaknesses in pupils' progress stem from inadequate knowledge and understanding of the human, physical and environmental processes which bring about changes. In both Key Stage 3 and Key Stage 4 many pupils do not sufficiently engage in the sort of discussions which help them to analyse, explain and reason, and there is little extended written work to move their thinking from description to explanation. Some learning is superficial because it is insufficiently rooted in practical work, for example with maps and aerial photographs; or in case studies which exemplify geographical principles and processes, for example relationships between climate, soils, vegetation and human activities. Although some schools make good progress with the use of IT in geography, a statutory requirement in Key Stage 3, there is still much to do in helping pupils to use IT to analyse and explain what they have studied. Too often the presentation of findings in a diagrammatic way is accepted without any explanation of what they mean. Problems in the use of IT also stem from the availability of equipment, the construction and organisation of the school curriculum and the competence and training of teachers.

Assessment practices

In Key Stage 3 one in five schools has unsatisfactory procedures for assessing pupils' attainment and two out of five use assessment unsatisfactorily to inform curricular planning. Overall, assessment practices for geography are unsatisfactory in one in four schools. Although many geography departments have comprehensive policies for many aspects of their work,

assessment strategies are frequently weak, and result in inconsistency in practice between teachers. Poor assessment practices are often found in departments where they are not systematically monitored by the head of department, resulting in partial or inconsistent implementation of policies. The position in Key Stage 4 improves, often influenced by examination board practices and requirements, and procedures are unsatisfactory in one school in four. But day-to-day assessment, as in Key Stage 3, is weak and the use of assessment to help the planning of future work is unsatisfactory in one in five schools. What is particularly lacking is marking which clearly informs pupils about the standards they have achieved in a piece of work, and what they need to do to improve; whilst marking needs to be supportive of efforts made, it also needs to be constructively critical, and diagnostic of both strengths and weaknesses. Although presentation is important it is often commented on to the exclusion of matters of geographical content. Not all schools have yet fully understood the ways in which the ongoing assessment and recording practices of the department relate to new statutory teacher assessments at the end of Key Stage 3.

7.7 HISTORY

Trends in history, 1993-7

Both the standard of pupils' achievements and the quality of teaching in history have been good in a high proportion of schools and have risen steadily, with particular gains in the last year of the cycle (see Charts 80 and 51). Almost 60 per cent of history candidates now achieve a higher grade (A* - C) at GCSE. One aspect of Key Stage 4 which appears to be especially successful is coursework. Much coursework is judged to be very good, particularly the detailed use of visits to historical sites as a basis for investigation. In the last two years, however, the number of pupils opting to study history post-14 has declined. At A level the picture is similar: standards of achievement and the quality of teaching are high and currently some 55 per cent of the entry gain a high (A - C) grade, but historians are beginning to form a decreasing proportion of A-level candidates.

The revision of the National Curriculum has brought significant benefits. Teachers have generally found the reduced body of historical content in Key Stage 3 more manageable. They have fewer anxieties about covering the subject matter in the time available – a reflection of growing confidence in working with history in range and depth. It remains the case, however, that not all parts of the Programme of Study receive parity of treatment, with departments tending to spend a disproportionate amount of time on the first four study units. Content apart, the revised approach to describing attainment and the introduction of the key elements have also been helpful in overcoming earlier difficulties. In most history teaching there is now a better balance between ensuring that pupils are taught a body of knowledge about the past and, at the same time, enabling them to understand and master the processes of enquiry and analysis by which that body of knowledge is arrived at. Concerns in earlier years that teaching too often over-emphasised one at the expense of the other - sometimes unhappily characterised as the "content versus skills" debate - have now mostly disappeared.

Pupils' achievements in history across the key elements are judged by the extent to which they show an ability to absorb and recall a body of historical information, and categorise and structure it in different ways to meet the specific requirements of a particular task. Can they make valid connections between, for example, discrete items of information, a range of written sources related to a given topic or sources of different kinds; and can they go beyond what is directly given and use the source to support an argument on the basis of inference? Is their work in history underpinned by effective language, communication and investigative skills? Inspection evidence over the last four years indicates that departments are increasingly successful in developing these abilities. Key element 3, interpretations, presents greater difficulties and in this aspect progress is slower.

Issues in history

Teachers' expectations in history

In the lessons where standards and the quality of teaching are low certain major failings persist. Because topics are treated in a perfunctory and sometimes inaccurate way pupils' knowledge of events is insecure and their grasp both of the period under consideration and of how it relates to other periods is weak. They undertake a

Chart 80 History

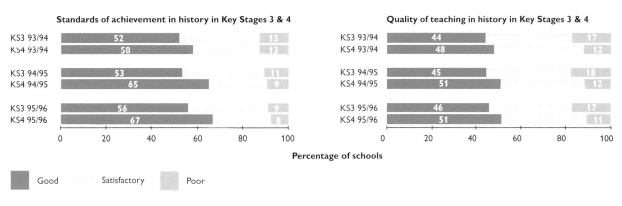

Standards of achievement in history in Key Stages 3 & 4

KS3 93/94	52	13
KS4 93/94	50	3
KS3 94/95	53	11
KS4 94/95	65	9
KS3 95/96	56	9
KS4 95/96	67	8

Quality of teaching in history in Key Stages 3 & 4

KS3 93/94	44	17
KS4 93/94	48	12
KS3 94/95	45	18
KS4 94/95	51	12
KS3 95/96	46	17
KS4 95/96	51	11

Percentage of schools

 Good   Satisfactory   Poor

monotonous series of mechanistic, source-related tasks which do little to further their understanding of historical evidence. Limitations in teachers' subject knowledge, or weaknesses in their planning and management, are reflected in a failure to provide a range of appropriate materials and activities, to ask probing questions or deal effectively with pupils' responses; to set tasks which are challenging and build on previous work; or to provide effectively for the ability range in the class. Such teaching frequently rests on an uncritical over-reliance on a single textbook or inadequate set of worksheets. As a consequence pupils' responses are weak and fail to develop either their knowledge and understanding or their evaluative and analytical skills. These problems are not restricted to Key Stages 3 and 4. In a small number of sixth-form lessons there is an overdependence on slow paced note-taking linked to poorly developed note-making skills; such lessons do little to develop a conceptual framework or, more broadly, to promote the historical enquiry and controversy which can make history at this level so compelling.

Up-to-date subject knowledge, a clear understanding of the nature of the discipline and a continuing engagement in some aspect of the practice of history are part of most history teachers' armoury. But, where the teaching is appropriately demanding, it is also based upon thoughtful planning, perceptive assessment of pupils' capabilities, a clear view of progression and a vigorous approach to the task in hand. The enthusiasm with which a teacher approaches a topic quickly establishes the right conditions for learning.

In a Year 10 class working on developments in medicine, the teacher introduced the lesson with a very good review of the work of Jenner, emphasising understanding. Excellent questioning reinforced knowledge, building concepts and eliciting extended responses from a wide range of pupils. Exposition was sometimes very funny, if inevitably macabre, with great expression and scene setting which created expectancy for what was yet to come. Written tasks were based on a good range of stimulus material. The tasks developed skills in evidence and enabled pupils to develop and deepen knowledge and understanding of Jenner and contemporary developments. Once pupils

had set to work, the teacher was active, intervening to support individuals and occasionally interrupting to provide whole class review of emerging issues. There was worthwhile challenging of misconceptions about sources. Pupils genuinely enjoyed the lesson, and the teaching in particular.

HMI INSPECTION 1996

Where teaching is good, questioning to review prior learning or analyse new material - whether a teacher's exposition or written or visual evidence - will seek to probe the limits of pupils' knowledge and understanding by, for example, asking open-ended questions, demanding justification for responses, or putting forward contentious viewpoints and counter-propositions. Teachers pose problems in ways which demand thought and not just memory to resolve, for example 'What were the most significant causes of the revolt?'; 'Why did Hitler stop the advance rather than allow his generals to complete the rout?'; 'What might have happened if all women had adopted the tactics of the suffragists?'. Additionally, pupils are presented with methodological puzzles, asking, for example, how conflicting eye-witness accounts can be reconciled; and are required to defend differing viewpoints or courses of action. Structure in the form of supplementary questions or additional guidance is given only sparingly and as it becomes necessary, rather than as a first resort. The resources used are of a kind which pupils, relative to their capabilities, have to work hard at to understand and they are regularly guided towards additional materials.

Good teaching builds on whole class, group or individual scrutiny and discussion of evidence to set a challenging written task. Sometimes this will be set as one of a regular pattern of homework tasks. Where pupils are closed down, it is often the written tasks which they are set which fail to exploit the stimulus of the lesson. Where open-ended tasks are effective, pupils and teacher share a high expectation for the end-product.

In addition, and especially with post-16 classes, the teaching creates an atmosphere of scholarly urgency. This is fostered by teaching which demands speed of thought whilst allowing time for reflection; which encourages pupils to question received wisdom and take risks in their thinking; which promotes a dialogue between pupils as well as between pupil and teacher; and which develops in pupils skills such as selective note-taking and skim-reading which allow them to move forward at pace.

Assessment and use of assessment information

Reports over the past four years have drawn attention to weaknesses in the strategies many history departments employ for assessing pupils' performance and in the use they make of the results - weaknesses which for the most part persist. Procedures for assessing pupils' attainment in history and the use made by teachers of day-to-day assessment in Key Stage 3 remain unsatisfactory or poor in nearly a quarter of history departments. Similarly, the use of assessment results to inform curricular planning is unsatisfactory or poor in over one-third of schools. Familiar weaknesses include the absence of a comprehensive departmental policy on assessment, recording and reporting; inconsistency of assessment practice across the department; marking which does not clearly inform pupils about the standard of their work or what they need to do to improve; and a lack of understanding of the relationship between day-to-day assessment and statutory end-of-key stage teacher assessment.

In Key Stage 4 the picture is somewhat brighter. Currently assessment procedures here are poor or unsatisfactory in only about one department in sixteen. But, even in Key Stage 4, the systematic use of assessment to improve pupils' learning remains the weakest aspect of much history teaching; and the use of assessment results to inform curricular planning or to monitor examination performance is still poor or unsatisfactory in a high proportion (almost a quarter) of schools.

The place of history within the whole curriculum

In too many schools history departments are only slowly coming to terms with all the demands of, and opportunities presented by, the National Curriculum. The history Order requires that pupils be taught to analyse the diversity as well as the characteristic features of past societies. Currently, there are few examples of history teaching where the social, cultural, religious and ethnic differences which existed in, say, medieval or Victorian Britain

are considered in any depth. It is important that this requirement is met if pupils are to acquire a balanced view of the past; and, from a wider perspective, if history is to play its proper part in the development of a sense of identity for all pupils and in the growth of their spiritual, moral, social and cultural understanding. History, too, could do far more to contribute explicitly to the development of citizenship and to environmental and economic and industrial understanding. And notably, despite some advances, much remains to be done in relation to IT in the study of history.

What has become the most pressing issue for many departments is anxiety about maintaining the place of history in the wider curriculum at Key Stage 4. The numbers taking history in the 1996 GCSE examinations fell by some five per cent on the previous year and the fear is that this trend may look set to continue. So far, any evidence that there will be a substantial decline in the near future in the numbers opting for history is inconclusive. But, clearly, history departments feel themselves under increasing pressure from such factors as the introduction of Part One GNVQ; the statutory requirement for schools to teach technology and a modern foreign language; the perceived difficulty of history compared with some of the alternatives; and, in some schools, an overall reduction in the number of GCSEs offered to pupils. Although not widely adopted, at least as yet, a small number of schools have attempted to preserve breadth of choice at Key Stage 4 by introducing GCSE short courses, in addition to the full GCSE course, in a range of subjects - including history. Where they have been taken up, history departments have generally opted for the two-year model and this has posed some problems of timetabling; for example where departments see pupils only once in a week. In addition, the demands on pupils in the reduced time available have been found to be relatively heavy; and there are concerns that the history short course may make the subject especially difficult for lower achieving pupils. Nevertheless, in the few schools where short courses are currently offered, pupils' favourable response to the opportunity to continue with history beyond the end of Key Stage 3 suggests that they warrant wider consideration.

Schools where history is thriving and where take-up is healthy in Key Stage 4 succeed because the subject is perceived as interesting, dynamic and challenging. The work they undertake extends the pupils' range of knowledge and the historical frame of reference within which they operate. It requires them to go beyond the superficial when analysing and using texts and sources and to cope with materials which are increasingly complex conceptually or linguistically. It forces pupils to structure their responses, both written and oral, and to base arguments or examine hypotheses upon available evidence. It gives them the opportunity to work in depth and produce descriptions, analysis and arguments of which they can rightly be proud. In such schools, history departments have also grasped opportunities offered by the whole curriculum. The great majority of history departments are attempting to secure the place of history in Key Stage 4 by making the Year 9 curriculum as appealing as possible. Arousing pupils' interest and motivation, and good examination results, remain the keys to a successful marketing strategy.

7.8 INFORMATION TECHNOLOGY

Trends in information technology, 1993-7

Pupils in Key Stage 3 have generally had greater access to IT teaching and facilities in the course of these four years than pupils before them. Many pupils show remarkable facility with IT, and in the half of schools which take the statutory requirements for IT seriously and which have made available the recommended time, progress and attainment in IT capability have shown significant improvement. However, in the other half of schools, which do not comply with National Curriculum requirements, pupils' progress is often unsatisfactory.

The already high profile of IT in the home and workplace continues to rise rapidly and affects young people's understanding of IT and their basic capability. Overwhelmingly, boys and girls respond positively to what school IT has to offer, and they co-operate readily and responsibly with one another in using it: the motivation to acquire relevant skills is high.

Beyond these observations, however, no simple generalisation about attainment can adequately describe the extraordinary range and variety of pupils' expertise in IT. While the National Curriculum sets out progressive, appropriate, age-related levels of competence in IT, individual pupils' progress is not necessarily linked to their age or general performance in the curriculum. Pupils' different experiences of IT in Key Stage 2 and the very varied opportunities they have for developing their interests in IT outside school mean that, in this subject, schools operate in a unique environment, and a very challenging one for teachers.

In many schools staff devote much time to ensuring that equipment and systems are available and functioning, and that pupils can have access to them during and out of school hours. There is a growing gap between schools in terms of provision of modern IT facilities, though pupils' progress is often determined more by the efficiency of use of available facilities rather than their quantity alone.

The teaching of IT skills, knowledge and understanding does not always do justice to pupils' varied backgrounds in IT. As noted in an earlier report[7], the pedagogy of IT as a subject is still poorly developed. The introduction of GNVQ has added further complexity to the work of the teacher of IT and to the assessment of pupils' work. Different expectations and styles of assessment of processes and outcomes are now required for a multiplicity of targets in IT - as a National Curriculum element in Key Stage 3; as a key skill in GNVQ at various levels; as a specialist vocational study at various levels; and as a subject at GCSE and Advanced level.

IT was the only 'new' subject to be introduced into the National Curriculum in 1990, and the original model was a cause of some difficulty. The National Curriculum review clarified some matters, in particular by uncoupling IT from design and technology and encouraging a mixed model of discrete and cross-curricular provision. The immediate trend was for subject teachers to see IT as largely a matter for IT staff, and they regarded the application of IT in their subject with less urgency than previously. Additionally, IT receives

[7] *IT in English Schools - A Commentary on Inspection Findings 1995–6,* National Council for Educational Technology with OFSTED, 1997.

Chart 81 Information Technology

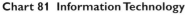

Standards of achievement in information technology in Key Stages 3 & 4

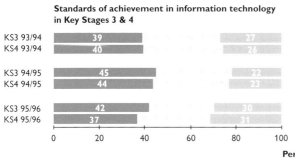

Quality of teaching in information technology in Key Stages 3 & 4

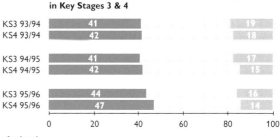

Percentage of schools

Good   Satisfactory   Poor

lower priority and more limited timetabled provision in Key Stage 4. Inspection 1995/6 showed that standards achieved by pupils in Key Stage 4 were polarising: those who studied IT continued to progress in the subject; those who had no timetabled or self-study facilities for continuing IT work made little progress and tended to fall behind unless they had access to IT at home.

Issues in information technology

Sustaining progress in IT

Many teachers have difficulty in assessing the levels at which pupils perform in their use of IT as they move from exercises developing basic competence to more significant problems and tasks. Too often only mechanical IT skills are taught and practised at the expense of some of the higher-order capabilities expected in the National Curriculum Order. Abler pupils, or those who experienced worthwhile work in the primary years, therefore often find that aspects of the subject lack challenge.

Teachers need to be alert to the relationship between pupils' prior experience of IT and the work in hand if they are to ensure that pupils make the progress of which they are capable. For example, in a class constructing and presenting an annual budget plan for the school tuck shop, a pupil familiar with a more advanced spreadsheet programme than that in use at school had not had to come to terms with nor had he understood securely some of the fundamental principles involved in using spreadsheets. Although he was adept at copying formulae and setting out captions and cell contents he gave insufficient thought to the structure of the spreadsheet and had no strategies for checking systematically the accuracy of the data entered. The pupil was approaching the construction of the worksheet purely as a problem of presentation, involving a few keyboard functions and display options, such as wrap-around. His progress in this lesson was therefore unsatisfactory. The difficulty for the teacher in this case was to spot that, notwithstanding his apparent fluency, he was working at only Level 3 or 4 of the National Curriculum; the teacher needed to raise his expectations in terms of detail in the budget lines, the use of accuracy checks and the design of layout, without affecting the central

thrust of the task for the rest of the class, who had not reached this level. A related and common difficulty for teachers is in ascertaining whether pupils who have accessed and retrieved information from a CD-ROM or Internet source have used good judgement in selecting and using material for the purpose in hand.

The review of the National Curriculum ensured that more pupils in Key Stage 3 receive satisfactory teaching. However, in Key Stage 4 many pupils have a very restricted programme. Most continue to use just one or two applications, notably wordprocessing, but have few opportunities to develop familiarity with more advanced or varied applications of IT, for instance, modelling or designing IT systems; nor can they develop greater independence in IT use. Many pupils in Key Stage 4 and post-16 have therefore tended to regress, doing work which is conceptually and practically no more advanced than work in Key Stage 3 or even Key Stage 2, unless they have access to IT outside school or follow specialist courses leading to external examinations or certificates.

Strategic use of resources

Overall, IT is less well managed in many schools than are other subjects, and this feature has become more pronounced over the inspection cycle. In most schools the IT strategy is included in the school development plan, but many plans focus upon the provision of more, or more up-to-date, equipment and software to improve availability of and access to IT without an accompanying evaluation of the impact of the IT resources already available within the school. In a third of schools there is good and careful financial management to ensure adequacy of IT resources, but even in many of these schools, less attention is often given to the detail of curricular planning to ensure good use of the available IT. The monitoring and evaluation of teaching and learning using IT and of the standards attained by pupils in IT are weak in most schools, and so the benefits of some of the costly investment in equipment and software are often not readily ascertainable.

In an increasing number of schools, many associated with nationally funded projects and industry partnerships, the commitment to develop IT is high. Given a clear educational vision by senior managers and strong curricular leadership and technical expertise, the potential to realise high standards of IT capability is evident. The main ingredients of successful management are: a clear strategy and the identification and training of members of staff to carry it forward into a viable plan; a well-informed review of available material resources and re-provisioning as necessary, on a phased basis, to ensure cost-effective access to suitable hardware and software (not necessarily the highest-specification facilities for all users, and not necessarily only fixed plant); and deciding on curricular priorities, for example resources for vocational courses in IT in Key Stage 4, or for technology-based approaches to literacy and numeracy, or for offering identified pupils advanced communications and Internet facilities. Additionally, schools are more successful where there is adequate technical support, information services and professional links and the targeting of such support to increase the likelihood that staff involved in applying or teaching IT are successful in their first attempts to do so, and gain confidence. Finally, ensuring the successful development of IT involves monitoring the developing curriculum in all subjects, ensuring that the programmes of study for IT are systematically taught, and that opportunities are available to pupils to apply IT in their studies at sufficiently high levels.

The role of IT managers and technicians

In most schools the role of the IT co-ordinator has been changing in the course of the four-year cycle. In 1994 it was not uncommon for the IT co-ordinator to be single-handedly responsible for technical services and support for colleagues. At the same time he or she had to negotiate with other staff which aspects of the IT programmes of study would be taught or reinforced in other departments, some of which contained staff who were at best reluctant partners. In a growing number of secondary schools the IT co-ordinator still has this dual technical and professional role, but is supported either by a technician or by an IT network manager. The latter's role is to ensure that the systems available to users function properly.

The importance for the school of support staff, such as a technician or network manager and a well informed and IT-trained librarian, cannot be underestimated. They have enabled some IT co-ordinators to function more effectively as professional leaders in a subject with many cross-curricular links. The technician can offer much first-line technical support to pupils and sometimes even instruction. Managers of schools without such technical support should weigh these potential benefits carefully against their other spending priorities.

7.9 MODERN FOREIGN LANGUAGES

Trends in modern foreign languages, 1993-7

Standards in modern foreign languages in Key Stages 3 and 4 have not shown the pattern of general improvement which has occurred in many other subjects. However, a modern foreign language was not a statutory National Curriculum subject in Key Stage 3 until August 1992. Following the review of the National Curriculum, its introduction as a compulsory subject into Key Stage 4 was postponed from August 1995 to August 1996. As the pupils following the National Curriculum in Key Stage 4 were only in Year 10 in 1996-97, it is too early to evaluate fully the impact of the National Curriculum on Key Stage 4. Generalisation over the period of this review should therefore be treated with caution.

Teachers had to face two major challenges during the period covered by this review. Firstly, they had to face the planning issues raised by extending the proportion and, in many cases, the ability range, of pupils taking modern foreign languages. Secondly, they had to implement a Programme of Study which is (potentially) more ambitious and demanding than what was previously expected in the vast majority of schools and which is required to be delivered through the medium of the target language. This requirement, together with the wide range of activities expected by Part I of the Programme of Study, represented a considerable rethinking of methodology for many schools. This double challenge has been met with considerable success. In the early 1990s only about half of all schools required all their pupils to take a modern foreign language in Key Stage 4. In the last year

before the National Curriculum requirement was introduced, 1995-96, about nine pupils out of ten in Key Stage 4 were taking a modern foreign language.

Although the use of the target language by teachers was already well established in some schools before the National Curriculum, it required a significant methodological shift for many teachers. As a result of their success in adjusting their approaches to cope with this change, teaching is now conducted predominantly in the target language, with evident benefit to pupils, not least in terms of listening comprehension. The pupils themselves have also been expected to make a major adjustment in their attitudes: to regard it as natural that pupils should continue with a modern foreign language until the age of 16 and that they should respond to the target language as the language of instruction.

Issues in modern foreign languages

Pupils' progress in modern foreign languages

After a good start as beginners in Year 7, pupils make less progress in Years 8 and 9 in their use of the target language, so that progress over Key Stage 3 as a whole is disappointing. Partly as a result of this, many go on to make insufficient progress in Key Stage 4. A major factor is that, over the two Key Stages, pupils rarely experience the full range of activities set out in the Programme of Study.

In Key Stage 3 pupils are usually able to understand the teacher speaking in the target language at normal speed for routine classroom business and to follow the recorded speech of native speakers on familiar topics. Their understanding is less secure when they encounter

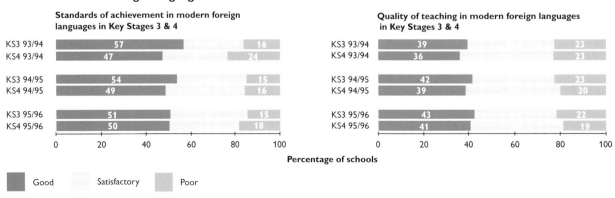

Chart 82 Modern Foreign Languages

Standards of achievement in modern foreign languages in Key Stages 3 & 4

	Good	Poor
KS3 93/94	57	16
KS4 93/94	47	24
KS3 94/95	54	15
KS4 94/95	49	16
KS3 95/96	51	15
KS4 95/96	50	18

Quality of teaching in modern foreign languages in Key Stages 3 & 4

	Good	Poor
KS3 93/94	39	23
KS4 93/94	36	23
KS3 94/95	42	23
KS4 94/95	39	20
KS3 95/96	43	22
KS4 95/96	41	19

Percentage of schools

Good   Satisfactory   Poor

new material or unfamiliar contexts.

Pupils can answer simple questions on matters concerning personal interests or basic transactions even in Year 7, but they lack the confidence to take the initiative in speaking. It is rare to hear pupils seeking clarification, as expected in the Programme of Study, using stock questions in the target language such as 'What does this mean?' or 'Can you repeat the question?'. Pupils speak with acceptable accuracy in routine situations. When required to speak at greater length or in new situations, their accuracy and fluency deteriorate, partly because their grasp of structure is usually less secure than their retention of vocabulary. In Key Stage 4, whilst pupils widen their range of vocabulary, many are still insecure in their grasp of tenses, idiom and other points of grammar, for example, when required to recount past experiences in areas previously covered in the present tense. The reasons include inadequate consolidation in Key Stage 3 of the basic structures needed to underpin communication, and insufficient account being taken of previous learning. Sometimes where pupils' grasp of structure and vocabulary in Key Stage 4 is secure, it is not channelled into more demanding or imaginative tasks, because of teachers' underexpectations of progression in its use.

Pupils' experience of reading the foreign language is frequently limited to a narrow range of short descriptions or dialogues in standard textbooks. Within this range, their understanding is usually adequate and they are able to extract basic details from texts. Their gist comprehension of longer texts is less effective, partly because they have limited practice in working out the meaning of unfamiliar material from contextual clues. Their ability to read more demanding texts is often not developed in Key Stage 4.

Writing activities such as gap-filling or adapting dialogues are usually completed accurately. Activities requiring pupils to use memorised language are less frequent, as are opportunities to undertake sustained writing about personal interests or projects such as creating a brochure to attract foreign visitors to their town. When available, such opportunities often lead to extended writing in which pupils are able to deploy effectively a wider range of structure and vocabulary. Written work is usually well presented,

but frequently pupils pay insufficient attention to accuracy. In Key Stage 4, where pupils have a sound knowledge of structure they produce writing which is formally accurate, incorporates appropriate idiom and shows a degree of awareness of audience.

Where pupils' use of the target language is well developed, this is usually due to good coverage of the Programme of Study Part 1, 'Learning and Using the Target Language'. If pupils do not experience the full range of opportunities and activities indicated, they cannot, for example, develop their skills and understanding sufficiently to take the initiative, cope with the unpredictable, and adjust language to audience and purpose.

During Key Stage 4 the range of experiences and activities is often not extended significantly, nor is the level of demand raised for many pupils beyond what they encountered in Key Stage 3. In the best cases, pupils can understand and use the target language in more mature contexts drawn from the full range of the Programme of Study. Where teachers continue to use the target language consistently and broaden the topics covered, for example talking incidentally about current events, pupils are able to grasp these and to respond. When the opportunity is created for pupils to speak at greater length, for example to 'hold the floor' on a familiar topic for several minutes, they show good recall and some capacity to order their talk into a continuous account. They also respond well to the challenge of activities which are interlinked and require them to use a range of skills.

A Year 11 French class carried out a class survey very responsibly. They interviewed their peers in the target language about a variety of sports and leisure activities, and reported back effectively using the third person. They expressed a wide range of opinions and reasons about preferences. Related listening and reading tasks about alternative sports involving a wide range of language provided an opportunity to build on this experience so that they were able to consolidate their knowledge and understanding of the perfect and conditional tenses.

HMI INSPECTION 1997

Teachers' command of the target language

Specialist teachers normally have a good command of their first foreign language: their accent and fluency usually present a good model for their pupils, although in some cases they do not insist consistently that pupils need to emulate that model. Many teachers show considerable skill in their use of the target language, particularly in the presentation and practice of new material, in exploiting visual materials, and in classroom management. Where expectations are high and the teacher has a confident command of the target language, pupils' positive response and good progress are sustained in Key Stage 4.

In a Year 10 German lesson, pupils were involved in a range of activities on the subject of 'Freizeit', including interviewing each other and taking notes on recorded interviews. Their excellent response was prompted by the high quality of the teaching and its preparation. The teacher had a very good command of the target language and used it exclusively and very skilfully. She generated an excellent atmosphere for learning, with 'larger than life' animation of activities, brisk pace, simple listening activities administered so as not to dilute the challenge; brief spells of pair work, for which intense practice had prepared pupils well; insistent but unthreatening pressure for grammatical accuracy (all via the target language); clear instructions and explanations, skilfully supported by gesture-voice-mime-singing; 'incidental' exploitation of topical references; and lots of patter in the target language at natural speed but understood sufficiently well for many pupils to appreciate the humour. A significant factor was the teacher's ability to sustain, in Year 10 pupils, the same enthusiasm as in Year 7.

HMI INSPECTION 1996

Non-specialist teachers, or specialists teaching their second (or third) foreign language, are usually less secure in their command and do not handle the target language with sufficient confidence or expertise, particularly in Key Stage 4. This can result in differences in the quality of teaching experienced and of language heard by classes in different languages, or even parallel classes in the same modern foreign language, particularly if consistent policies are not followed by all the teachers concerned. In some cases individual teachers may present an imperfect model of the foreign language for pupils to imitate so that errors in pronunciation and accuracy are passed on and may become difficult to eradicate later.

The linguistic updating of teachers is an important staff development issue if all pupils are to be provided with a good model of the modern foreign language(s) they are learning. The benefits to pupils' experience of the target language when teachers improve the quality of their second foreign language can be considerable. However, systematic approaches to the linguistic updating of teachers, including experience abroad, are rarely found. Linguistic updating usually requires more time out of school than other subjects and is therefore relatively more expensive in teaching cover than other forms of staff development.

7.10 MUSIC

Trends in music, 1993-7

There has been a steady improvement of standards in music in Key Stage 3. Improvements are evident in composing, performing on instruments, listening and appraising, but are most noticeable in singing. Schools where pupils rarely sang at all in 1993 now sing frequently, and to an ever-rising standard. Teachers are building up a repertoire of songs that are suitable for boys and girls to sing in Key Stage 3, and developing their ability to help pupils improve the quality of their work. More pupils now use their voices in their compositions.

The improved standards in music are mainly the result of better teaching. Most teachers have worked hard to implement the requirements of the National Curriculum in music. Lessons contain more practical activity that is likely to motivate pupils to learn than was the case in 1993. Listening and appraising are being taught effectively through performing and composing when this is appropriate. Pupils are taught to use their performances and compositions as a springboard for developing knowledge that they can apply when appraising music, and learn to apply to their own work knowledge developed when appraising other people's. There is an emphasis on teaching pupils the technical instrumental and vocal skills that they need to express themselves when performing, and when playing their compositions. The range of composing activities that pupils undertake has broadened beyond the melodic invention that dominated the curriculum in 1993 to include experience of some of the processes undertaken by contemporary professional composers. There is a

growing understanding that aspects of composing have to be taught: they do not just happen.

Music teachers who have effected these changes have been able to argue for increases in taught time and improvements in resources and accommodation from a position of strength. Since 1993 the resourcing and accommodation in many schools have improved. Taught time for music has increased, and carousel timetables that fail to provide pupils with a weekly opportunity to practise and develop their musical skills have become very rare. However, there remain schools where the impact of good teaching is constrained by insufficient taught time, or inadequate resources or accommodation.

Issues in music

The variable quality of music provided by schools

Despite sustained improvement, music in Key Stage 3 continues to compare poorly to other subjects with respect to standards and teaching. There is undue variation between schools both in standards and the quality of teaching. There are almost as many schools with good standards and lessons with good teaching in music as in other subjects. However, in music there are markedly more schools with unsatisfactory standards and lessons with unsatisfactory teaching; this applies particularly in Year 9.

In the schools where music is good the teaching encourages pupils to learn the skills that they need to express themselves, involves content that stimulates pupils to increase their attainment, and includes good modelling of the technical vocabulary of the subject. Pupils respond to this teaching with enthusiasm, even excitement on occasions, and make good progress. The

Chart 83 Music

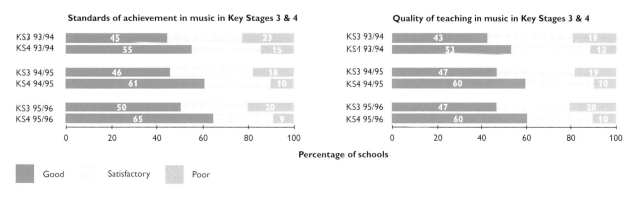

curriculum is underpinned by a clear view of progression, and is organised to build on all pupils' prior attainment, and move them forward as musicians from their first lesson in Year 7 until their last lesson in Year 9. All aspects of the programmes of study of the National Curriculum are visited and revisited in an organised manner that promotes learning. Where published materials are used, they are applied selectively and strategically to enhance progress. Day-to-day assessment is managed well, and the results are used when planning further teaching. Procedures for meeting statutory requirements concerning reporting to parents and assessment at the end of the key stage are planned thoroughly, and fulfilled in a manner that adds quality to pupils' education. Despite the fact that the music accommodation is unsatisfactory in many of these schools, the spaces that are available are used effectively. The resources, including musical instruments, in some of the schools are of inadequate quality, range and quantity, but teachers have agreed priorities for purchase or repair of resources as funding becomes available. They communicate these priorities clearly to the senior management of the school, but meanwhile use the resources of the school effectively and efficiently.

Such schools that provide a firm curricular base in music for all pupils in Key Stage 3 are well placed to move beyond their core responsibility of teaching the National Curriculum and increase the opportunities that they offer to all or some pupils. In some schools there is well-planned promotion of pupils' spiritual, moral, social or cultural development through music. Other schools offer opportunities for pupils to take lessons from peripatetic instrumental teachers on a range of instruments that may include steel pans, Asian instruments or pop music instruments as well as the more traditional range of orchestral and band instruments. The work of peripatetic instrumental teachers is monitored, and they follow a scheme of work that is agreed with the department and dovetails with the National Curriculum. Many departments also run ensembles outside taught time for pupils with particular interests, and encourage pupils who wish to form their own ensembles to use the school's facilities. Some schools buy in musicians to take rehearsals of school ensembles. This can be a constructive development, because it frees the school's music teachers to spend more time preparing their

lessons and playing a full part in the management of music in the school.

In these schools, it is usual for the proportion of pupils who wish to continue to study music at the end of Year 9, usually by embarking on a GCSE music course, to be higher than average. In some cases it exceeds 20 per cent, and occasionally 30 per cent. The interest of pupils with a wide range of prior attainment in music has been captured during Key Stage 3, and they wish to continue to feel the satisfaction of making progress in music during Key Stage 4. Pupils who take lessons on instruments from peripatetic or private instrumental teachers understand that these lessons will complement, but not be a substitute for, a curriculum with the breadth of GCSE. Pupils who do not take instrumental lessons still feel that they have something to offer in music, and that a GCSE music course has much to offer them.

At the other extreme, some schools have unsatisfactory standards and teaching in music, and are not improving. This includes some schools with good standards in most other subjects, and a few with a good reputation for music in their local community, perhaps because some pupils are members of bands or choirs that perform locally, nationally, and also sometimes internationally. In these schools most, and in some cases all, pupils are failing to make the progress of which they are capable. The curriculum is often narrower than the National Curriculum. Opportunities to play instruments in lessons may be limited to descant recorders, or electronic keyboards. The forms of notation used may be limited to staff notation. When composing, pupils may only rarely be given the opportunity to draw on the resources of a full chromatic scale. When listening, they may be limited to the light classics, or pop music of the 1960s and 1970s. The repertoire for singing may be over-specialised, and not lead pupils to make progress. Some lessons are musically silent: pupils may complete worksheets about staff notation, copy text from the board, or research instruments or pop music with access to neither. Teachers' expectations may be low, or inappropriate to pupils' ages. For example, work related to Prokofiev's "Peter and the Wolf" in Year 8 may focus unduly on the story, which clearly was written for a younger audience.

There lie between these extremes schools where the standards and quality of teaching are barely satisfactory, but where there is discernible improvement. Typically, teachers in these schools followed a published scheme of work literally for two or three years, but by 1996-7 were starting to use it more flexibly, adding some of their own materials, and adapting or missing out some parts of the published materials, in an attempt to build on the prior attainment of pupils in their school. Even so, pupils in these schools do not as yet receive a music education of the quality that will enable them to make the progress of which they are capable.

Accommodation and resources for music

The accommodation for music in many schools is unsatisfactory. The main music classroom is often too small, or there are too few overflow spaces where groups of performers and composers can concentrate on refining and improving their work, without disturbing or being disturbed by other music. Too often, however, departments fail to use the existing accommodation to its best advantage. For example, the main music classroom is cluttered with tables that get in the way of most musical activities; groups of performers and composers are not organised to use the overflow spaces that are available; resources such as headphones and headphone splitters are not used to try to reduce noise levels and help pupils concentrate on their work; the storage of resources is organised poorly, with the result that time during lessons is wasted on the distribution of resources, or pupils repeatedly limit themselves to using the musical instruments that are readily at hand; and there is little in the way of display that establishes the identity of the music accommodation, stimulates and celebrates pupils' work, broadens pupils' musical horizons, or links music at school with the music in pupils' homes and the community. In the short term such deficiencies should be addressed, and will add weight to legitimate claims for better resources.

Peripatetic teaching in schools

Local Management of Schools has bitten hard on the free provision of peripatetic instrumental lessons over the last four years, and charging, albeit often subsidised, has been introduced in the great majority of schools. External surveys suggest that as many pupils as ever are taking peripatetic lessons at school, and the issue is whether they are the right pupils learning the right instruments, for example, whether pupils from poorer families have been further disadvantaged, and whether we should have quite so many aspiring flautists. However, there are examples of schools that provide good advice to pupils about which instrument they should learn, and subsidise or pay for the tuition of pupils in financial need.

7.11 PHYSICAL EDUCATION

Trends in physical education, 1993-7

Standards in PE are generally high and have improved steadily. In 1995/6, achievement in both Key Stages 3 and 4 was good or very good in two-thirds of schools.

A strong feature of secondary PE is the rapid expansion of GCSE Physical Education, from 38,000 candidates in 1992 to 87,000 in 1997. This is having a very beneficial effect on programme structure and higher achievement in Key Stage 4 in an increasing number of schools. A move away from the 'recreational activities' and 'activity choice' approach is also raising achievement levels in Key Stage 4. It is too soon to be able to judge the longer-term effects of the introduction of the GCSE (Short Course) PE, but a number of schools are showing interest. The short course may give better structure for the large majority of pupils for whom PE is compulsory to the end of Key Stage 4 but who have only 5 percent of timetabled curriculum time each week. A qualification designed to provide a limited range of activities in this shorter time may prove to be highly motivating for pupils.

Rising standards overall in PE are a reflection of the improving quality of teaching. The incidence of poor lessons has fallen steadily from one in six in 1993/4 to about one in twelve (see Chart 51) in 1996/7; the proportion of good or better teaching has risen steadily during the same period. The most effective teaching provides well-targeted and carefully matched challenge to pupils. However, not all teachers reach this high standard and, in a small proportion of less successful lessons, slow pace and poorly differentiated tasks leave pupils either under-challenged or out of their depth. Skilful teachers are able to ensure that the needs of all pupils in the class are catered for with tasks differentiated by demand or outcome. In some lessons, however, this essential ingredient is neglected and pace and learning suffer.

Where PE departments have carefully considered the effects of mixed or single gender teaching groups across all the areas of activity, and have moved to single gender teaching at Key Stage 3, the effect on standards has been positive. Similarly, ability grouping in PE appears to lead to better achievement and is increasingly used, but still only in a minority of schools.

Issues in physical education

Higher-level skills in PE

The most able pupils develop confidence in the use of technical language, show mastery of technical skills, and understand and use scoring systems as appropriate in games. The ability to analyse and reflect on their performances, and to understand and apply the principles of play in games, is shown by these able games players, and they can usually devise their own training drills. Many pupils show good use of space and awareness of different roles in the game. Most have a good understanding of the rules and conventions of fair play.

In gymnastics, the most able show good understanding of sequence development and good awareness and skill on the floor and on apparatus, and in flight, rotation, balance and inversion. These pupils have good sense of line and of body tension. They show understanding of the factors that affect quality in their work. Although dance is included in only a minority of schools, where it is a

Chart 84 Physical Education

Standards of achievement in physical education in Key Stage 3 & 4

	Good	Poor
KS3 93/94	60	9
KS4 93/94	54	9
KS3 94/95	62	7
KS4 94/95	59	8
KS3 95/96	67	6
KS4 95/96	66	4

Quality of teaching in physical education in Key Stages 3 & 4

	Good	Poor
KS3 93/94	49	15
KS4 93/94	45	17
KS3 94/95	50	14
KS4 94/95	47	14
KS3 95/96	53	13
KS4 95/96	52	12

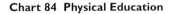

Percentage of schools

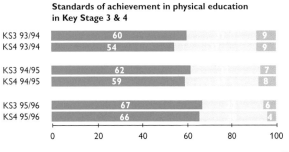

Good   Satisfactory   Poor

chosen activity it is often taught very effectively and standards of achievement are high, particularly for girls. The ability to create and develop motifs, to show a good sense of rhythm and timing, to work co-operatively in groups, to interpret mood effectively and to respond sensitively to accompaniment are all positive features of the work of the highest attaining pupils. Swimming is included in the curriculum in a small minority of secondary schools; where it is included, attainment is usually good and pupils demonstrate confident and fluent stroke production in a number of styles. Almost all pupils have a good understanding of safety matters in PE. Many are aware of the importance of exercise and know the fundamental principles for warming up, cooling down and making gains in strength, stamina, speed and flexibility.

However, many pupils are not successful in the development of higher-level skills in PE. Some can plan attacking and defensive strategies in games, and are aware of appropriate tactics, but many cannot reach this standard and have limited tactical awareness. Most do not reach high standards in gymnastics and their movement lacks the quality required; their body awareness is weak and their movement vocabulary limited. It is a cause for concern that achievement levels in gymnastics are so variable between schools, and between genders even within a school: girls' achievement can be high but the achievement of boys, and of girls taught in mixed gender groups, is too often relatively poor.

The most persistent weakness over the four years is the inability of a large proportion of the pupils to plan for and evaluate their own work and that of others in order to improve their attainment. Much of the weakness in pupils' understanding of the essential process skills of planning and evaluating in relation to performance can be attributed to the failure of teachers to give sufficient emphasis to this central requirement of the National Curriculum in PE. Some teachers, however, do this very well.

In a dance lesson with a mixed Year 10 class the teacher organised the warm up and body training parts of the lesson and also taught the GCSE directed study from the front with considerable focus on detail and precision. Pupils then had to work in pairs, and later in

groups. They repeated and analysed each other's movement, observing with care and commenting freely and intelligently on how to improve it. They later used video to correct problems and check progress.

HMI INSPECTION, 1997

The PE curriculum

The revision of the National Curriculum in PE was undertaken against a background of pressure towards traditional games in schools; this adversely affected the internal logic of the original curriculum which balanced the six areas of activity. The outcome was an over-narrow curriculum experience, especially for boys. Typically for pupils in Key Stage 3, games now occupy between 50 and 70 per cent of the available time. The other three chosen areas of activity required by the National Curriculum are squeezed into the remainder, leaving too little time to develop them fully.

In particular, the Key Stage 3 programme must include only a minimum half unit of the body management activities of gymnastics or dance. In 1993, a valuable outcome of the introduction of the original National Curriculum was the substantial number of men teachers who willingly undertook in-service training in dance. Since the review of the National Curriculum, whilst most girls have a sustained programme in both activities throughout the key stage, in many schools dance has been omitted from boys' programmes and gymnastics has been restricted to only a few lessons. As a result standards in boys' gymnastics have fallen considerably over four years when compared to those of girls.

Additionally, over the past decade there has been an increasing tendency towards short, blocked units of work in physical education. The length of the unit depends on timetable and other factors but it often settles at around a lesson per week for half a term. A unit of six or seven double periods - around five to six hours of working time after changing and preparation time is deducted - is typically devoted to an area of activity or a major game. It is increasingly clear that in many schools these units are too short to allow effective learning and the development of appropriate skill levels. Shallow coverage and superficiality result from the introduction of too many activities in Key Stage 3 in short bursts of time, and with lengthy periods before the same activity comes into the programme again. This militates against continuity and progression. Some thoughtful departments have arranged for fewer activities to be covered and are successfully experimenting with longer blocks of time. This allows a greater depth of knowledge, better understanding and higher skill to be achieved.

One good department had given much thought to the planning of a balanced curriculum, and to the games activity area in Key Stage 3 in particular, in the light of the revised National Curriculum. They sensibly decided to devote games lessons in Key Stage 3 to the teaching of traditional team games, thereby avoiding the dangers of introducing too many new games before skills in traditional team games had been established. They had identified this weakness in their previous planning and felt that the introduction of too many new activities coinciding with puberty or early adolescence had led to many pupils failing to make progress in the new activity. They had judged that excessive self-consciousness and rapid loss of self-esteem had resulted, with a consequent loss of motivation or poor behaviour in lessons.

'PHYSICAL EDUCATION AND SPORT IN SCHOOLS: A SURVEY OF GOOD PRACTICE', OFSTED, 1995

PE accommodation

Resources for physical education, with the exception of books for examination courses, are generally satisfactory. However, the provision and maintenance of accommodation and facilities for physical education are probably the most significant issue affecting standards of achievement in many schools.

Access to indoor accommodation for some required areas of the National Curriculum, and in inclement weather, is essential if the full Programme of Study is to be taught. Often, however, indoor spaces are unavailable because they are being used for internal or external examinations, school productions or other functions. With the introduction of national testing in Key Stage 3, this burden has been increased and some PE departments lose access to their specialist space for up to 70 days per year or about a third of the working time.

Some schools - particularly those with shared community facilities - have outstandingly good, effectively managed and well-maintained accommodation. In others, however, provision of PE is restricted by the inadequate size of outdated accommodation from a different era; for others the decline in standards of maintenance of indoor accommodation and outside facilities has continued steadily to the point where some areas are taken out of commission on health and safety grounds. Indoors, where they exist, sports halls are usually well-maintained facilities, but gymnasia often have inadequate heating, neglected floors and drab decor, which is made worse by ingress of water from more recently constructed flat roofs. More often the major problem is cramped, dirty and poorly ventilated changing rooms with an inadequate number of hooks for the pupils' school clothing to be kept in reasonable condition. The absence of well-maintained showers obstructs the development of good attitudes to personal hygiene. Older, open, run-through showers are generally regarded as unacceptable for adolescent secondary pupils and there is an increasingly urgent need for the installation of individual privacy cubicles or curtains in school showering facilities.

Greater difficulties can be found with outdoor facilities in some schools. Hard areas with disintegrating surfaces, or damaged surround netting, present dangers for pupils and restrict both curricular and extra-curricular use. Ageing dri-play surfaces are often in need of extensive maintenance. Acceptable sand-filled jumping pits and hard run-up areas for athletics are now almost unknown in schools. About a third of the playing fields are judged to be in poor condition for several winter months each year. Physical education teachers in some schools have to adjust curriculum arrangements to maximise the learning opportunities provided by the more readily available accommodation. Relatively few schools have access to outside playing space which they can use throughout the most difficult weather conditions. Where schools have access to a floodlit artificial turf area, it is usually in constant use by the school and the community for up to thirteen hours per day.

7.12 RELIGIOUS EDUCATION

Trends in religious education, 1993-7

The proportion of schools where standards in RE are satisfactory or better in Key Stage 3 has increased, but there remains considerable scope for further improvement. The lowest standards occur where RE is taught within Personal and Social Education. There is evidence that this practice is declining, but it still exists in nearly half of schools, particularly in Key Stage 4. The highest standards in RE lessons are found among pupils preparing for public examinations.

Over the first inspection cycle there have been several important initiatives in RE. Since 1993 all LEAs have been required to produce a new agreed syllabus to take account of the 1988 Education Act, and syllabuses are now subject to a five-yearly review. In 1994 SCAA published two Model Syllabuses for RE. These were not statutory, but have been used as guidance for most of the agreed syllabuses produced subsequently. Public examinations have also been subject to new developments. In 1996 GCSE (Short Course) syllabuses in Religious Education were introduced. Schools have used this course to provide accreditation for pupils in Key Stage 4 who did not wish to follow a full GCSE course, or as an alternative to non-examination RE; as a result the motivation, standards and progress of pupils have improved.

Even so, at the time of their inspection over half of all secondary schools either failed to provide RE for all pupils or provided insufficient time for the agreed syllabus to be taught. Non-compliance occurs most frequently in sixth forms, but many schools are not making adequate provision in Key Stage 4. It is a matter for the headteacher and governors to ensure that the school complies and that sufficient time is made available for the agreed syllabus to be taught.

Issues in religious education

Teachers' expectations in RE

There is more unsatisfactory and less good teaching in RE than in most other subjects. In particular, teachers' expectations of pupils are low. Many RE departments assume that pupils come from primary schools with little or no knowledge, understanding or skills in religious education. This gives pupils a poor start, repeating work which they have done before and offering little that is new or challenging. Additionally, most RE lessons are taught to mixed-ability classes, but appropriate strategies to provide challenge across the whole ability range are rare. The use of a single text-book is commonplace, as is the use of common tasks of a mundane nature. This includes closed comprehension exercises, which restrict writing to one sentence answers, and activities such as drawing and word searches. Much of the work seen in Key Stage 3 would be more appropriate for Key Stage 2, and urgently requires review. At the same time, there is an overemphasis on learning about the phenomena of religion and too few opportunities for more challenging work that extends pupils' learning from religion by asking more fundamental questions. Work of this kind is most likely to contribute to pupils' spiritual development, which in turn contributes to their progress by causing them to think more deeply about religious and philosophical questions.

In general, teachers need to give more thought to

Chart 85 Religious Education

Standards of achievement in religious education in Key Stages 3 & 4

	Good	Satisfactory	Poor
KS3 93/94	39		20
KS4 93/94	37		26
KS3 94/95	46		20
KS4 94/95	43		23
KS3 95/96	48		18
KS4 95/96	42		21

Quality of teaching in religious education in Key Stages 3 & 4

	Good	Satisfactory	Poor
KS3 93/94	40		19
KS4 93/94	45		16
KS3 94/95	42		21
KS4 94/95	45		16
KS3 95/96	43		20
KS4 95/96	47		17

Percentage of schools

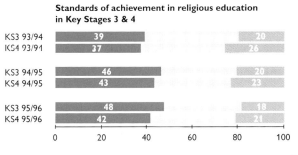

Good   Satisfactory   Poor

the types of activity which enable pupils to progress from initial knowledge about religions, such as the analysis and synthesis of evidence from a range of sources and traditions, to making associations between aspects of the same religion (e.g.between the rite of baptism, the theology of redemption and the community basis of Church life), and making significant comparisons between religions (e.g. comparing and contrasting the role of iconography in Orthodox churches and Hindu temples).

In a Year 7 lesson pupils were fascinated by a local woman priest talking about her job and, with the help of members of the class, demonstrating the Eucharist. The speaker had been well briefed by the class teacher - the talk was lively, amusing and at the right level for the pupils. There was good involvement of members of the class, good use of artefacts in context, and clever strategies for demonstrating theological links between the Eucharist, Moses and the Exodus (and hence between Christianity and Judaism). The presentation to the whole class was an effective and appropriate way of teaching, and pupils made regular and intelligent use of opportunities for asking and answering questions. Many pupils, especially girls, stayed behind during break to take the discussion further. The clear structure and interesting presentation enabled pupils to make progress in their knowledge and understanding of the Eucharist and the historical origins of Christianity within Judaism, and in their thinking about the issue of women priests. The class teacher played an effective role as 'devil's advocate' in raising controversial questions which took discussion onto a higher level when it could easily have become mundane.

HMI INSPECTION 1997

Where progress is satisfactory or good, pupils improve their evaluative skills. They develop the ability to justify their points of view by reference to evidence and argument, and to balance differing points of view. They develop the understanding that religious and ethical debates are of a different kind from, for example, the historical and scientific. They are also aware that what may count as evidence for a religious point of view (for example, personal experience) may not be acceptable in scientific debate. They recognise the need for respect and sensitivity in discussing the beliefs of others, and feel confident and secure enough to draw upon their own faith backgrounds. For example, pupils in a number of schools carry out surveys and questionnaires to discover variations in belief about God, or current moral and spiritual issues. They then categorise answers according to religious affiliation (or lack of it) and draw conclusions about the extent to which members of each tradition hold the same or different beliefs. A few pupils begin to refer to the work of scholars in support of arguments. In these cases pupils are constantly challenged by RE and make good progress.

The use of agreed syllabuses

Agreed syllabuses form the legal basis of RE in schools and as such should both meet legal requirements and promote religious education of the highest standards. The quality of agreed syllabuses is, however, variable. Some of them lack clarity, making it difficult for teachers to use them to plan schemes of work, and in particular to plan for progression and continuity. Most identify progression as increasing pupils' amount of knowledge about religions or themes rather than developing their conceptual understanding or their ability to use skills such as analysis, interpretation and evaluation. Relatively few give help in the areas of assessment or provision for pupils with SEN, despite the fact that these have been identified as areas of particular weakness in RE teaching.

There are, however, some new agreed syllabuses based on the SCAA models which include attainment targets, notes on progression and examples of tasks to promote learning. These help teachers to make more appropriate and increasing demands of pupils as they grow older. Some schools already use these syllabuses well, but in general more needs to be done to ensure that the agreed syllabus supports effective planning.

Staffing and resources

The qualifications and experience of staff have a direct impact on standards and progress. Where teachers of RE are well qualified and experienced, pupils' progress in RE is good or better in over half of schools, and unsatisfactory in only one per hundred; by comparison, where teachers' qualifications and experience are weak, progress is poor in nearly half of schools. Although most secondary schools have at least one RE specialist, most use some non-specialist teachers. While non-specialists can, with training and experience, become good RE teachers, inspectors frequently comment on the detrimental effect of using different staff each year to 'fill in' their timetable with RE lessons. It is important that non-specialists receive training and that, wherever possible, there is continuity in their deployment.

There is a strong positive correlation between poor resources in RE and unsatisfactory progress. Conversely, where resourcing is good, pupils in six out of ten schools make good or better progress. RE is poorly resourced in comparison with other subjects, and senior managers need to give the subject higher priority if standards in the subject are to improve.

7.13 CLASSICS

Trends in classics, 1993-7

Pupils' attainment is high, especially in the classical languages, and their progress is generally good. In Key Stage 3, pupils often demonstrate secure knowledge of tense and case, and are able to translate accurately and fluently; they successfully relate their studies to the modern world. They are able to use Latin vocabulary to illuminate the meaning of words in English and often in other European languages. In Key Stage 4, many pupils have a sound grasp of the structure of language, understand and translate complex texts accurately, and show understanding of the cultural context. They show their knowledge of history, appreciate literature and literary techniques, and use dictionaries well.

In the sixth form, students often have a good degree of accuracy in translation and are sensitive to nuances of language and style. They have an analytical approach to literary criticism and historical evidence, they explore ideas and they are competent in research and the use of libraries. Many who study classical civilisation have developed the skills needed for effective research and critical analysis. Written work is generally well focused and well structured. Pupils are confident in expressing their views and often engage in mature debate. For example, in one lesson pupils joined in an animated, informed and detailed discussion of their set texts, using Aristotle's Poetics as their framework.

Classical subjects are judged in most schools to contribute significantly to the spiritual, moral, social and cultural development of the pupils through the exploration of Greek and Roman thought, literature, religion and culture. Pupils are given opportunities to reflect critically on their own attitudes, values and beliefs through comparison with those in the classical cultures.

In over eight out of ten of the schools that offer classical subjects, the teaching in these subjects is good, and it is unsatisfactory in one in twenty. In a significant minority of schools, Latin is taught partly outside the regular curriculum; occasionally it is clear that time constraints adversely affect attainment and progress. In all types of schools, there continues to be a fall in the numbers of pupils entering A-level and GCSE examinations, apart from a significant increase in entries for GCSE classical civilisation, which, unlike classical languages, tends to be open to pupils across the ability range.

Issues in classics

Lesson planning and teaching

Occasionally planning fails to take sufficient account of the range of ability in the class and teaching approaches are not broad enough. From time to time, in both key stages, higher-attaining pupils make less progress than they could because their needs are insufficiently recognised; lower-attaining pupils, too, are presented with inappropriate tasks and materials so that their progress is hampered and their motivation reduced. In the small minority of lessons where progress in Latin is unsatisfactory, pupils in both key stages remain too dependent on the teacher, have a poor grasp of the essential structure of the language, know little vocabulary and fail to recognise case and verb endings. Occasionally the teacher's narrow linguistic focus, for example an excessive concentration on the minutiae of grammar, prevents pupils from appreciating broader and more important aspects of language and understanding. A general weakness in the teaching is a failure to exploit the potential of information technology to enhance the learning and motivation of pupils. Another shortcoming is that few schools give sufficient help and opportunity for pupils to develop their skill in reading Latin aloud.

By contrast, many lessons are well planned to realise the richness of the linguistic, cultural and literary aspects of classical subjects.

In a Year 9 Latin class, the pupils did a vocabulary test which included questions on English words derived from Latin. Then the teacher read them a passage of Latin which was set in a Romano-British religious context. The reading was clearly pronounced with variations of pace, emphasis to stress the meaning and helpful use of gesture. The pupils showed their understanding by eagerly answering questions on the story and its cultural context. They then worked hard in pairs, using a word list to aid their translation of a further paragraph of the text. The lesson concluded with a class summary of the work covered, in which the pupils read short extracts aloud and asked and answered questions on the meaning of the story, its cultural significance and its grammar and vocabulary.

HMI INSPECTION 1997

In a Year 11 classical civilisation lesson on Sophocles' Oedipus Tyrannus, the pupils discussed the character of Oedipus. They supported their opinions with close reference to the text, which they knew well. Their level of concentration was very high and they were ready to volunteer their own observations and ideas. They showed maturity of approach in discussion and grappled with the moral issues of the play, such as Jocasta's suicide. As the discussion developed, they kept systematic notes in preparation for an essay.

HMI INSPECTION 1996

The place of classics in the curriculum

Classical subjects continue to struggle to keep their place in the curriculum. They are accommodated in a variety of ways, many of which are an indication of the difficulty which schools have in finding adequate curricular time. Sometimes, in Years 7, 8 or 9, the subjects are offered to all pupils for one or more whole years, and sometimes as a part of a rotation of courses. Latin is frequently offered as an option against a second modern foreign language. In a significant minority of schools, it is taught partly at lunch-times or before or after school. Occasionally pupils are extracted from other subjects to study Latin. In Key Stage 4, classical subjects are usually offered among other options, but occasionally Latin (and almost always Greek) is taught outside the normal school day. In a few schools, the time allocated to Latin is very little: for example, 35 minutes a week in Year 9, or two half-hours at lunch-time. Such arrangements make progress difficult, and where they work it is because of the additional commitment of the pupils and the teachers.

This continued curricular pressure on classical subjects is reflected in public examination entries from both maintained and independent schools. In the GCSE for summer 1997, a year in which entries for English and mathematics declined by about 2 per cent and 1 per cent respectively, the number of candidates in Latin and Greek was about 4 per cent lower than in the previous year.

However, there was an increase of nearly 6 per cent in entries for classical civilisation. The decline in the numbers of candidates for classical subjects at A level, 12 per cent, was particularly marked.

7.14 VOCATIONAL COURSES

Vocational GCSE courses

631 Vocational GCSE courses in Key Stage 4 and post-16 allow pupils to undertake new areas of study which have vocational relevance. As indicated in the 1996 OFSTED report *A Review of Vocational GCSE Courses*, pupils' progress is generally good in courses such as Business Studies, Electronics, Media Studies, Child Development and Travel and Tourism, which are broadly based, providing a general education related to a sector of business or industry. These include the majority of vocational GCSE courses, with combined annual entries above 250,000 each year. Progress is generally less good in courses such as Horticulture, Agriculture and Motor Vehicle Studies which are more concerned with the development of workplace skills; here understanding is less secure and standards are lower. Such courses are generally declining in popularity and attract below 40,000 entries per year. Overall, in Key Stage 4, pupils often make more rapid progress in GCSEs with vocational relevance than in other GCSEs. Pupils' response across the ability range is characterised by high motivation, application and commitment. Pupils take independent initiative and work successfully in teams on tasks modelled on industrial and business activity. However, overall the quality of teaching in these courses is slightly lower than that found in Key Stage 4 as a whole.

In general, these courses provide pupils with a widely transferable introduction to business and industry, and some usefully promote skills of direct relevance to the workplace. Some courses have found their candidate numbers decline with the introduction of GNVQ. It remains the case, however, that they offer a flexible 'single option' alternative for pupils and maintain a standard commensurate with other GCSEs.

Theory and practical application

Subject knowledge and understanding of the theory and concepts associated with the vocational field are often given less emphasis in lessons than practical applications. Where basic subject knowledge is fragile pupils are unable to develop an understanding of the principles underlying the vocational activity, to generalise, to interpret, to plan and solve problems, and more broadly to predict and adapt to the likely effects of change. For example, some pupils studying electronics could not design and adapt electrical systems because of an insecure grasp of science. However, where knowledge and understanding are well founded, standards are high. In a minority of courses, theory is emphasised at the expense of practical applications, with a consequent limiting impact on motivation and standards. For example, some media studies courses are overly academic and as a result pupils have insufficient understanding of applications, such as making a media product, and are disappointed in their course.

Applications of IT

Standards in IT within vocational GCSEs are generally unsatisfactory. This is particularly disappointing in courses which in other ways seek to provide up-to-date treatment of a field in which IT is prominent, such as engineering, electronics and photography. There are exceptions in some courses and in their treatment by some schools. Good standards in applications of IT can be found, for example, in the completion of coursework, involving selection of software, planning its application and manipulating data. IT is also used effectively and appropriately in some media studies, travel and tourism and other courses for wordprocessing and desktop publishing, for example in drafting and presenting assignments.

Knowledge of industry

The understanding of roles, responsibilities and decision-making within business and industry organisations, for example the factors influencing decisions about the running of a business in a particular vocational area, is broadly sound. High standards were demonstrated, for example, when pupils discussed the conflicting priorities facing a business in reaching a decision over the disposal of environmentally hazardous material. However, in a number of courses, including agriculture, building construction and commerce, analysis of decision-making receives limited attention and standards are consequently lower. Knowledge and understanding of working practice in business and industry are often unsatisfactory. In many lessons and in some courses as a whole standards are limited by the exercise of skills in isolation from the real world of enterprise, business and industry. Many schools capitalise insufficiently on the goodwill of local industry. Too often, work experience is not drawn upon either in course objectives or in lessons in order to sharpen understanding. Standards are usually higher where work is closely linked to business and industry and draws upon the expertise of practising industrialists. For example, pupils studying art & design: photography, have benefited from contact with local practitioners by gaining an understanding of how technical and creative skills are applied in a commercial and business environment and from an awareness of the often rapid pace of change.

GNVQ

Standards of work in Advanced GNVQ have mostly been satisfactory since the introduction of the courses in 1993, but with considerable variations between schools. The amount of good work seen in schools showed a slow but steady improvement from 1993 to 1996, but this improvement was not sustained in the work seen in 1997, when the proportions of distinction and merit level work which were judged to be of a standard comparable respectively with higher grade and middle grade GCE A-level performance fell from approximately three-quarters to two-thirds. Work was judged to be broadly equivalent in quality to that of GCE A-level grade E or above in 80 per cent of completed portfolios in 1996 and 1997, and in all but a few cases the quantity of work produced was comparable with that which could reasonably be expected from a student taking two A-level subjects.

Overall, the prior GCSE attainment of GNVQ students is not as high as the average for those taking GCE A-level courses, but there are some very able students now choosing to take Advanced GNVQ, often together with an A-level or AS course. The progress made by the large majority of Advanced GNVQ students is at least satisfactory, and from relatively modest starting points some students are making very marked advances in the achievement they demonstrate. More than three-quarters of the students whose work was inspected in 1997 had achieved more in GNVQ than they could reasonably have expected to if they had studied GCE A levels, on the basis of their prior GCSE results. Most students show that they have

developed the skills and knowledge needed for effective progression to higher education or employment. A large proportion of those students who achieve an Advanced GNVQ at merit or distinction level, and who apply for higher education, obtain places on degree courses.

There has been an improvement in the quality of Intermediate level work since its introduction in 1993. Standards were initially very variable and, overall, barely satisfactory. By the summer of 1996, the majority of work was satisfactory, but with a greater consistency of achievement in art and design, business, media and science than in health and social care and in leisure and tourism. Work was judged to be comparable in quality to at least GCSE grade C, and equivalent in quantity to four or five GCSE subjects in nine out of ten completed portfolios inspected. The proportion of very good work is lower at Intermediate than at Advanced level, with a correspondingly smaller proportion of distinctions and merits awarded.

Students make good progress in their vocational work in about two-thirds of Intermediate courses; in one-tenth, however, progress is generally poor, usually because students are slow to hand in work, so building up a backlog of unfinished assignments. In a few cases, students make marked progress from modest GCSE results to merit or distinction grades at GNVQ. For example, one student on a media course, who had previously achieved nothing higher than a grade D at GCSE, had responded much better to the style of working in GNVQ; he had produced a portfolio which had reached merit grade, and he had also successfully completed some Advanced level media units. An increasingly large number of students, on completion of the Intermediate GNVQ, are going on to Advanced level courses, usually GNVQ or NVQ level 3, but occasionally also GCE A levels. The Intermediate GNVQ is therefore fulfilling an important function in providing a progression route for students who would not otherwise be able to qualify for this next stage of formal education.

In several schools where results are poor, some of the students would have been better suited to a Foundation rather than to an Intermediate level course. However, very few schools are now offering Foundation level GNVQ post-16.

In the main, students tackle the courses in a

purposeful and diligent way but at Intermediate level there are examples of students lacking maturity, problems with attendance, and excessively relaxed attitudes to work. For many, GNVQ has resulted in an increase in confidence and self-esteem, in some cases following disappointments at GCSE.

GNVQ assignments

The best work in portfolios is almost always the result of imaginative assignments devised by the students' teachers, which are conceptually demanding in relation to the subject matter, and encourage students to make maximum use of their contacts with local employers, so that they can base their studies on realistic, relevant and up-to-date information.

For example, excellent work took place in an Advanced business class where one group of students simulated the purchase of a hotel by raising capital from a local bank, based on a business plan they had developed to underpin the entire running of the hotel. Through direct contacts with the bank, the estate agents and the small business advisory service in the locality, they researched and went through all the stages necessary to open a new business. They also reported on and presented their work in an exemplary manner, so that the bank manager was able to comment that it was the best business plan he had ever been presented with.

In another school an extremely able student was encouraged in her GNVQ art & design course to produce work of extraordinary range and depth, which went beyond the scope of A-level art; this included a unit of study on 20th century sculpture, where in response to a commission from the headteacher of her school, she carried out extensive research in visits to art galleries, and produced a large metal sculpture of exceptionally mature quality. This student's work was good enough to obtain her direct entry onto a degree course in design and applied arts, without having to do an art foundation course.

HMI INSPECTION 1997

However, some of the poorest work occurs where teachers do not give their students specific assignments, but just leave them to produce

reports and summaries based on the evidence indicators outlined in the GNVQ specifications. Where use is made of assignments or case studies from books or produced by the awarding bodies, work is usually satisfactory, but since tasks are not tailored to local opportunities and individual circumstances, the potential for really good work is often limited.

Completion rates

Completion rates, as well as quality of work, depend very much on strong and well-informed course leadership. The best courses are led by relatively senior staff who have sufficient authority to direct and monitor the work of other colleagues. They ensure that teachers work well together as a team, sharing materials and co-operating closely in assessment and verification. Courses are carefully planned and organised, with deadlines clearly identified and enforced.

The extremes of performance are illustrated by an Advanced business course in one school where 17 out of 19 students completed the course, with eight obtaining distinctions and seven merits, and in contrast, a leisure and tourism course in another school where none of the 13 students achieved a full GNVQ. The issue of non-completion in GNVQ has to be treated with some caution, however; since, although the intention is normally to complete in two years, students can quite readily return for more time in the sixth form, if necessary, and a number do so successfully.

Business studies

Business studies continues to be the most popular optional subject both in Key Stage 4 and post-16 in many schools. Most secondary schools offer business studies to pupils in Key Stage 4 either as a single subject or combined with design and technology. In schools where Part One GNVQ has been introduced, many continue to offer GCSE business studies, with some examples of excellent linking of topics across Part One GNVQ and GCSE.

Standards of achievement in Key Stage 4 are satisfactory or better in eight out of ten lessons and good or very good in over one-quarter. In sixth forms they are satisfactory or better in eight out of ten lessons and good or very good in one-third. In the best lessons, students demonstrate a good knowledge of terminology, a growing understanding of business concepts and an ability to apply these to real-life situations. The quality of teaching in Key Stage 4 and in sixth forms at Advanced level is satisfactory or better in nine out of ten lessons and good or very good in well over half.

Knowledge and understanding of business and economic concepts

Where pupils and students are attaining highly, they demonstrate a knowledge and understanding of a range of business and economic concepts and are familiar with the decision-making techniques used in business. Responses are accurate and students are able to discuss a wide range of economic and business issues, making detailed use of topical business and economic examples.

Year 13 students were able to use their business knowledge to explore the issue of branding effectively. They explored the power it gave to producers in the market-place and were able to produce reasoned explanations for consumer and product behaviour in such circumstances.

HMI INSPECTION, 1996

The written work arising from such decision-making exercises is generally of a good standard and sometimes excellent, cogently argued and making good use of current newspaper articles and a range of appropriate texts.

Such high standards are achieved by teachers providing a good balance between developing pupils' knowledge and understanding and their ability to apply these concepts to real and unfamiliar situations. Where such a balance is not present, work tends to be superficial, lacking in analysis and showing little understanding of important interrelationships, such as, for example, the strength of the pound and changing levels of exports.

Business studies and industry links

Progress in both Key Stage 4 and post-16 business studies is good where teachers build on pupils' and students' own experience of business.

In a simulated reaction to a hostile takeover, pupils in a Year 11 class were able to evaluate the takeover well, and, as a board of directors, give a reasonable and sophisticated response to the company initiating the takeover. Another

group, asked to react to a production problem for an internationally known company, were able to produce a mature press release which revealed a good knowledge of company image and personnel problems.

HMI INSPECTION, 1997

Most schools make use of links with industry but they are not always sufficiently developed or exploited. Industry is often used superficially as a source of information rather than as a context for investigative work, problem-solving and decision-making. In some lessons, particularly in the sixth form, there is also underuse of Young Enterprise projects, role play, case studies and business simulations. More broadly, including in GNVQ courses, insufficient use is made of work placements, industrial visits and visiting speakers, thus denying those on business studies courses the opportunities to learn through the direct and practical experience of the business world. Where such opportunities are absent, and this is often linked with over-reliance on a textbook or note-taking, and with over-directive teaching, pupils' learning is insecure and often unenthusiastic.

The place of business studies in the curriculum

Not all schools have a comprehensive plan for business studies and there are examples of disjointed delivery and management of economics, business studies, GNVQ business, EIU, business links, and work experience. There has been a fall in recruitment to economics courses both in Key Stage 4 and post-16. In order to arrest this decline and to delay the time when students need to specialise, some schools have chosen to offer combined economics and business studies courses. In other schools a wide choice of business courses post-16 is offered including GCE A levels in economics and business studies, together with GNVQ courses in business and leisure and tourism. An increasing number of school sixth forms offer Advanced and Intermediate GNVQ courses in business but some fail to offer a GNVQ foundation course. This leads to some sixth formers following inappropriately difficult courses. Part One GNVQ, as a vocational alternative at Key Stage 4, has been generally well received by pilot schools and increasingly other schools are showing interest in introducing some Part One GNVQ provision into their curriculum. However, the progression routes for GNVQ students, particularly those who fail to complete some units, need to be carefully considered. Schools need to audit and evaluate the place of business studies in the curriculum in order to ensure that the pathways for those who specialise in business studies are clear.

7.15 PERSONAL AND SOCIAL EDUCATION

Personal and Social Education (PSE) is a timetabled part of the curriculum in Key Stages 3 and 4 in most secondary schools. It is provided in a very wide range of ways, through combinations of timetabled PSE courses, tutorial periods, National Curriculum subjects, assemblies, extra-curricular activities and residential experiences. Despite its importance, however, the teaching of PSE is too often unsatisfactory and the status of courses with pupils is often low.

Most schools see their tutorial and PSE programmes in Key Stages 3 and 4 as having a vital part to play in securing a whole curriculum which fully meets the needs of young people. At the **Richmond School, North Yorkshire**, Personal and Social Development has the following aims:

a) to work on areas of content which are not specifically covered through the subject-based lessons, for example health education, careers education, work experience, economic and industrial understanding, multicultural education, equal opportunities and environmental education;

b) to help develop approaches to learning and social skills which can be of benefit to each student in the wider curriculum and in life after school, for example decision-making skills, communication skills, assertiveness, working with others, study skills, and personal organisation;

c) to help bring together an understanding of issues and topics which are covered by a variety of subjects but in a fragmented way, for example an appreciation of how others live in society, environmental concerns, health issues, awareness of individual needs.

Richmond School was inspected in 1997 and was described as a school where 'the very good behaviour and positive attitudes of pupils result in good progress throughout the school leading to good examination results'. Amongst the factors contributing to the school's success, inspectors noted that 'great importance is placed on personal and social education and a carefully structured programme is in place for each year. It is valued by the majority of pupils, particularly at the upper end of the school.'

Although similar programmes exist in some sixth

Chart 86 Personal & Social Education

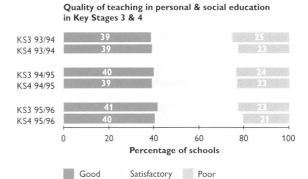

Quality of teaching in personal & social education in Key Stages 3 & 4

	Good	Poor
KS3 93/94	39	25
KS4 93/94	39	23
KS3 94/95	40	24
KS4 94/95	39	23
KS3 95/96	41	23
KS4 95/96	40	21

Percentage of schools (0, 20, 40, 60, 80, 100)

Good   Satisfactory   Poor

forms and schools accept the importance of "enrichment" studies, the range of this additional provision and the time allocated for it vary widely, and few schools have a clear rationale for defining the content provided. Programmes often include general studies, sports studies, courses in IT, modern foreign languages and drama, as well as activities suggested by the students themselves.

Monitoring and review of PSE

Schools are under increasing pressure to include new or extended topics within their PSE programmes - particularly in Key Stage 4. However, this is unhelpful and courses are becoming overcrowded and, as a result, less effective. This is reflected in too many schools by a fall in the quality of the teaching, poor responses from the pupils and a lower level of attainment as less and less time is devoted to any one topic. In order to improve the quality of PSE there is a need to review and consider the content, teaching and structure of PSE courses. Such a review should be informed by improved monitoring of the outcomes of PSE provision so that it more closely meets the identified needs of the pupils.

Torquay Boys' Grammar School has an effective monitoring and evaluation programme in place. Informal evaluation takes place through discussion between the head of PSE, her deputy and the year tutors, and enables teachers to keep progress under review and to identify targets for future development that would further good practice. At the time of the end of year review, the views of both teachers and pupils are sought on the overall programme. This is in addition to the reviews that take place at the end of each module of the programme. All such reviews involve pupils and staff. The co-ordinator also seeks advice from outside agencies at the time of the annual policy review to ensure that resources are up to date.

The PSE co-ordinator and her assistant also monitor classroom practice. To this end they have set down the criteria they will use for deciding whether the classroom teaching is effective or not. These criteria are shared with the teachers. The work of all staff in all year groups is monitored on an annual basis. In addition the co-ordinator carries out spot checks to ensure that the programmes are underway. Overall the monitoring and evaluation processes are extremely thorough and are effective.

HMI INSPECTION 1996

Non-specialist teaching

Schools continue to be divided over the question of the relative merits of teaching the PSE programme by specialist teachers or by form tutors. Inspection provides strong support for the use of specialist teachers wherever possible. Many tutors do not have the necessary levels of knowledge of a range of topics in order to teach PSE effectively. Additionally, many are understandably reluctant to become involved in the teaching of sensitive issues such as sex education. Numbers of teachers see their academic subject teaching as their first priority, not their tutorial role. This lack of commitment on the part of some tutors is reflected in the poor responses and low level of achievement of many pupils. Additionally, where PSE is taught by tutors it is often in an extension of registration time and the time available is frequently insufficient.

Index

Printed in the United Kingdom for The Stationery Office
J46782 C80 5/98 13110